D1562831

# GURINDJI JOURNEY

Minoru Hokari (1971–2004) was a brilliant and pathbreaking young scholar who passed away in his early 30s. He made outstanding contributions towards 'cross-culturalising' historical practice and towards developing a respectful collaborative research strategy with Indigenous Australians. A graduate of Hitotsubashi University (MEc 1996) and the Australian National University (PhD 2001), Minoru conducted fieldwork among Gurindji elders, whom he acknowledged as exceptional historians in their own right. His untimely death in 2004 curtailed a very promising career. He had a profound impact on a wide range of people, including many fellow students. As a result, there are scholarships named in his honour at both the University of New South Wales, where he started his PhD, and at the Australian National University, where he completed it.

See 'Being connected with HOKARI MINORU':
www.hokariminoru.org.

# GURINDJI

**A JAPANESE HISTORIAN IN THE OUTBACK**

# JOURNEY

## MINORU HOKARI

University of Hawai'i Press
Honolulu

10 9 8 7 6 5 4 3 2 1
First Published in Australia by UNSW Press
University of New South Wales
Sydney 2052 New South Wales
AUSTRALIA

Published in the United States of America and Canada by
University of Hawai'i Press
2840 Kolowalu Street
Honolulu, HI 96822 USA
www.uhpress.hawaii.edu

Library of Congress Cataloging-in-Publication Data

Hokari, Minoru, 1971-2004.
    Gurindji journey : a Japanese historian in the Outback / Minoru Hokari.
        p. cm.
    Includes bibliographical references and index.
    ISBN 978-0-8248-3614-6 (pbk. : alk. paper)
    1. Gurindji (Australian people)--History. 2. Gurindji (Australian people)--
    Historiography. I. Title.
    DU125.G8H65 2011
    305.89'915--dc22
                        2011006890

*Design* Avril Makula
*Cover* Nada Backovic Design
    *Front cover photo* 'On the way to Gurindji country, 1997'
    *Back cover photos* Main and top left from 'The Call of the Living Earth:
    Photographs of Indigenous Australians by Minoru Hokari' (exhibition
    catalogue); centre top 'George Sambo pointing at Seale Gorge, 2000'; top right
    'Presentation at Daguragu, 2000'.
*Printer* Ligare

This book is printed on paper using fibre supplied from plantation or sustainably
managed forests.

This book contains names and images of Aboriginal people of Daguragu and
Kalkaringi who have since died. This may cause unintended offence to some
people. The author thanks their communities for allowing him to use their names
and images in the making of this book, and for their ongoing support to publish.

The author's family and friends acknowledge with gratitude the considerable
support provided by the Australian National University Publication Subsidy
Committee, and the Australian Academy of the Humanities and the Australian
Centre for Indigenous History, Australian National University.

# CONTENTS

# A SUPERVISOR'S REFLECTIONS

Ann McGrath

In the mid-1990s, while working at the University of New South Wales (UNSW) in Sydney, I received a letter from a prospective Japanese doctoral student. Introducing himself as Hokari Minoru, its author apologised for his broken English, and signed in an awkward hand. With Japanese students very rare in Australia at this time, it was surprising to hear that a young man had read my book on Aboriginal cattle workers at all, let alone that he actually wanted to come here to study Australian Aboriginal history. Some months later, he advised me that he had successfully stitched together a number of scholarships. My academic colleagues were bemused, presuming the language difficulties alone would make a PhD impossible. However, something about his letter made me believe in him already.

Brimming with enthusiasm and excitement at his proposed project, Minoru – or Mino to his friends – showed an eagerness to learn, and a flexible, open-ended approach to his research thinking from the moment of his arrival in Sydney. Although his spoken English was basic, he picked it up quickly, greeting his own mistakes with infectious laughter. He also asked very tough questions about the discipline of history.

Soon after Mino arrived, we had a party at our home to welcome him. When served sushi, which had just started to become popular in

Sydney, he was taken aback – somehow he had overestimated the cultural gap. Mino was eager to embrace Australia and things Australian, and was full of youthful rebellion against his own country. Although friendly, he did not bother too much with small talk, preferring to spend the evening at the back of the room, purposefully going through our entire CD collection.

Mino's most annoying trait was not turning up for our meetings on time. Sometimes he was an irritating half an hour or more late. He would arrive puffing, flustered, and with wild hair and ruffled clothes. He would whisper effusive apologies and bow deeply. I was uncomfortable with the excessive deference *and* the lateness. One day he explained that he usually slept all morning. He was passionate about music, and stayed at clubs and music venues until the early hours. Subsequently, we adjusted our meeting times to suit his night owl habits.

Minoru often had trouble with his eyes in supervisory meetings. His contact lenses would somehow stick onto his eyeballs and he would try to dislodge and adjust them. He would get embarrassed – he told me that this did not happen anywhere else. Perhaps it was nerves that made them dry out, or perhaps it was because he was always straining to see things in new ways.

Supervision meetings combined his reports of research progress with brisk and stimulating insights. We laughed a lot. He was very excited about his long-held dream starting to eventuate, and he actively sought out new friends and advisers among Aboriginal scholars. At the university I often saw him in a coffee shop with one pretty girl or another, and they would always be giggling flirtatiously. He rarely introduced them, dismissively explaining that Chinese-speaking students bothered him by asking for help with Japanese, and he couldn't meet the demand. He also commented that he wanted to mix with non-Asian people. Clearly, there was more to this than language lessons – and I am sure he made many girls cry.

When I tried to suggest how he could use his Japanese background to advantage – for example, by comparing Aboriginal sensibilities with Japanese, rather than with the homogenous 'western' ones – I hit one of his rare conceptual walls. Perhaps his self-imposed rupture from his home country and all his friends was too great to acknowledge, but it was as if he did not want to think of Japan again.

While Minoru was receptive to most advice, he could also be stubborn. When I told him he should read more anthropology to understand Aboriginal cultural precepts, he made only a perfunctory effort. Always honest, he declared that he didn't like reading this difficult English. Besides, it was too dull and it gave him a headache. In another instance, when I advised him to give a paper based on his research at a particular history postgraduate conference, he obliged. Afterwards, when I asked how the conference went, he hesitated. 'Hmmmm,' he said, looking up and down and rubbing his eyes anxiously, creating extra time to deliberate. Then, looking at me rather sheepishly, he said in a deliberative tone: 'Ann, I'm sorry, but historians are … *very boring*.'

At Japan's elite Hitotsubashi University, where he studied economics, Mino was well aware that this competitive journey was supposed to lead towards his becoming a wealthy businessman. Following his acceptance into the elite stream of the Japanese school system, his parents had high hopes. Yet Minoru, apparently perversely, yearned to live with an Australian Indigenous people. His 1996 Master of Economics research was called 'Aboriginal economy and cattle labour: economic history of the Gurindji people' – surely a bizarre choice at the renowned business-oriented campus of Hitotsubashi. It was also an extremely challenging path to follow. In the days before digital books and articles, little relevant literature on Aboriginal history was available in Tokyo or other Japanese libraries. But nothing could stop him. He made friends with Australian Embassy staff, who were so captivated by his passion for knowledge that they ordered an extensive specialist research library of books and articles.

Minoru Hokari had obtained prestigious scholarships to study in Australia. In 1991, he won an overseas education grant from the Josui-kai Committee of Hitotsubashi University, then in 1994, a first-category scholarship from the Japan Scholarship Foundation, followed in 1996 by a Rotary Foundation multi-year ambassadorial scholarship, and a research fellowship for young scientists from the Japan Society for the Promotion of Science. While his parents worried about whether this path would lead to a secure future, they never stood in his way, but instead provided funds, computers and much-needed practical support to enable him to continue his work. Commencing his Doctorate in Philosophy at UNSW, he completed his thesis – 'Cross-culturalizing history: Journey to the Gurindji way of historical practice' – in January 2001 at the Australian National University's (ANU) Centre for Cross-cultural Research. The examiners, Dipesh Chakrabarty, Henry Reynolds and Greg Dening, considered the thesis outstanding. Mino's parents flew to Canberra to attend Minoru's graduation.

Certain celebratory Mino moments stand out in my mind. In the early 2000s, I was working at the newly opened National Museum of Australia. I had recently employed Mino to do some part-time research on Ishikawa Goemon for an exhibition on outlaws, and was still rehearsing aloof management behaviour in the public eye – in an open plan office. Minoru burst in, looking and sounding like a madman, shrieking and choking on his words in Japanese. The tall, rampaging young man dashing through the aisles of the staid workspace, waving his arms to the ceiling with excitement, was heading my way. There was no stopping him, and my workmates took on their long-practised pretending-not-to-look-up mode. Talking over-excitedly, his normally deep voice was raised several octaves: 'I have my results! I've passed! And you should read what they said!' He couldn't contain himself within normal speech or demeanour. Tenor cries vibrating across the workstations, he rushed towards me, encircling me in a joyous bear-hug. It was as though he could have embraced the whole world.

Mino's graduation ceremony was almost as memorable. His parents had travelled from Japan for this formal occasion and it was a great honour to meet them. Despite his nervous excitement, when it was Mino's turn to accept his degree from the Chancellor, he made the most of his moment on the stage, defying decorum by holding his degree up high in a victory gesture. One of those Mino moments of uninhibited style and panache.

When I visited Tokyo in 2001, Minoru was also in Japan doing some research, and we arranged to meet at the railway platform near the national museum. Goggle-eyed in disbelief, it was as if I had stepped out of the wrong movie: 'I can't believe you're here! In *my* country. At *my* train-station,' he said. As he shook his head trying to take in the apparition, I consciously tried to be cool and supervisor-like. Once a supervisor, always a supervisor. Minoru had the capacity to experience the fullness of the moment, and had a sure confidence in himself. Rather than feigning worldliness, he was uninhibited and self-confident enough to express his wonder.

Mino had a spirit of adventure and a creative intellect marked by a flexible, imaginative style. His modes of fieldwork transport amused the Gurinjdi community, as he first arrived across great distances on a small motorbike, and then, on a later visit, turned up in a bright orange four-wheel-drive Landcruiser he had dubbed 'Pumpkin'. After immersing himself in the Gurindji world, and much hard work, Mino made exciting breakthroughs in understanding their historical stories. Mino never ceased to be amazed that the Gurindji had enabled his far-off aspirations to come true; he viewed his learning experiences from Indigenous teachers as one of his life's great privileges, with great transformative potential.

As a talented young man, Mino's life travels drastically diverged from a journey that was ordained to lead towards the sought-after professions of economist or businessman. Mino patiently requested of Aboriginal communities that he be allowed to sit with them on desert ground. He listened in a respectful fashion to Gurindji teachers, learning their language, and collaborating with their elders as equals. Mino was willing to live for lengthy stints in very basic conditions alongside his new teachers – fellow historians, he called them – in remote areas of northern Australia. Although not seeking religious beliefs (indeed, he was even sceptical of them), Hokari was humbled and thrilled to be invited to watch Indigenous ceremonies and to be taught and mentored by their leading philosophers and historians.

One of Mino's main teachers was Jimmy Mangayarri, affectionately known as 'Old Jimmy', who passed away just before Mino's thesis was examined. Mino had relied upon him as his main teacher and the top historian of the community. I believe that before Mino went back to attend the funeral; I recall his tears when he told me that attending Jimmy's funeral must come ahead of his academic commitments. Jimmy taught Minoru a great deal of Indigenous knowledge and interpretive insight, but he also taught him how to learn about himself. This learning transformed not only Mino's thinking for his doctorate, but also his thinking about life and his own journey.

During Mino's final illness, a particularly aggressive form of lymphoma, he asked his mother to bring in a photo that he had taken of Jimmy Mangayarri, his 'number one' teacher, that old Gurindji man who seemed to know the full extent of Mino's mission long before Mino did. During those last weeks, Minoru spoke to Jimmy often.

The Gurindji people had been pleased to have this young Japanese man in their midst.

Minoru was quick to learn some of the Ngumpin language spoken at Daguragu. Jimmy explained that his country had 'called' Mino in order for him to take their stories and their messages back to Japan and Asia. Mino had replied that he hadn't heard anyone calling, to which Jimmy said that he needed to 'wake up his memory', his mind, and that he had to learn to listen. Mino cherished the way Aboriginal people told even disturbing histories in a humorous, entertaining style. He had learnt from them that history should be fun.

Minoru charmed almost everyone he met. His sense of enjoyment of life and his own opportunities made him popular in any company, whether he was among leading scholars, Indigenous university students or Gurindji elders. He was also intensely serious, passionate, sincere and conscientious. Open to new people, experiences and cultures, he was deeply committed to historical scholarship.

It was my great privilege to act as Minoru's supervisor throughout his thesis. Deborah Bird Rose, Professor Ann Curthoys and Dr John Docker also played key roles as formal and informal supervisors, and many other mentors also assisted.

Minoru's peers who joined him in a postgraduate writing workshop at the Centre for Cross-cultural Research remarked that he was 'cool' … possibly the 'coolest'. This workshop and its peer encouragement enabled Minoru to find his own powerful writing voice and to embrace his own 'difference' and unique, individual Japanese perspective. He had a certain charisma or magnetism that one cannot explain in words; there was a style about him, and a *joie de vivre* that was palpable. Greg Dening, who met Minoru during that course, described him as a 'handsome' and 'elegant young man'. Other students at International House at UNSW so relied on Mino for generous assistance (including in their Japanese studies) and for friendship that they named a scholarship in his honour. After Mino graduated, he enjoyed meeting Tessa Morris-Suzuki, whose work showed him new pathways to connect his Japaneseness with his Australian interests. Now he readily agreed to mentor Japanese students at ANU. He had many close friends in

Australia and Japan whom he greatly valued. In his last year, on a huge email network that his sister Yuki dexterously managed, and in deeply inspiring words, he warmly thanked all for their friendship.

Minoru had organised a diverse range of conferences and programs: in Japan these were the All Japan University Business Strategy Conference (1991) and the Annual Conference of the Research Institute of Universities, 'Towards multi-ethnic and multi-cultural Japan' (2002). At the Humanities Research Centre of ANU, in Canberra, it was 'Locations of spirituality: "Experiences" and "writings" of the sacred'. He worked as an interpreter and as a translator of several academic texts for Japanese and English audiences. The Daguragu Community Government Council asked him to act as their historical consultant. He was a research assistant for the Asahi Shimbun newspaper company, an editorial supervisor and a research consultant and interpreter for the National Museum of Japanese History, the Kampo Museum in Kyoto, the National Museum of Australia and for Dr Caroline Turner in Canberra. Research topics ranged from history, nature and curatorial research on Indigenous art to the pop-culture surrounding the Japanese outlaw Ishikawa Goemon, who was executed in a cauldron of boiling oil.

Minoru's writing was in strong demand in both Australia and Japan, and in the few years after he completed his doctorate, he published numerous academic articles in leading journals, in both English and Japanese. Themes ranged widely, from the Gurindji mode of historical practice, anti-minorities history, globalising Aboriginal reconciliation, and reading oral histories, to 'history happening in/between body and place'. His writing was clear and to the point, but it could also achieve a poetry, a gentleness and wisdom that was profoundly moving. He was an energetic paper-giver, and although he eschewed reading theory himself, his work was often praised for its breakthrough theoretical insights.

Minoru initially had a conception of Japan and Australia as being completely disconnected, but following the Gurindji's plan, he became a conduit between the two places, someone who enabled both voices to be heard across the seas. Determined to fulfill not only his own dreams, but also his ordained mission to take the Gurindji story back to Japan, Mino worked with incredible drive and determination until the very last days before his passing. He died at 32 years of age at St Vincent's Hospice in Fitzroy, Melbourne. The passing of Dr Minoru Hokari, one of the brightest and most innovative young scholars working in Australian Indigenous history research, was a tragic loss to the field.

Although Dr Hokari gained Australian residency, and published his innovative writing in both Australia and Japan, it is significant that his first book, *Radical Oral History: Historical Practice of Indigenous Australians*, was published by Ochanomizushobo in Japan, in 2004. It reached the Japanese-speaking people of the world first. A playful, whimsical opus of integrity, imagination and breath-taking audacity, it has had a significant interdisciplinary impact. Fortunately, due to the wisdom of Phillipa McGuinness, UNSW Press and its anonymous readers, Minoru's writing and creative thinking can finally become available to an English-speaking audience.

Minoru Hokari learnt how to communicate across multiple languages, across multiple cultures, and across many historical trajectories. His sense of fun and his humility will not be lost, for they are clear in his writing. He speaks to us. He appears. He challenges and changes things. He unsettles our usual framings, opening up new vistas.

In 2006, Minoru's sister and father came to ANU for the launch of a scholarship in his honour. They saw where Mino had written the last chapters of his PhD thesis. When I visited Japan a few years later, as part of a film we are making about Minoru, I saw many sides of Minoru that I had not imagined. Travelling to Niigata, where Minoru grew up, in 2008, I found out just how exceptional he was; from kindergarten age on, he had been admitted into the most elite schools available at every level. We met his teachers and his friends. They all had stories to tell. He was a rebel and he did things that young Japanese schoolchildren did not dare to do. He walked to the ocean alone, climbed its rock wall, sat on rocks and fished in the rough ocean near dangerous rocks. He challenged his teachers at school. Rather than being relegated to outsider status when he questioned the rules, he became the school captain and used his position to bring lasting change. Rather than ridiculing the rule-makers, he would question and debate with them. He did so respectfully, but created a mini-revolution. One of his teachers explained how Minoru had convinced him to change his view, and what a rare thing that was for a student to achieve. His classmates loved him, for although he was bright, he worked co-operatively, wanting to share intellectual exchanges rather than show superiority. He called for teachers to have greater respect for and trust in the students.

He had very clever friends, humble, ambitious friends, shy friends, lonely friends and popular friends. He knew homely girls and stylish girls. He had friends who were computer people, bankers, bohemians, academics, professors. One of his Hitotsubashi lecturers declared that he had 120 top students to teach every year, yet Minoru remained his best student ever. Minoru went way beyond what he was told to do; he had an exceptionally vigorous mind, posing the toughest questions and pushing beyond the limits.

Minoru established strong connections with and cared deeply about people. Nobody wanted to let him go. Girls loved him, guys loved him. But it went beyond this. It was as if everyone who knew him had also been changed by him. Their thinking had changed, and their world had been slightly realigned.

In his work with the Gurindji, something changed for Minoru too: rather than creating a conceptual revolution for others, he handed the baton to Old Jimmy, who led Minoru to his own personal revolution, his own personal transformation. In a model of collaborative Indigenous scholarship, Mino worked with Jimmy and the whole community respectfully, collaboratively, fruitfully and creatively. As well as spending time living together, on more than one occasion on desert journeys the water ran out, the heat made their limbs melt, and they almost died together.

# A CONVERSATION
# WITH MINORU HOKARI

Tessa Morris-Suzuki

Somewhere in the long-forgotten lower depths of my email inbox there is an email dated 5 November 2000 which begins with the words: 'Dear Tessa, Mino again, sorry for suddenly appearing in your life frequently these days ...' Mino Hokari, who was then completing his PhD on Aboriginal history at the Australian National University (ANU), had first 'appeared in my life' a few weeks earlier. He was helping a Japanese journalist who had come to Australia to write about the far right-wing One Nation Party. He was also eager to discuss his own research. At first I felt a little hesitant, doubting whether I would be able to give him any useful advice on his topic.

Very quickly, though, I was won over by the ebullient prose of Mino's emails. Ten days later he emailed to say that he had secured a meeting with a leading member of the One Nation Party. 'Gonna be exciting!' he wrote. And when I met him, I quickly found that we had very many things to talk about. Mino, I realised, had a passionate and wide-ranging interest in problems of historical understanding. I might not be able to provide much advice on his research, but I could certainly learn a great deal from long and enjoyable conversations about our common interests, and from reading his work.

His research is about Australian Aboriginal history. However, as Mino himself repeatedly stressed, it is not an attempt to explain 'how

Aboriginal Australians understand history'. There is, of course, no single Aboriginal understanding of history. This book is about a view of the past presented by certain Aboriginal people whose knowledge is widely respected by other members of their community.

It is also a book that brings its readers face to face with a whole range of questions whose implications go far beyond the boundaries of 'Aboriginal history' as it is normally understood: What is history? Who is a historian? How do we communicate knowledge? How do we experience the past? How do we 'do history'?

Let me here attempt to explain some of the things that I learnt through conversations (both face-to-face and through the written word) with Mino Hokari. These are, of course, the thoughts of one person writing at a particular point in time. Other readers will discover their own insights and ideas in this book. The text is not difficult to read, but the messages it conveys are deep and complex. I shall come back to this book many times, and I think that I shall find new meanings and gain new understandings on each reading.

The years when Mino Hokari was conducting his doctoral research, from 1996 to 2001, were momentous times in Australian Aboriginal history. In 1993, the High Court of Australia had recognised the traditional ownership rights of Indigenous Australians. Until then, Australian courts had refused to acknowledge the ancient and enduring Indigenous connection to the land as a basis for legally valid ownership. But the 1993 ruling led to the passing in the same year of a new Native Title Act, making it possible for some Aboriginal communities to reclaim formal ownership of their land.

Even though the process for claiming native title was complex and surrounded by restrictive conditions – and even though the Howard government in 1998 made the conditions more restrictive than ever

– the High Court's formal recognition of Native Title was nonetheless a milestone. From 1995 to 1997 Australian society also began to confront another long-neglected legacy of colonialism: the issue of the stolen generations, the generations of Aboriginal children removed from their families as part of the state policy of assimilation. The final report of an official inquiry into these stolen generations, published in 1997, was a searing indictment of government policy, and demanded an official apology and compensation for the victims.

The Howard government made only minimal responses, and refused to apologise to the stolen generations. However, the report sparked widespread public debate throughout Australia, and created greater public awareness of the long history of injustices against the Aboriginal population. In 2000, hundreds of thousands of people took part in demonstrations supporting a new process of reconciliation between Indigenous and non-Indigenous Australians. At the same time, though, a conservative backlash was gathering strength. From the late 1990s onwards, a number of right-wing historians (actively encouraged by Prime Minister Howard) attacked what they called the 'black armband' view of history, which emphasised the suffering and destruction caused by colonisation. In particular, former Marxist sociologist turned revisionist historian Keith Windschuttle produced a series of writings arguing that stories about massacres of Aborigines were vastly exaggerated, and that Indigenous people had benefited rather than suffered from the coming of 'civilisation'.[1]

It was against this background that Mino, and a growing number of other scholars, turned their attention to Aboriginal oral history, often using it as a source to verify or disprove claims about massacres and colonial acts of violence. For some researchers, the key problem was the place of oral history in establishing the facts of the Aboriginal confrontation with colonialism, including massacres and other forms of colonial violence. In exploring this issue, a key question was how to distinguish the elements of 'myth' from the elements of 'history', thus turning oral accounts into 'usable' historical source material.

Mino Hokari's approach to Aboriginal history was startlingly different. He listened to Aboriginal oral history, but did so in an unfamiliar way. This approach is uncomfortable for someone like me, who likes to imagine that they have freed themselves from the colonial prejudices which once dominated the study of indigenous societies.

There is a Gurindji Aboriginal elder (says Mino Hokari) who insists that the Wave Hill flood of 1924 was caused by a man called Tinker giving rainstones to the *kurraj* (rainbow snake). Do you believe him? Can you accept this story as part of your understanding of modern Australian history?

My immediate answer, of course, is 'no'. I respect the elder's right to his own beliefs. I do not laugh at him or dismiss him as stupid. But I do not believe him in the same way that I would believe an agronomist who told me that the flood was caused by bad land-management practices, or a meteorologist who told me that it was caused by unusual weather patterns.

But then, says Mino Hokari (not aggressively, but with feeling, for he himself is struggling with the same problems), you are not being honest with yourself. You are still really treating the Gurindji elder's story as a myth. You are still claiming that you know how to determine 'truth', and can therefore say that his knowledge is false.

Confronted by this dilemma, my response is to pose a whole set of questions of my own. If I accept 'irrational' Aboriginal accounts of the powers of the rainbow snake as literally true, how can I argue with Christian fundamentalists who tell me that God really made the world in seven days? If I agree that Gurindji elders have their own interpretation of their own history, and that this interpretation is as 'true' as anyone else's, how can I disagree with Japanese revisionists who deny events like the Nanking Massacre, and then claim the right to their 'uniquely Japanese' interpretation of Japanese history?

These questions do not have simple answers. And, to be honest, I must admit that I still have not come to believe that the 1924 flood at Wave Hill station was really caused by rainstones or the rainbow snake. But over the years I have gradually come to see the profound importance of continuously asking the uncomfortable question, '*Why not?*'

*

When I moved from England to Australia in 1981, I discovered two things which I had never experienced before: silence and darkness.

Going into the Australian bush, away from the towns and cities, I was overwhelmed by the experience of a place where you could hear no human sounds at all – no cars, no aeroplanes, no distant buzz of the city. Just the wind and the occasional cry of birds. And at night, when darkness falls, that darkness is total; there is only the light of stars hanging in the deep, deep black of endless space. This is the world as it was experienced by most human beings for the past hundreds of thousands of years.

But these are experiences which most modern urbanised communities have lost. Not only have we lost them; we have forgotten the fact that we have lost them. It is only when, for a moment, we visit places where we can recapture this experience of the world that we also recognise the experience of loss. Returning to our noisy, endlessly neon-lit world, we suddenly begin to see it with new eyes.

Mino's approach to history, it must be emphasised, does not present a romantic or nostalgic image of Aboriginal society. He does not offer 'Indigenous wisdom' as a panacea for the problems of the contemporary world. It would be absurd to imagine that people from completely different social backgrounds could ever fully enter the world of the Gurindji historians whose words are recorded by Mino Hokari.

Instead, he suggests something different and more profound. The intellectual and institutional frameworks of modern scholarship have produced what may be called 'monocultures of the mind'.[2] In the effort to create all-encompassing, universal narratives of truth, modern thought has also created a kind of mental uniformity, by which, all over the world, certain canonical texts, and certain ways of thinking and of producing truth, have been authorised as the only basis of valid 'knowledge'. All aspects of knowledge and experience which fail to fit into this modern edifice of truth are consigned to the realms of 'myth', 'superstition' or 'ignorance'.

In recent decades, of course, postmodernism and post-colonial thought have criticised this tradition. But the postmodern and post-colonial critiques have their own limitations. They have emerged and flourish within the same system of knowledge production as modern thought: in universities, academic conferences, refereed scholarly journals, etc. For that very reason, they tend to replicate some of the problems of the modern knowledge system even as they criticise it. They too have found it difficult to take seriously the challenges offered by types of knowledge created in quite different ways, in places far removed from the lecture theatre and the university library.

Mino Hokari's work demands above all that we – that is, people who have grown up within the 'monoculture' of the modern academic tradition – should take the Aboriginal history of the Gurindji elders seriously. This does not mean that we must come to believe all the things that Jimmy Mangayarri, Mick Rangiari, Billy Bunter and others believe. But it does mean that we must listen carefully to what they have to say.

\*

The most important thing I learnt from encountering Gurindji elders through Mino Hokari's writings is the importance of 'listening' or 'paying attention'. Just as modern societies have lost the experience of silence and darkness, so too they have lost the capacity for listening. And just as the loss of silence and darkness can only be recognised when we unexpectedly rediscover them in places like the Australian bush, so it was the encounter with the Gurindji elders through the pages of Mino Hokari's work that made me conscious of the absence of 'listening' and 'attention' in the world in which I live.

We tend to assume that 'listening' is easy, passive, something that comes naturally. The experience of the Gurindji elders, however, suggests that this is a complete misunderstanding. To listen, to pay attention, requires much time, skill and preparation. If you doubt this, try an experiment: try spending just one whole morning sitting still, or walking quietly around, listening and paying attention to the world around you. I suspect that you, like me, will find this virtually impossible.

Listening to the Gurindji elders' accounts of history also requires time, skill and preparation. For listening is not a purely receptive practice, in which we simply open our ears to all the sounds around us. As we listen, we must classify and make sense of sounds ...

*That was a bird. That is the sound of a car starting. That is the voice of my next-door neighbour.*

But the skill of listening also requires sensitivity to new and unexpected sounds, to sounds which do not fit any of our existing categories. Unexpected sounds should not merely be filtered out. And if they are persistent enough, they must lead us to rethink our knowledge of the world ...

*What was that? There is something out there that I have never heard or seen before.*

Taking Gurindji history seriously means hearing its unfamiliarity, and allowing that unfamiliarity to reshape our vision of what is possible in the world. When rainbow serpents and other unexpected presences are no longer safely confined to the category of myth, but are recognised as actors in a very unfamiliar sort of history, we can begin to get a glimpse of ways of experiencing the past which we have never imagined before.

The wonderful achievement of Mino Hokari's work is that it creates a space for dialogue between utterly different worlds of historical understanding, and in doing so opens windows on such unfamiliar experiences. In his work we encounter forms of history which involve bodily experience – history which can only be 'felt' in certain places. We discover ethics embedded in the landscape, so that 'goodness' is inseparable from the way we move over the surface of the earth. We learn about a history in which the earth itself, the rocks, plants, animals and spirits as well as people, are participants.

Listening to unfamiliar ideas is a deeply disconcerting experience. What matters is that we should neither reject these 'dangerous' ways of understanding history out of hand nor (and this is equally important, I think) instantly accept them as exotic new revelations of truth. These concepts of history are not new material to be hastily packaged into neat academic gift-boxes which will enjoy a passing popularity at next year's international conferences; nor are they new-age remedies for a troubled society, to enjoy a brief vogue in the pages of weekly magazines.

Rather, Mino Hokari invites us to enter into a long, slow conversation with unfamiliar experiences – a conversation to which we bring our entire memory and experience of life, thus deepening our own pursuit of historical truthfulness.

He invites us to embark on the difficult and demanding task of re-learning the skill of listening, so that little by little we may become more deeply engaged in ongoing conversations 'across the gap'.

\*

In the middle of 2003 Mino was suddenly and unexpectedly stricken with a life-threatening illness. In his approach to illness, as in his approach to history, Mino drew on resources which came from his encounters with Jimmy Mangayarri and the other elders of the Gurindji country. He listened to his own body, and to its relationship with the world around. And he faced pain and illness with audacity, refusing to be overawed by their demands on his life, refusing to grow solemn in their imperious presence.

He continued writing up to the moment of his death, working to complete a version of his research which was published in Japanese in 2004. It has proved profoundly influential. In a country where the discipline of history has traditionally focused overwhelmingly on the use of documentary archives, and where oral history was for long relatively marginalised, Mino's work has helped to inspire a whole new generation of researchers to set out on the path of exploring the riches of oral history.

How often have I wished that Mino was still here to read and enjoy and debate their work. And how much did I wish he were here in February 2008, when the newly elected Rudd government finally issued its statement of apology to the stolen generations. On the late afternoon of that day I walked across the lawns outside Parliament House, where the celebrations were quietly subsiding. Small groups of people of all ages were sitting around in the shade of awnings set up on the lawn, laughing, talking. Under one awning, a woman and a small child were intent on adding pieces of coloured tile to large mosaic. As I stopped to admire the work, the woman said, 'Come on, love. Give us a hand.' So

I carefully picked out the brightest and squarest blue chips of tile from their plastic bag and added them to the design. The picture they were making was of a flag emblazoned with one word: 'Sovereignty'. It was slow work adding the pieces, and they still had a very long way to go before the picture would be complete.

I thought then about how Mino would have reacted to the apology – with delight, but also with sharp and amused perceptiveness, appreciating the emotion but not being swept away by the rhetoric; recognising the significance of the step forward, but seeing it too (I think) as a small chip in a vast and yet incomplete mosaic of history.

Mino Hokari was always conscious of the difficulty of conveying the experience of conversation and companionship with the Gurindji elders in a written text. Written words can never convey the presence of the person, the sound of that particular voice, the expression of that face. Yet written words have their own magic. They endure through space and time, reaching those whom we will never meet, and whose lives we can never even imagine. To decode the marks on the page, you, the reader, must 'awaken' your own knowledge, memory and imagination, and reach out across the gap in time and space. The gap cannot be closed. But by speaking and listening across the gap, we take part in the extraordinary experience of doing history.

So find a quiet place to sit down. Be still. Pay attention.

It is time for you to enter into conversation with the Gurindji elders, with Mino Hokari and with others: a conversation which begins, but does not end, in the pages of this book.

## NOTES

1  Keith Windschuttle, *The Fabrication of Aboriginal History, Vol. I: Van Diemen's Land 1803–1847*, Sydney: Macleay Press, 2002; see also Robert Manne, *Whitewash: On Keith Windschuttle's Fabrication of Aboriginal History*, Melbourne: Black Inc., 2003.
2  I borrow this phrase from Indian scholar and activist Vandana Shiva. See Vandana Shiva, *Monocultures of the Mind: Perspectives on Biodiversity and Biotechnology*, London: Zed Books, 1993.

# BEING CONNECTED WITH MINORU

Yuki Hokari

It was July 2003. I received a call from my father in Japan: 'Minoru has been hospitalised in the middle of the desert. His doctor needs to speak to you.' ... What? ... I did not know what to think. I did not know what would happen to my brother, my parents and myself. It took quite a while for us to find out that he had lymphoma. It was cancer.

He declined my offer to fly from the US to Australia right away, even as the doctors and nurses wondered why no family had shown up. I understood that he needed space to think through what was happening to him. We talked on the phone every day. While we were waiting for a diagnosis, he said, 'Yuki, even if I had to die right now, I'd have no regrets. I spent an amazing 10 years with the Gurindji people.'

I went to see him soon after he was moved by flying ambulance from Alice Springs to Adelaide for treatment. He asked me to organise the move to Melbourne, where he had more friends who could help him. During the following months I made three trips to Australia, leaving my 2-year-old son at home. I never thought that Minoru was going to die.

During his last 10 months, he communicated with all of his friends, a few hundred people, through emails. Sometimes when he was not feeling well enough to write I wrote to them on both his and my behalf; he had so much more to think about regarding his situation as the days passed. Being away from my dearest brother – in the US, the farthest country from Australia – I felt very close to his friends who could not come to see him. I could not stop writing to them.

Although I was a match for Minoru as a bone marrow donor, his doctor gave up on treating him. He was in the final stages of cancer. I stayed for one month with my son in Melbourne after Minoru moved to a hospice. His doctor told us that he had a few months to live, but none of us believed it. We believed in a miracle. He could not die. No way. That wasn't possible. Minoru started working on the Japanese manuscript of his book.

*

My brother and I had always been very close. People told my mother that it was as if he had two mothers. He followed me everywhere. He listened to me and always followed my instructions. I protected him. I was always there for him. We rarely fought. The only fight I remember was when I made fun of his 'big nose' and of his Scrooge-like money-saving habit.

When Minoru was a high school student, a teacher who had taught me before him said to me, 'Yuki, you were an excellent student, but your brother is even better.' I was not jealous at all. I could not stop smiling. I was so proud of my little brother.

We both loved reading books, especially historical novels. Ryoma Sakamoto was our all-time favourite historical figure. Ryoma, who lived in an era when Japan was forced to open itself up by the American navy, after having shut its doors to the rest of the world for centuries, was probably the first Japanese in history to look at Japan from the outside while living there. He convinced two powerful feudal states, Satsuma and Choshu, to work together to bring down the Shogunate system. However, he did not stay in the newly established government

– he wanted to go overseas to see a different world. But he was assassinated, at the age of 32.

Minoru often said he wanted to live like Ryoma. He was very sensitive and accepting, yet very critical of what went on around him and in the world. He could talk about anything – politics, economics, social issues, food, music, movies and other arts … anything. His interest in and curiosity about the world was endless.

＊

It was 10 May 2004, in the middle of the night. I was in Melbourne with my son, Kyle. We were in bed when the phone rang. It was my mother: 'Yuki, please come right away. There is something wrong with Minoru.' I woke up Kyle, dressed him and impatiently waited for a cab, as they had told me not to walk to the hospice. I got out of the car and ran to Minoru's room, carrying my son in my arms. Outside the room, someone told me he had just passed away. I don't remember what I did with Kyle. I threw myself onto my brother, whose eyes were closed, and screamed his name.

My parents told me that I had come into the room just as he stopped breathing, and everyone assured me that he had heard my scream and had known I was there before he left this world. I was also told that he had shouted my name twice before he lost consciousness.

That same day, I sent his friends the terrible news, along with Minoru's last message (written in Japanese):

> Although I know this is selfishness on my part, I cannot begin
> to tell you how much comfort I take in feeling connected with
> all of you, my dear friends. So please stay connected with
> me, whether by remembering me in your prayers, by simply
> thinking of me, or by mentioning me in conversation – it
> doesn't matter how. Please do not abandon me to my isolation.

Who I am now exists in being connected to you, and that connection is what has supported me all these years and is supporting me now.

After he passed away, I finally had a chance to read his PhD dissertation, the basis of this book. I could picture him smiling while writing, listening to his favourite music. I came to believe that what he had said to me was true: 'Yuki, I have no regrets. I've had a fulfilling life.'

For the six years since his passing I have devoted myself to keeping his connection to the world expanding. Here is a brief chronology of events and developments:

I created a memorial website, 'Being Connected with HOKARI MINORU' (www.hokariminoru.org), which tells the world not only of his academic life, but also of all 32 years of his life, from his childhood in Niigata, our home town, to his university days in Tokyo, to his work in Australia. Many people searching for Minoru Hokari have come to this website and found him there.

On 19 June 2004, about 100 of his Japanese friends and teachers met at Hitotsubashi University in Tokyo for 'Talking with Minoru Hokari', a gathering to share our precious memories of Minoru. In July 2004, his Australian friends gathered at ANU to do the same.

The two universities that he attended in Australia, the University of New South Wales and the Australian National University, founded the Minoru Hokari Memorial Scholarship Funds. These scholarships have been providing young international students and scholars with support to achieve their academic goals and dreams. A fundraising entity in Japan has raised almost 2 million yen (US$20,000) as of 10 May 2010, not including donations from the family.

In November 2004, a few months after his passing, Minoru's Japanese book, *Radical Oral History: Historical Practice of Indigenous*

*Australians*, was published. He had finished the manuscript a few days before his passing. He had hoped to sell at least 5000 copies – so far 4000 copies have been sold. Many favourable reviews have been written from the perspectives of history, anthropology, sociology, philosophy and even feminism. A roundtable discussion entitled 'Exploration of Historical Practice: The Work of Minoru Hokari' was held on 23 April 2006 at Keio University. The book has been used as a textbook at many universities, and it has established its status as a 'long-selling' book at major bookstores.

On 5 April 2005, my daughter was born. We gave her the middle name 'Minori', which is a female version of Minoru.

In mid-2005, Minoru's estate donated his recorded tapes of Gurindji oral history to the Australian Institute of Aboriginal and Torres Strait Islander Studies (AIATSIS), as my mother remembered that Minoru had planned to donate them, eventually, to a museum.

In late 2005, the publisher of Minoru's two translations, *Nourishing Terrain* (Deborah Bird Rose) and *White Nation* (Ghassan Hage), planned to dispose of the remaindered copies. Minoru's estate purchased as many copies as possible, and I called for help to purchase them from the estate. To date, more than 100 people have purchased books and proposed that local libraries do the same. As a result, more than 300 copies of the books have survived. The proceeds have been donated to Minoru's memorial scholarship fund at ANU.

I asked Kyoko Uchida, a friend and translator, to translate into English the columns that Minoru had written about the Gurindji for *Niigata Nippo*, our home town newspaper; Professor Tessa Morris-Suzuki helped me to publish them in an academic journal, *Conversations* (Summer 2006), under the title 'The Living Earth: The World of the Aborigines'.

An Australian production company, Ronin Films, and Professor Ann McGrath started working on a documentary about Minoru. They mined every opportunity to track Minoru's life, and in May 2008 I arranged for the filming of interviews with his friends in Japan. They are still working toward the film's completion.

On 5 July 2006, the CD 'Locations of Spirituality' was launched in conjunction with ANU's inaugural scholarship award ceremony. The CD includes a collection of papers submitted to the conference 'Location of Spirituality', which Minoru had organised with Dr Linda Bennett in 2002.

On 29 April 2010, a photography exhibition entitled 'The Call of the Living Earth: Photographs of Australian Aborigines by Minoru Hokari' opened at the Hokkaido Museum of Northern Peoples in Abashiri, Japan. Although it was a long process to find and reach the right contact person and receive permission from the Gurindji people to show the photographs, I somehow knew it would happen; we were prepared to postpone the opening until we could obtain permission. Special thanks to Sean Heffernan and Roslyn Frith, to whom Minoru's fax requesting permission for his last stay at Daguragu, which did not happen due to his illness, led me! This was such a rare exhibition for the museum. It was not about Northern Peoples; instead, it introduced the Gurindji people's story and Minoru's analysis (as excerpted from the Japanese edition of his book) along with his photographs. The idea for the exhibition came from a friend and curator at the museum, Irumi Sasakura. She believes that 'just as Hokari-san had been "called by the Country", I too was "called" by some place to put on this exhibition'.

For all these years, I have continued to write to his friends, his readers and donors on the anniversary of his passing in May, on his birthday in July and at Christmas time every year. I always have something new to share. None of the above events could have been organised without the help of numerous friends, both his and mine. I wanted as many friends as possible to be involved in these processes because it is all about being connected with Minoru. However, I have to mention two people who have always been a great help and support to me: Ann McGrath and Tessa Morris-Suzuki. Without their love, help and support, I could not have done any of the above, especially from the US.

I shall continue in my work for and dedication to Minoru's cause to make sure that he keeps meeting new people and telling the Gurindji people's story.

We Japanese often wonder how Ryoma Sakamoto would have lived and what he would have brought to Japan if he had not been killed. But we all know what Ryoma achieved in his short life. Modern Japan would not exist without his life. We always say how much more Minoru would have done if he had lived longer. I hope this book will have an impact on the world. History will tell. Following Professor Greg Dening's advice, Minoru Hokari wrote his PhD dissertation to change the world, not simply to present it to the three thesis examiners.

Mino, my dearest brother, I've done it. I've finally published your book. I am sure you knew I would do it for you. You had full faith in me and I will never let you down. Please go ahead and tell Old Jimmy that the Gurindji people's history and teachings will be heard.

Now, what do you want me to do next?

# INTRODUCTION TO
# THE JAPANESE EDITION

## translated by Kyoko Uchida

### DID PRESIDENT KENNEDY MEET ABORIGINAL PEOPLE?
### – SPEAKING FROM THE IMAGINARY BOOK LAUNCH[1]

## 1 Oral history and fieldwork

Hello, nice to meet you. My name is Minoru Hokari. Thank you very much for picking up this book. If you've paid for it, thank you very, *very* much. This is the first book I've authored (not counting translations), so naturally I'm pretty nervous, but in any case, I'm thrilled that my book has caught your eye. I hope you'll enjoy it, and I look forward to getting acquainted.

I recently received my doctorate from a university in Australia, where for my doctoral thesis I studied Indigenous Australian history through the methodology of oral history. With the publication of Paul Thompson's *The Voice of the Past: Oral History* in Japanese translation,[2] currents in oral history research in the United Kingdom and the United States are being introduced to Japanese audiences. But in the case of Australia, especially since the Indigenous peoples have not kept written accounts, oral history research has long been well established as a matter of necessity. That said, with regard to the methodologies used, I'm not entirely satisfied with the research conditions in Australia (and probably elsewhere as well), and I'd like to start by talking about that. I want to clarify something first, though, because this becomes important later on: I am a historian. People often insist that I'm an anthropologist, and it's true that my methodology has been greatly influenced by anthropology. Yet I myself conduct my research as a historical discipline. Sometimes I half-jokingly, half-seriously refer to myself as a 'strategic historian'. It should become clear as we go along what I mean by that.

By listening to the oral histories of these Aboriginal peoples, we come to realise that academic historians are not the only ones producing and maintaining 'history' – in fact, each of us is engaged in historical practice in our day-to-day life. My goal in this book, more or less, is to highlight the need to be attentive to our own historical practice and to value it. In this chapter, I'd like to map out the book's overall trajectory by summarising what I've been thinking about, over the course of my doctoral research, about the methodology of oral history.

In my view, there are roughly three methodologies in oral history research. One is for scholars to access existing archives of tapes and documents, that is, oral accounts – and I think it's wonderful that there's talk about creating an oral history archive in Japan – and to conduct research using these as documentary material. Anthropologists who do not conduct fieldwork are ridiculed as 'armchair anthropologists', so perhaps we can call these oral historians who do not themselves conduct interviews 'armchair oral historians'. That said, accessing past oral accounts that can no longer be obtained is undoubtedly one important method of researching oral history.

The second methodology of oral history research, which is the most popular in Australia and also commonly used worldwide, is the interview method. The historian personally meets with people, records their oral histories by taking notes or taping or videotaping the interview, and then analyses that material on his/her own. This most 'orthodox' method is discussed in detail in *The Voice of the Past: Oral History*, and I have a feeling that plenty of books about this methodology of oral history research will be coming out, so I won't take it up in this book.[3]

Now, the method that I have chosen is neither of the above, but a third alternative. What kind of method is it? I myself rarely conduct interviews. It's not exactly that I never interview people; at times I do turn on the tape recorder. But I avoid setting a specific time to ask people to answer a set of prepared questions within a set amount of time. Instead, I ask permission to stay in their communities and, in living among them, I share in their historical practice. In other words, I strive to 'do history' along with them. Of course, during that process I occasionally say, 'Hey, could you elaborate a little on that for me?' and turn on the tape recorder. I have not, however, made appointments to meet in some 'interviewing room' – that is to say, an artificially created time-space – to ask people to speak of the past. Instead, I've focused on experiencing history according to the historical practice that they engage in as part of their everyday lives. I call this the fieldwork method.

In practical terms, I was probably conducting the same kind of fieldwork as that of an anthropologist: entering a community with permission, learning the language, and living among the people. Essentially it was 'participatory observation', although I'm not fond of that term. (Personally, I don't understand how you can both participate and observe at the same time. When I lived in that community, I was unable to participate when I was observing, and unable to observe when I was participating. Just as we can't see both figures in a 'double-image' picture simultaneously, I suspect that it's impossible to participate in and observe a practice simultaneously. Furthermore, it troubles me that the term 'participatory observation' doesn't take into account at all the local people's perspective: namely, that they too are observing and testing you.) Specifically, between 1997 and 2002, I spent a total of about a year in an Aboriginal community called Daguragu (and Kalkaringi) – almost two years altogether if I include the time I spent roaming around northern and central Australia – researching oral history strictly from a historian's perspective, while undertaking the same kind of fieldwork as that of an anthropologist.

## 2 The Gurindji country

I should explain a little about the Gurindji people and the Daguragu community. The community of Daguragu is located in the northwestern part of the Northern Territory, within the Gurindji country. Gurindji is one of the approximately 600 different language groups among Australia's Indigenous peoples. Each language group has its own 'country' – a defined area of land to which they are economically, socially and spiritually connected. In the Gurindji country, there are two communities, Kalkaringi and Daguragu, situated only about 10km apart, and the residents frequently go back and forth between the two communities. These two communities are currently self-governed by the Daguragu Community Government Council. Most of the residents are Gurindji. Naturally, many people from surrounding areas who are related to the Gurindji by marriage also live there, but all the residents of Daguragu (and Kalkaringi) know they live in the Gurindji country, so even those who are not of the Gurindji people, strictly speaking, are generally referred to as Gurindji.

The Gurindji country lies in the upper reaches of the Victoria River. To the south of the Gurindji country lives a desert people called the Warlpiri. At the mouth of the Victoria River lives a coastal people. The Gurindji are a river people. The Gurindji country is neither as mountainous as the middle and lower reaches of the Victoria River to the north, nor as flat as the desert region to the south. Low hills rise here and there, and evergreen trees grow lushly along the riverbed; otherwise, the landscape consists mainly of vast grassland plains. The climate is divided into a wet season and a dry season. By the calendar, the wet season lasts approximately from October through March, the dry season from April to September. But there are significant variations from year to year, and calendars aren't used much in Daguragu, so the residents' sense of seasons may be closer to something like: 'When it starts raining, it's the wet season; when the earth begins to dry out, it's the dry season.' During the wet season, there is heavy rainfall, the rivers overflow, and the roads are flooded and cut off in many places. In 2001, the Daguragu community was almost inundated, and all the residents evacuated to the town of Katherine, about 450km away. During the dry season, by contrast, the tributaries of the Victoria River dry up, cutting off the flow and creating billabongs. The country – green and lush as far as the eye can see during the wet season – turns brown as the vegetation fades and dies over the dry season, until the only greenery is the trees along the river.

Here, briefly, is what's known about the Gurindji society that can be confirmed by 'the published literature'. Like all other Aboriginal societies, the Gurindji had been a nomadic, hunting-and-gathering people. It is thought that the first human habitation on the Australian continent dates back 40,000 to 50,000 years, but we have no way of knowing when people began to live along the Victoria River and what their relationship to the Gurindji people of today is. In any case, the so-called modern history of the Gurindji country – that is, colonisation – began in the second half of the 19th century. As you know, in the second half of the 18th century, the Australian continent was colonised by the British. The Gurindji country and the surrounding areas in northern Australia were settled largely as cattle ranches. Starting from Queensland in the northeast and from South Australia, land cultivation for cattle grazing expanded rapidly. The first cattle station in the Gurindji country was established in the 1880s. Named the Wave Hill station, it was bought at the beginning of the 20th century by British agribusiness giant Vesteys, and quickly grew to 25,000 square kilometres of grazing land carrying 50,000 head of cattle by the 1930s. At first, the white cattle station owners killed many Aborigines and ran others off the land; later they lured them with beef, flour and tea to the stations and exploited them as a source of cheap labour. Thus the Gurindji and many other Indigenous Australian communities whose countries are in northern Australia came to live at the cattle stations, working as stockworkers under poor labour conditions.[4]

The Gurindji are quite well known in Australia for the Wave Hill walk-off in 1966, when they left the cattle station in a pastoral strike against poor working conditions and established their own community at Daguragu, about 20km away. They carried out a nationwide campaign for their 'land rights', demanding that the station owner return their traditional land. Supported by a journalist and labour unions sympathetic to their plight, the Gurindji people's movement garnered national attention. Finally, in 1975, the rights to land encompassing Daguragu and surrounding areas were handed over to the Gurindji elders in a grand ceremony, attended by then-Prime Minister Gough Whitlam, to commemorate the return of their traditional land. This successful land claim is widely recognised as an enormous achievement in the Indigenous civil and land rights movement, which continues to this day.[5] Therefore the Daguragu community was established in a somewhat different context from other Aboriginal communities; furthermore, the Gurindji people are very proud of this aspect of their history. It would be a good idea to keep this in mind as you read on.

## 3 Who is a historian?

One question that I thought deeply about throughout my stays in the Gurindji country is: just who is a historian? If, instead of only us academic historians collecting the stories of informants, we were to consider the informants themselves to be historians, what kind of historical practice might they be engaged in? I am one example of a historian, but they, too, are historians. By shifting our thinking this way, how might we see history differently? That is, more or less, our starting point.

What happens is that it calls into question what history itself is. The stories the Indigenous Australians tell as historians involve one bizarre episode after another, and the researcher ends up in an apparently impossible position. Shall I give a quick example? First of all, before we can discuss history, we must listen to the earth. The earth will teach you many things. So the elders say, but I can't hear anything. Yet they are listening to the voice of the earth. And, according to what they hear from the earth, they relate that 'The white man died at that cattle station because he violated the law and the country punished him.' How should we understand this Aboriginal story? Would it be possible to receive this history not by saying, 'Oh, in the Aboriginal worldview, that's how they interpret that incident of the white man's death at the station', but as the words of historians – that is, *as a historical analysis by a historian*, just as we would the studies of E.H. Carr or Hisao Otsuka? Let's say we were to make an effort to listen in such a way.

What happens then? Inevitably, we would have to accept 'the voice of the earth' as a historical agent. In the fields of anthropology and historical anthropology, it seems that such supernatural narratives and accounts have been analysed as some kind of metaphor. Wouldn't you agree? Various theories about metaphors have developed in recent decades to the point that these days, claims such as 'All is metaphor' no longer seem outlandish. That said, the argument that I'd like to develop in this book is, in a sense, the flip side (but not the opposite!) of such theories of metaphor. In other words, at the risk of being misunderstood, I propose the thesis (and question): (What if) there were no such thing as metaphor? When the Aboriginal people's historical analysis is that the earth punished the white man, what if this 'earth' were not a metaphor for something to explain the historical incident in which the white man died at the cattle station, but rather a historical agent of a historical fact? Stated even more bluntly: *What if we were to understand that the earth did punish that white man, in truth?* Would it be possible for me, an academic historian, to make such a statement? Could non-human beings become agents of history?

Shall we frame this question as an issue of the historian's 'speaking position'? Let's imagine that Gurindji elders were invited to an academic conference on history or anthropology and there told the story of how 'the earth punished the white man'. The entire audience would probably 'accept' this claim with hearty applause. No one is troubled when an Indigenous Australian speaking from the position of Aboriginal culture talks about the voice of the earth. Why? Because academics these days are able to practise cultural relativism and be respectful of other cultures. But what would happen if I, reporting on my research at a conference from my speaking position as a research fellow of the Japan Society for the Promotion of Science, were to state, 'The white man died at the cattle station because the earth punished him'? I think everyone would be rather vexed. Could I blame them for thinking I'd lost my mind? They might say, 'That is the Aboriginal people's belief; you don't mean that you yourself believe in it?' or at best, 'That may be their truth, but it can never be our truth.' Personally, I would hope that they'd go so far as to say, 'How dare you try to appropriate the Indigenous Australians' belief system as well!' That history and truthfulness become plural and multi-dimensional or are made 'other' according to the speaking position is not problematic. The problem is this: why, when placed in the speaking position of an academic researcher (academic historian), does it suddenly become unacceptable for us to present a non-human historical agent?

Perhaps 'listening to the voice of the earth' sounds alluringly mythical and mysterious enough for you to empathise. The problem is that the Gurindji elders I learned from also say that the late US President Kennedy visited the Gurindji country. Of course I know for a fact that the president never visited. But the Gurindji have their own historical context. The story goes that before the start of the 1966 Wave Hill walk-off that I briefly described, President Kennedy came to visit the Wave Hill station. He came to the Aboriginal people and asked, 'Why are you being treated so badly by the whites?' The elders explained, 'This and this happened, and the colonists from England have been treating us terribly.' President Kennedy told them that he was the 'Big American Boss' and he would start a war against England and support the Gurindji people in their struggle. And this is how the walk-off began, backed by a powerful ally, the Americans.

Now, as in the case of the voice of the earth, the question arises whether an academic researcher can accept this oral history enthusiastically narrated by the Aboriginal elders at face value in the context of academic historical disciplines. Any researcher working in the field of social humanities has been told over and over again of the plurality of history, the multiplicity of voices, the instability of truth, the disintegration of the self, the overcoming of dichotomies. So, given these premises, how is a research fellow of the Japan Society for the Promotion of Science to engage with the Gurindji elders' historical narrative that 'President Kennedy visited the Gurindji country and met with the Aboriginal people'? As I said before, I reject the analysis that 'President Kennedy' is a metaphor for '...', because the Gurindji elders don't think of JFK as a metaphor at all. If we reduce him to a metaphor, it means that we haven't listened seriously to the Gurindji historians' historical analysis. It would mean, moreover, that history would continue to be centralised. This would be nothing other than the one-sided and violent appropriation of the Aboriginal belief system. Yet, at the same time, we historians know that JFK never visited the Gurindji country and that the US never fought a war against the British in the second half of the 20th century ... Are the Gurindji historians telling the 'wrong history' then? Is it possible that I, an upstart academic historian from Japan, 'know' more about Gurindji history and am 'right', whereas the Gurindji people themselves, who were born and raised in the area and who have been passing down their historical reality and experience through their oral tradition, 'do not know' and are 'wrong'? Are academic systems of knowledge really so unshakeably superior? Let's not rush to conclusions, but first repeat like a mantra, 'The plurality of history! The multiplicity of voices! The instability of truth!' before asking ourselves deliberately: *What if, just maybe, President Kennedy did meet the Gurindji elders?* If that doesn't work, try also repeating a few times, 'Hybridity! Ambivalence! Subalternity!' If there's still no effect, next try calling out, 'Cross-culturalising knowledge! The implosion of knowledge! The colonisation of knowledge!' ... Is it working yet? Even if it's impossible, under present circumstances, for the Aboriginal peoples' knowledge, experiences and beliefs to occupy academia's rigid, modern system of knowledge, isn't it possible at least to put a dent in it? Can we be absolutely certain that President Kennedy never met the Indigenous Australians?

Let me give you another example, just to be absolutely clear. Back when the Gurindji people were still working at cattle stations run by whites, torrential rains caused a flood. The old Wave Hill station and its cattle were washed away. This occurred in 1924, and I was able to read about the specific damage the flood caused to the station in newspaper articles from the time. The question is: why was the Wave Hill cattle station washed away? Obviously it was because there was a great flood, but why did it occur in that particular area in that particular year? Here is what happened: one of the Gurindji men had caused it. A great serpent called the rainbow snake (rainbow serpent) reigns over the waters, and apparently a Gurindji elder had asked it to bring heavy rains and wash away the cattle station. I analyse this incident in detail in Chapter 9, but here I'd like to bring up again the question of how we academic historians are to handle this history. The issue is: if the Indigenous Australians are historians – that is, if those who narrate this oral history are not simply informants but historians themselves – and if this is their historical analysis, what does that mean for us academic historians?

Until we researched the Gurindji people's oral history, *we academic historians did not know that the flood had been caused by the rainbow snake.* Now that *we know*, we academics are forced to choose – perhaps we can call it a responsibility to respond – whether or not to accept the Gurindji's historical analysis. If we do accept it, we must clarify in what way; if we do not, we must clarify why not. To put it differently, we're being asked whether we are prepared to treat their historical experience and our epistemology on equal terms. If we are, we must be able to demonstrate the specific ways in which we are giving them equal status. To push the question further, it is a matter of whether we accept hybridisation not as an issue for 'their practice', but as a challenge for 'our own practice as academics'. The question is whether we are serious about promoting the pluralisation of history.

What I wanted to do in my doctoral thesis was abandon, deliberately, the attitude of 'we' academic historians listening to the stories 'they' the informants tell, or fitting and categorising their historical narratives within the histor(iograph)y we're familiar with – in other words, the effort that powerfully maintains 'us academic historians' as agents of the construction of history. What happens once we put our own agency in parentheses and hand agency over to them? I am interested in what limitations of existing methodologies of history become apparent then.

I don't know if this is characteristic of Aboriginal societies, but things quickly get chaotic from the perspective of academic historical disciplines. Animals speak to us, plants speak to us and, in some cases, even stones narrate history. At this level, perhaps we are beyond the realm of 'oral history' – these histories are not only 'oral', given that historical narratives emanate from all kinds of objects and places. At one point I even considered renouncing the phrase 'oral history'. Toru Shimizu, who is studying the history of the Indigenous peoples of Mexico, calls his method 'field-school history', and I thought of calling my approach fieldwork history or field history, too. But when I met oral history scholar Junko Sakai, who also translated *The Voice of the Past: Oral History*, she suggested that it was possible to think of oral history in broader, more encompassing terms. And in that context, what I was pursuing was a radical, extreme form of oral history. So I decided to call my methodology 'radical oral history', and used it for the title of my Japanese book. Of course I am using the word 'radical' with all its multiple meanings and ambiguous connotations in mind.

## 4 Our historical practice

You may not be aware, but we're all actually 'doing history' in various moments of our everyday routines. To help us become conscious of that and consider anew what that means, I'll explain a little further what kind of historical practice the Indigenous Australians are engaged in. As I'll discuss in more detail in Chapter 2, academic historians are usually 'searching for history'. What I learned from the Indigenous Australians was the importance of 'paying attention to history', instead of, as subjects, searching for history. In fact, history is everywhere around us. We need to listen carefully to what it is telling us. That was the kind of historical practice that was taking place. To put it another way, we academic historians write books about history, and this means that we are constructing and producing history. There are other expressions, such as 'weaving history', but it is difficult for us, as subjects, to avoid writing and producing history. In contrast, in Daguragu, where I stayed, history was being maintained. History is always present, and the community as a whole takes care to pay attention to it. They all participate in maintaining their history. That is the form of their historical practice. To describe it yet another way, we could say that they live their day-to-day lives 'dipped' in history – steeped in and surrounded by history as a lived experience.

I wonder why this practice should necessarily be limited to the Aboriginal peoples. We, too, must be maintaining history in our daily lives. When Grandpa, sipping his green tea, starts grumbling about 'young people these days', and you sit listening to his stories of 'the good ol' days' while having a snack, you are practising history with Grandpa. When, on a trip with a boyfriend or girlfriend to the hot springs, you visit the local historic sites, you two are practising history. You are practising history when you visit your ancestral grave at Obon, the Buddhist festival; when you attend a class reunion; when you listen to a classic jazz album; when you reminisce about the old scars on your body. Even by just watching period dramas on television, playing video games involving medieval warlords, reading historical graphic novels, debating the logic behind the 'galactic century' of an animé series, or even dancing at a retro club that plays Eurobeat or rockabilly, we are engaging in historical practice. History is everywhere, flooding every aspect of our daily lives. It's just that we usually, and in part correctly, don't think of such activities as practising history. If you suggest a trip to the hot springs, you may not be thinking, 'Hey, let's do history together!' but instead have an ulterior motive, as in, 'It's too far for a day trip, so we'll have to spend the night ...' Similarly, you may be playing a video game simply because you want to play a video game and not because you want to practise history. That's certainly true. But if I may be so bold as to ask, just how many academic historians could engage in historical practice in the total absence of salaries, reputations, status, promotions, and other goals and incentives? There are professional historians, but there are no 'pure historians', are there? It's the normal state of historical practice to co-exist alongside and proceed simultaneously with other quotidian practices. I am simply focusing on historical practice as one aspect of our day-to-day activities, practised within the complex web of our primary objectives, might-as-wells, whatever happens to be convenient, coincidences, and duties – how we interact with or connect with the past, bodily, mentally, spiritually; through localities and objects; or in a utilitarian way.

Aren't we a little too easily convinced that history is something to be discovered or produced by academic historians? Perhaps we should begin to acknowledge the fact that all human beings (and perhaps other beings as well) participate in maintaining history. Why are we under the impression that historical practice is something stuffy that only scholars do in archives and research facilities? That the only historical practice others engage in is taking history courses? If such preconceptions are hobbling contemporary perspectives on history (and historical studies), we need to loosen these shackles little by little.

I'll sum up what I've said so far, in the spirit of, 'It won't be easy, but I think it's worth trying, so won't you join me?': if we academic historians put aside the preconception that we and only we are historians, then various other kinds of historians will begin to speak to us. More precisely, we academics will become more aware of how beings other than academic historians are maintaining history. That said, it'd be pretty hard to make the huge leap all at once and start listening to histories told by stones or to the voice of the earth. So how about we begin by listening sincerely and faithfully to what people who are not academics have to say as historians? How about we engage with all kinds of 'historians'? To go even further, if academic historians truly succeeded in suspending their position as subjects searching for history, then 'history' in turn might begin speaking to us. The expression 'to tell the history of', based on historical facts and documents, seems to have been around for a long time. The context is slightly different here, but my goal is to destabilise the privileged status of the academic historian as the subject searching for history. I'm casting about for a way to enable us to put aside for now our 'academic historian-centrism'. This is the intention behind my (radical) oral history research.

I can guess that such talk will elicit the response, 'But that's nothing new; it's all been said before.' And that, too, is true in a way, so I'll have to explain a little. Remember the histories I introduced earlier of President Kennedy visiting the Aboriginal community and of the rainbow snake causing the flood that washed away the cattle station? Within the normal – although I'm not sure that's the word – naïve framework of positivist historical discipline, such histories would be excluded. Why? Because they are not historical facts. I probably should take up the question of how to define 'fact' here, but I'm afraid we won't be able to get past that question to the next argument, so for now I'll just say that perhaps we need to explore historical methodologies that are no longer under the binding spell of historical 'factuality' ...

*Question #1 (from positivist academic historian A):*
For a historian like myself grappling with Japan's responsibility for atrocities committed during World War II, the question of historical factuality is of utmost seriousness. Especially given the search for and pursuit of reconciliation and co-operation in Sino-Japanese relations, clearly there are situations in which the verifiability of people's

memories must be closely examined. What are your thoughts on such real and pressing demands for historicity?

*Hokari:*

Well, I agree with you that in some cases history absolutely must hold up to positive verification. In such cases we *should* conduct positivist research. I'm not arguing at all that we should abandon positivist research because it's old-fashioned.

In the case of Indigenous Australian history, there is a heated debate over the mass killing of Aboriginal people by white settlers. For example, when Indigenous Australians say that several hundred were killed at a certain location, in the absence of documentary material, what happened there is called into question. Those who take the so-called revisionist-denialist stance insist that such mass killings are mere fabrications by leftist historians and that very few Indigenous Australians were actually killed. Many simply died because they were constitutionally weak, they say, and even in cases in which the whites did kill them, it was in self-defence because the Indigenous Australians had attacked first. Academic historians who have collected Aboriginal oral histories, including myself, have recorded many, many stories about specific locations where people were killed. Yet the positive verifiability of those stories is questioned. Typically – and I think this is also the case with the Rape of Nanking controversy – the debate centres on the 'numbers'. Personally, I wonder if it isn't futile to debate the numbers of victims, but perhaps the numbers are important in and of themselves. If so, then please go ahead and pursue positivist research. Let's find out exactly how many people were massacred. But that's not the only mission of historical scholarship, is it? That's what my argument boils down to: that's not our only mission. If there is a need for positivist research, by all means, let's do it. But that's not all our work is about, is it?

*Question #2 (from positivist academic historian B):*
What you're saying is rather problematic. It wouldn't be going too far to say that 'histories that cannot be exhibited as evidence in a trial cannot be studied in modern academic historical disciplines'. The story of the rainbow snake causing the flood cannot be treated as fact or evidence in a court of law. Therefore, it cannot be considered in historical research.

Besides, if academic historical disciplines ignored historical factuality, wouldn't it descend into a free-for-all? Anyone and everyone would be able to fabricate whatever history suited them. As an academic historian, I couldn't possibly accept such a development.

*Hokari:*
This will overlap a little with my response to the previous question, but I don't think at all that we should quit the kind of academic historical discipline that can be exhibited as trial evidence. Of course there's room for that kind of academic history, and there will always be a need for it. We shouldn't underestimate the power of the notion of 'authentic' truth – modern, rational and scientific. No matter how loudly intellectuals in the humanities shout, 'Postmodernism!', there remain plenty of established systems where such arguments carry no weight. While there may be some flexibility in legal philosophy, the realities of today's courts may represent the worst of such establishments. But my question is: in this age of globalisation, when Western-centrism is persistently criticised, the exhaustion and limitations of modernism are expounded upon, multiculturalism is proclaimed, 'fundamentalism' becomes visible as a contemporary phenomenon, and ethnic culture is increasingly cross-culturalised, is the mode of history that can be used in a trial really the *only* kind of history needed?

One more point: my call for historical methodologies that are no longer under the binding spell of historicity has nothing to do with a 'free-for-all'. That interpretation completely misunderstands the historical practice that Indigenous Australians are engaged in. I can say this with conviction: the Aboriginal historians I dealt with never 'fabricate whatever history suits them'. Their history is shared across the Gurindji country and passed down from one generation to the next. If someone suddenly were to fabricate a story, no one would take such a made-up story seriously. Not one person thinks to himself/ herself, 'Let's see, what historical event shall I think up today?' and then starts telling a new narrative. It's true that the historical practice that takes place in the Gurindji country is conducted according to different rules from those of the academic mode of history. We might say they are different ways to approach the past or different historical philosophies. But that doesn't mean that past events are fabricated at will. The Gurindji people are historians in that they re-narrate past incidents and experiences in the present, re-enact them, apply their moral, political, spiritual and philosophical analyses and thereby try to learn something from history and communicate that something. It's true that their historical practice doesn't meet modern academic history's criteria of positivist historical 'factuality', but to dismiss it as a 'free-for-all' is too barbaric and quick a judgement.

In any case, as long as academic historians remain bound by historicity, they will continue to exclude the history of JFK's visit to the Gurindji community. To be sure, there are several groups who say, '*We* won't exclude it.' Typically, they are the ones who are studying the theory of memory or of mythology; the latter has been around for a while, mainly in the field of anthropology. While these researchers don't exclude such histories, the problem is that they subsume it instead. In other words, theories of memory and mythology render harmless the experience that the Indigenous Australians insist they actually experienced. What does it mean to make an experience harmless? Essentially, they say, 'That is not factual, but it is nonetheless significant', and they 'rescue' it. None of it happened as far as they're concerned, but they assume there's something important there, so they 'rescue' it, or are respectful of it. I think that we need to question the politics of this act of 'rescuing and being respectful of' the Aboriginal experience.

What does it mean to be respectful of that experience? For example, it would certainly be possible to state, in academic history or anthropology, 'The Aboriginal people believe that President Kennedy met the Gurindji elders.' In fact, most anthropology researchers on magic and belief systems often write of spiritual, magical or divine experiences using such phrases as 'it is considered that ...' or 'it is said that ...' or 'it is believed that ...' This tradition, presumably passed down from the days of J.G. Frazer and Lucien Lévy-Bruhl, remains a strong current within ethnography even today, apparently unaffected by postcolonial criticism. But doesn't this way of writing unconsciously conceal the power imbalance between the two systems of knowledge? While such statements do respect the belief system in question, in the end this act of subsuming in the name of 'being respectful' may be merely a skilful way to dismiss it. After all, none of these researchers believes that JFK actually met with the Aboriginal elders. They don't believe that it happened, but they make the token gesture of saying, 'We still value it for what it is.' If I may borrow from the study of speech acts, as a constative utterance, the statement 'it is believed that ...' communicates that 'the Indigenous Australians have a different and unique belief (system)'; at the same time, as a performative utterance, the speaker is implying in this perlocutionary act that 'I, as a researcher, naturally do not believe such things.'

Would it be possible, then, for an academic historian – or an anthropologist, for that matter – to write that President Kennedy visited an Aboriginal community? I'm not saying unequivocally that it is. What I do believe is that delving deep into this question may be the next challenge for historical and anthropological study. The question is: are there methods of historical writing or ethnography that neither exclude nor subsume? What if we were to explore ways in which different historical spaces could connect with and resonate with one another in dialogue? The historical spaces in which people experience their pasts are deeply plural; therefore there will always exist a clear, undeniable gap that cannot be filled between our experiences, which can neither be replicated nor fully understood. We can accept that for what it is. Hence the call for pluralism in recent years. At the same time, while recognising the existence of the gap, I believe in the possibility of communication over the gap. This is not to say, 'You may believe that this happened in reality, but it's actually a myth, right? But okay, I'll respect your myth', but to say instead, 'I may not be able to share deeply in your experience, but I understand that this is your historically truthful experience. So let's consider together the possibilities for connections and dialogues between your historical experience and my historical understanding.'

I'd like to introduce a few people who will be helpful in this endeavour. First, Morris Berman discusses what he calls 'the re-enchantment of the world' in his book of the same name.[6] To borrow from Max Weber, modernism has always been a project of disenchanting the world. The field of history has contributed a great deal to this process of disenchantment. Do we not, however, live in an age in which the brutality of such processes as secularising the world and colonialism are called into question? I would, therefore, rather pursue the possibility of 'the re-enchantment of the world' (I even considered using this phrase as the title for my book). I believe that secularism is the last remaining bastion of modernism. It's fairly easy for anyone to criticise the concept of the modern nation-state or family structures. Benedict Anderson or Chizuko Ueno, among the most well known, and many, many others have also criticised the nation-state or the patriarchal system as constructs over the years. Yet when it comes to secularism, everyone pulls back. Is it possible to take up once again what lies beyond secularism – the world of spirits and gods – in the framework of academia or, more broadly, in the public sphere, in a real sense? This, I feel, may be one of the big challenges before us. Berman thinks very seriously about this question. His arguments are quite general, and digress into Jung's interest in alchemy, and may give the impression of being an extension of theories that were popular in the 1960s, but as a primer it's quite good and I recommend it.

Next, William E. Connolly, who is a political philosopher, proposes something called 'post-secularism'. Although he is fairly well known, the book I have in mind, *Why I Am Not a Secularist*,[7] is not. In it he discusses the concept of 'deep pluralism'. Generally speaking, multiculturalism and cultural pluralism take a stance along the lines of: 'There are many different cultures, so let's all respect one another.' Yet even the people who champion this stance never break out of the framework of secularism itself. Connolly, by contrast, insists on the need to explore the possibility of pushing pluralism further, deeper, to the point of not excluding spiritual experiences and religious cosmologies.

Last, Dipesh Chakrabarty is a historical theorist and author of the book *Provincializing Europe: Postcolonial Thought and Historical Difference*.[8] He is known for his postcolonial criticism, but his views on this issue, which is connected to the work of religious scholar Mircea Eliade, are as follows: in the world of academia, we are performing secularism: that is to say, we are studying history solely through secularist methodologies. Yet in our actual everyday lives, spirits and gods continue to have a meaningful existence. Therefore, if we were to focus our academic consciousness not only on secularist historical methodologies but also on the world of our daily lives, we would not fall into simplistic dichotomies such as 'The Indigenous Australians are superstitious, whereas we are advanced.' He formularises this concept as 'doubled consciousness'. This, too, is worth paying attention to. There are several other works that I would like to introduce, but I will leave off attempting to organise my theoretical underpinnings until Chapter 9.

*Question #3 (from a grassroots activist/sociologist):*
I understand very well what you're saying, and I think the issues you raise are important. Nonetheless, I want to ask you about the meaning of oral history to the struggle for equal rights for minorities. Oral history research, or interviewing people, has been a way to listen to those who have been voiceless until now and to make their voices heard by the power structure; it's taken on the aspect of a means of resistance, a means of political protest. Against this background, it's also true that there are many minority groups who find validity and legitimacy in oral history, as well as many academics who support them. My concern is that the post-secularism you spoke of could undo this basic foundation of oral history.

If secularism is the last bastion of modernism, the political struggle of Indigenous Australians is itself an extremely modern movement. The rights that it claims and the value systems that it relies on are based on human rights, civil rights and land rights – all very modern values. In that context, it could be dangerous to call for post-secularism. By insisting on post-secularism, we could inadvertently undermine oral history's validity and legitimacy, quite apart from the intentions of the very people for whom it is a hard-won political means. For if the historicity and verifiability of oral histories could no longer be trusted, the government might use that as a reason to reject all claims based on oral histories. Don't academic sociologists and historians have an obligation to maintain the validity of oral history as a means of resistance?

If I may add one more point, won't your argument for liberating academic historical disciplines from historicity lead to the accommodation of the so-called revisionists' claims that the Holocaust never happened or that the history of 'comfort women' is a fabrication? Here, too, I'm afraid there's a risk of your argument being manipulated in a way you never intended.

*Hokari:*
First of all, I realise this is very utopian, but I think we need to take a two-pronged approach. By a two-pronged approach I mean that while we remain involved in the kind of struggle that would hold up in a court of law within the framework of secularism, we should also be able to take a 'truthful' attitude towards what lies beyond that framework. In other words, if we were to make 'experiential historical truthfulness' a key concept in our work, we should be able to engage simultaneously with both claims based on modern values and those that lie beyond the boundaries of modernism. This is related to Chakrabarty's concept of doubled consciousness, which I introduced earlier. There are human experiences that can be defined by modern rationalism, and there are others that cannot be defined in those terms. As historical experiences, they are connected, yet in the context of specific political struggles or trials, it inevitably becomes necessary to sort out 'historical facts' that can be 'proven or verified' in a 'modern, rationalistic' way. If we must sort them out, then let's sort them out. But I believe we also need to accept those experiences that don't fit that definition as historical experiences that are equally important. That's my first thought, utopian as it is.

But that's not how things are in reality. We face, as a very real problem, revisionist histories that deny that the Rape of Nanking or the mass killing of Indigenous Australians ever took place. Or that claim that oral histories and testimonies are all made-up lies.

Perhaps I should explain a little about the connection with revisionist history (or rather the lack thereof). In my understanding, the revisionist-denialist historians who deny the Holocaust or the Rape of Nanking make their arguments 'based on historicity'. It is precisely around the debate over this 'historicity' that they deny and/or fabricate history, so they're on a completely different trajectory from my argument, which is for not being bound by historicity, isn't it? I'd like to make that distinction clear. That's one point. Another important point is that when the Aboriginal elders claim that President Kennedy visited the Gurindji country, it's not to reject a previously narrated history. They don't insist on JFK's visit as a way to deny the established historical narrative. They teach us 'the history we do not know', but they never narrate history in order to refute 'the history we know'. In connection with this, I'd like to raise a final point: the issue of universalisation. I think many historians, not just revisionist historians, have as a general rule tried to 'universalise' their historical writing – that is, they strive for historical statements that can be verified objectively by anyone at any time, so it can be said that whatever it was 'actually happened'. I have no intention of universalising the history the Gurindji people tell in that way. On the contrary, I'm calling for accepting Gurindji history truthfully in order to seek the plurality, the individuality, and the situationalised and localised aspects of history-spaces.

There's a lot more I could say about revisionist history, but to be honest, I don't want to take part in such idiotic debates. As historians we have so much work ahead of us, and it's extremely frustrating to have to waste time responding to revisionism when we should be concentrating on developing plurality-oriented historical studies. So I can't help but say, quite irresponsibly, that I leave it to our distinguished, eminent elder intellectuals to deal squarely with such idiocies as revisionism. We'll follow the developments with interest, but with all due respect, my fervent wish is that we younger scholars be allowed to move on.

## 5 Meeting Old Jimmy Mangayarri

To be sure, I did not set out to do fieldwork in the Gurindji country to examine such questions as 'Just who is a historian?' or to take the approach of focusing on everyday historical practices. Reading over the research project proposal that I wrote at the start of my doctoral research, I see that originally I'd planned to do fieldwork to study how the Indigenous Australians' 'walkabout economy' had evolved with the influence of colonialisation – by taking down oral histories and observing and analysing their current economic activities. After all, at graduate school in Japan I had studied economic history and economic anthropology. But after meeting a certain elderly man, I lost interest in my original research project and decided to focus on the Gurindji people's historical practice and analysis.

My encounter with Jimmy Mangayarri changed my perspective dramatically enough to shift my relationship to the Gurindji community from the third-person 'me and them' to the second-person 'me and you'. In explaining it this way, I have no intention of ignoring the power dynamics of a Japanese researcher's act of interviewing an Indigenous Australian – a project made possible by the world's colonial power structure: that is, the global imbalance of economics and systems of knowledge. That said, between Old Jimmy and myself such structural imbalances never became a significant issue. Old Jimmy's interest was in making sure that I, as I sat across from him, was listening attentively to his stories and that I truly intended to pass on his words throughout Australia and Japan. In this sense, for Old Jimmy, I was not 'him (them)' but rather 'you'. As for me, I was profoundly struck by Old Jimmy's unique and detailed analysis of Australian colonial history. I came to understand him not so much as an informant but rather as a 'historian' from whom I should learn political philosophy and historical analysis. In this sense, for me, Old Jimmy was not 'him (them)' but rather 'you'.

Don't get me wrong: I don't claim to be the only one who has been able to forge an especially friendly relationship with 'the locals'. Not at all. In fact, some Aboriginal elders refused to speak a word to me. Instead, I'm simply trying to describe in a realistic way the kind of profound encounter and strong rapport that any researcher conducting fieldwork experiences with certain people. From fieldwork locations to faculty meetings to parties, we meet some people with whom we develop friendships and mutual trust, and others whom, unfortunately, we come to ignore or dislike. The more problematic issue here, I think, is that even as we spend more time in their communities, and our mutual trust deepens and we no longer see the people as 'them' but 'you', we nonetheless believe that we must analyse those people as 'them'. Shouldn't we question this coercive 'third-person plural'-ism – the academic self-consciousness that takes a form of communication that is going relatively smoothly with 'you' but still believes it to be a 'discommunication' with 'them'?

Let's take a concrete example. Consider a scenario in which 'the locals' taught you a magic spell to cure an illness. Let's say that, not when you've just met them, but after having lived with them for a long time and having become familiar with the local language and customs, you fall ill, and someone with whom you've developed a rapport, friendship, and mutual affection teaches you their precious healing magic. Do you really not believe in it at all? I would think that dismissing it 100 per cent would be just as difficult as believing in it 100 per cent. Wouldn't you agree? Have the researchers who write academic papers about the magic they've been taught never performed it themselves? And if they never have, why do they obstinately refuse to believe in or use what they've learned? Or perhaps they actually do sometimes use it. If so, why do their papers never reflect that fact? It seems that the demands of modernism, academicism and secularism not to believe in supernatural phenomena forcibly deny the 'authenticity' of what researchers actually (or supposedly) experienced or felt in the field.

But I digress. I was introducing Old Jimmy. Unlike in Europe, various African societies, Japan or China, in Aboriginal societies there were apparently no professional or specialised historians for a long time, whether as scholars or storytellers. Today there are Indigenous historians who are active in academia, but at the time that I visited the Gurindji country, there were no professional historians in the community. I'd like it to be clear that Old Jimmy and the other historians I discuss in this book do not specialise in narrating history for their livelihoods. As I explained earlier, I engaged with these Gurindji historians by paying attention to the practice of maintaining history that they took part in throughout their daily lives. The historian I spent the most time with while in the Gurindji country was Old Jimmy, so in this book I focus mainly on his historical analyses.

Old Jimmy's country was located about 100km west of Daguragu, in the area around the Limbunya cattle station. As Limbunya remains a station managed by whites, he had no land rights to his own country and lived in Daguragu instead. He belonged to a language group called Malgin, which is referred to both as a proximal language to Gurindji and as a dialect of it. So, broadly defined, he was Gurindji, but strictly speaking, he was Malgin. His precise age was unknown, but based on the name of the Limbunya cattle station owner he'd worked for, he might have been over 80 at the time. In terms of age, Old Jimmy was the most senior elder in the Daguragu community.

That said, I don't think such details are all that important to my book. E.H. Carr taught that when reading a history book, one should be sufficiently aware of the background of the historian who wrote it, but in reality, this rule is not always followed. I don't place too much emphasis on it, either. The fact that Michel Foucault was homosexual likely had some impact on his historical theories, but I don't think it's useful to over-emphasise its significance. The same goes for Old Jimmy. The fact that in his final years a young man from Japan came to listen enthusiastically to his stories may have influenced his historical analyses in some way, but I worry that focusing too much on that aspect would shift the act of listening truthfully to historian Jimmy Mangayarri's analysis of colonial history to a 'discourse analysis of Old Jimmy's narrative'. I am not an ethno-methodologist. In this book I plan to consider in various ways how we can accept and engage with the historical analyses of Old Jimmy and other Gurindji historians as real histories, but I'd rather steer clear of analysing the Gurindji historical narratives. I do realise, of course, that inevitably the distinction between the two will become blurred at times.

In any case, what I want to emphasise here is that I do not intend to present 'the historical perspective of the Gurindji society' as a single static epistemology. I will be introducing the historical analyses of one extraordinary historian named Jimmy Mangayarri, and there is no doubt that his analyses take place intertextually: within the context of historical practices that have been passed down and performed continuously in the Gurindji country. But this does not mean that Old Jimmy's historical analyses represent all of Gurindji society, just as E.H. Carr's historical perspective, while born in the context of the traditional Western views of history, does not represent those views. Naturally, Gurindji women, Gurindji youth, Warlpiri elders related to the Gurindji by marriage, etc all have their own distinct consciousness of history, and it is precisely in the co-existence, connection and sharing of these various senses of history that historical practice occurs, that history is maintained – a point I will discuss in more detail in Chapter 2.

Before submitting my PhD thesis, I returned to Daguragu with a draft and made presentations on it. I describe this process in Chapter 10. Of course the Gurindji people knew that my thesis had been written with a non-Aboriginal audience in mind. To put it another way, they would not have told me their stories if it had been otherwise. 'The *kartiya* [whites] and the Japanese will read the stories that we tell him' – it was precisely because of this hope that they had narrated their history for me, and this is why I've prepared my book – based on my doctoral thesis – in both English and Japanese. In that sense, if I were to address the fashionable question, 'To whom are we speaking?', the answer would be 'to an audience unfamiliar with the Indigenous Australians' colonial experience'. Yet this is precisely where the problem arises: how should I communicate to white Australian and Japanese audiences the history of President Kennedy visiting the Aborigines? Is there a language that enables us to share truthfully the Indigenous Australians' historical analyses? This becomes a huge issue. Do you see what I've had to struggle with?

## 6 Alternative experientialism

As I mentioned at the beginning when I talked about relationalising historical agents, I believe that we need to learn from all kinds of beings other than academic historians about the question: just what is history? We could learn from random passers-by, our grandmothers, the Aboriginal peoples, and if all goes well, maybe non-human beings such as animals and plant life and insects as well. We might even be able to contemplate what history is in dialogue with stones and buildings. We could ask the question 'What is history?' of people other than academic historians and of inanimate beings. I am interested in exploring how far the possibilities of opening up history extend. Is there a more effective methodology for pursuing such a project than oral history in the form of fieldwork?

It seems to me that one group supports memory and narrative and another group supports historical fact and truth, and they stand in opposition to each other. Isn't this rather futile? I tend to get pigeon-holed as belonging to the memory/narrative group, but I am actually concerned with neither narrative nor memory, but with experience. I am focused on the historical experience of human beings, and in examining the human experience of history, it seems to me that the dichotomy between memory/narrative and fact/truth becomes less meaningful, even though I have to admit I'd be hard pressed to prove that at this stage, without further research.

'Experience' is one of the key words in my work. My criticism of postmodern historiography is that academic historical disciplines must return once again to experience. Since the so-called linguistic turn, it has been argued passionately that histories are first and foremost narratives. That in itself has been interesting and informative in many ways, but I'd like to think of the study of history as the study of experience – historical scholarship that is truthful to experience. By 'truthful' I mean both 'faithful' and 'truthful'. Shouldn't we pursue research methodologies that value experiential historical truthfulness, that analyse seriously the historical narrative of President Kennedy meeting the Gurindji elders? Shouldn't we be seeking a history that allows for a faithful examination of the plurality of historical experience and of history-spaces? Therefore I don't consider myself as theorising memory or narrative; rather, I could say I am pursuing a new kind of empiricism. I sometimes use the term 'experientialism' in place of 'empiricism' to suggest the need for an alternative theory of experience. If a historical discipline based on an alternative experientialism existed, what kind of historical writing might become possible?

With references to Walter Benjamin, Tadao Uemura discusses 'the defeat of 'experience'.[9] He highlights 'the poverty of experience (Erfahrung)' as wisdom passed down from one generation to the next as a condition of 20th century history following two devastating world wars and the Holocaust, and I sincerely appreciate this outstanding historical theorist's insight and acute sense of crisis. And yet, even then

I feel the urge to say, in the face of this undeniable global condition of 'the poverty of experience': 'That may be so, but let's not concede defeat just yet.' Perhaps 'experiences' have not declared unconditional surrender yet. Might they not be continuing their guerilla-like resistance throughout the world, even as we speak? These 'experiences' have long been exiled from the Broadway of history and now have been shut out of even the seedy cabaret shows, and precisely because they are grassroots guerillas with no hope of an absolute victory, I imagine they could function as one channel that enables pluralistic accounts of history-spaces.

I feel that oral history is positioned closer to these various issues than any other history methodology is. That's my point about the possibilities for oral history. I would like nothing better than to be able to shape the methodology of oral history, beyond merely adding another method and more documentary material to the historiography, into a force that calls into question once again just what history is.

*Question #4 (from a postcolonial critic):*
I have no expertise in oral history, but I was struck by how your interest is focused not so much on the 'oral' but more on the 'history' aspect. I suppose there are possibilities for oral history, but what's needed is a consideration of how to cross over the various dichotomies, such as between listener and speaker, injury and aggression, primary language speakers and peripheral language speakers, orality and literacy or, these days, the righteous and the terrorist. Against this background, you propose this very interesting concept of experience. At the same time, I think it's essential to envision diverse levels of agency on the side that accepts those experiences, such as academics, historians and those who are neither, and to relationalise agency, to put aside the hierarchy of agency. But in doing that, we need to examine what we call experience in a more fundamental way.

The main achievement of cultural studies and postcolonial studies, the lesson we've learned, is that as long as experience is considered to be a product of an individual's life, it remains problematic. It's the issue of individualistic liberalism. Experience cannot but emerge from the relationality between oneself and others. And the experience that emerges to confront us, as is salient in the case of the so-called comfort women, is not something that we can just 'rescue' and subsume or accept, because it's too shocking. I believe that it's essential for historians to deal with the way in which experience emerges out of the relationality between the self and others to confront us, so in my philosophy, or to my thinking, when we talk about oral history, we need to deepen our understanding of these fundamental issues.

### Hokari:

I completely agree with you. I think the questions I've brought up are, in the end, connected to the issues you raise. There was one point I wanted to address – what was it? Oh yes, the term 'experience'. I'm always trying out different terminology. Today I discussed the term 'experience', but there are others – 'reality', for example. There is the question of what 'historical reality' is. By the way, my usage of the word 'truthful' is borrowed from Tessa Morris-Suzuki. By emphasising 'truthfulness' instead of 'truth', we are overlaying the meaning of the word 'faithful' onto the word 'truth'. So one way to frame the question is whether academic historians can narrate histories that are oriented towards, and open to, this 'truthfulness'. I think we need to experiment with different key words like this. I'm sure you all have experimented with various terms as well, and I'd be interested in exchanging information and continuing the debate.

### Moderator:

I would like to thank Dr Hokari, those of you who asked questions and everyone in the audience. I hope you'll pick up a copy of *Radical Oral History* and consider these arguments for yourself. Thank you all for coming today. We hope to continue to host debates about historical practice and the definition of history in the future.

## NOTES

1   This chapter is loosely adapted from a report given at a symposium of the Centre for Documentation and Area-Transcultural Studies entitled 'Listening to Fading Voices/Envisioning the Invisible – The Possibilities of Oral History and the Challenges for Archives', held on 15 March 2003 at the Tokyo University of Foreign Studies (and published in the *Journal of the Centre for Documentation and Area-Transcultural Studies*, vol. 2 [2003], pp. 57–65). While the audience members asking questions in this chapter are fictional characters, the questions themselves are all based on actual questions posed at the symposium in response to the report.

2   Paul Thompson, *The Voice of the Past: Oral History*, Oxford: Oxford University Press, 1978. Japanese transalation: Junko Sakai, *Kioku kara rekishi he – Oraru hisutori-no sekai*, Tokyo: Aoki Shoten, 2002.

3   To cite a few examples of excellent references on oral history (life history), albeit in the field of sociology: Tomio Tani (ed.), *For the Students of Life History Method*, Kyoto: Sekai Shiso-sha, 1996; Suguru Nakano and Atsushi Sakurai (eds), *The Sociology of Life History*, Tokyo: Kobundo, 1995; Atsushi Sakurai (ed.), *The Sociology of Interviewing – How to Listen to Life Stories*, Tokyo: Serika Shobo, 2002.

4   I have considered the living conditions of Gurindji and other Aboriginal stockworkers from the angles of both documentary evidence and oral history. See Minoru Hokari, 'Reading Oral Histories from the Pastoral Frontier: A Critical Revision', *Journal of Australian Studies*, vol. 72, 2002, pp. 21–28.

5   For more details on the Gurindji people's Wave Hill walk-off, see Minoru Hokari, 'The Walk-off Movement by Indigenous Australians: An Oral Historical Approach', *Rekishigaku Kenkyu*, no. 783, December 2003, pp. 1–18.

6   Morris Berman, *The Reenchantment of the World*, Ithaca, NY: Cornell University Press, 1981. Japanese translation: Motoyuki Shibata, *Dekaruto kara Beitoson he – Sekai no Sai-majutsu-ka*, Tokyo: Kokubunsha, 1989.

7   William E. Connolly, *Why I am Not a Secularist*, Minneapolis: University of Minnesota Press, 1999.

8 Dipesh Chakrabarty, *Provincializing Europe: Postcolonial Thought and Historical Difference*, Princeton, NJ: Princeton University Press, 2000.

9 Tadao Uemura, *For the Critique of Historical Rationality*, Tokyo: Iwanami Shoten, 2002, from the Introduction.

# AUTHOR'S PREFACE

This is a history book. This book explores histories of the Gurindji people of Indigenous Australia and their country. Even though I am delighted to admit that my research method heavily relied on anthropology as much as on historical disciplines, the interdisciplinary nature of my study does not change the simple fact that this is a history book.

Exploring history to me is like dancing with openness. Therefore I wrote this book with openness. This is because there is no history without openness. Just as there is no world without earth, history is not possible without openness. History happens within this openness. As far as I am concerned, everyone tacitly knows this nature of exploring history.

Radical oral history: I did not treat the Gurindji people's oral histories either as simply their life histories or as private/public memories. The value of oral histories is not restricted to just exploring people's life stories or knowing what they remember or forget. I propose that oral historical studies hold the possibility of exploring alternative modes of history, which may be able to interact with, destabilise, and also expand the academic notion of history and historical reality.

\*

I am not a postmodernist. This is because I am not interested in the linguistic turn or deconstruction. I am studying the historical reality of the Gurindji people and their country. In other words, my aim throughout this book is to learn from their experiences of/from/about the past. I am interested in writing the Gurindji people's experiences because they were what they told me. How simple is that?

\*

The real question may not be how we explore history, but how history finds us.

\*

After all, WHAT IS HISTORY?

# AUTHOR'S ACKNOWLEDGMENTS

This book owes itself mostly to the Aboriginal people of Daguragu and Kalkaringi who kindly accepted me as a person learning their histories. I would like to acknowledge their generosity and support. I especially thank my main teachers – Jimmy Mangayarri, Mick Rangiari and Billy Bunter. Their friendship was as important to me as the teacher–student relationship. George Sambo, Peter Raymond, Violet Donald and Peter Mick were great hunting and fishing friends while I was staying in the Gurindji country. I would also like to thank the Gurindji country and Dreaming for letting me stay there. I especially thank *Jurntakal* and *karu* Dreaming, which directly affected my life and being.

I am also grateful to the members of the Daguragu Community Government Council, who always approved, helped and encouraged my stay and study in the Gurindji country. I would especially like to thank Community Presidents Helen Morris, Barry Wardle and Justin Paddy, Vice President Roslyn Frith, and Town Clerks Kim Muhlen, Gary Cartwright and Sean Heffernan. I also thank Tommy Wajabungu, Harry George, Roy Yunga, Thomas Mungka, George Karlipirri, Teddy Crew, Harry Sambo, Stanly Sambo, Banjo Ryan, Victor Vincent, K.J., R.R., K.K., Erika, Freeman, Daniel, Roark, Bob and Jo, Jim and Coleen for their friendship and support in the Gurindji country.

Ann McGrath has been a constant source of advice, support and encouragement. I have no doubt that I could never have completed this project without her generosity and sensible advice. Debbie Rose

66

has been a great inspiration since my first encounter with her. I am grateful that she always made time for me to discuss a number of issues. Koichiro Fujita and Toru Shimizu have supported and encouraged me from the time I was in Japan and trying to find a way to continue studying Aboriginal history. Thanks are also due to Darrell Lewis, Ann Curthoys, Patrick McConvell, Lyn Riddett, Greg Dening, Dipesh Chakrabarty, Peter Read, Nic Peterson, Ian Keen, Howard Morphy, Chris Watson, Donna Merwick, Joan Kerr, John Maynard, Geoff Gray, Christine Winter and Vern O'Brien in Australia as well as Seiji Suzuki, Komei Hosokawa, Shigenobu Sugito and Sachiko Kubota in Japan for their support and helpful suggestions.

There are many teachers and friends who kindly read the manuscript and made a number of helpful suggestions. Ann McGrath, John Docker and Philippa Webb read every chapter and made grammatical corrections and other numerous valuable suggestions. Linda Bennett, Ann Curthoys and Carolyn Roberts are the 'runners-up' who read most parts of the manuscript and gave me great feedback. Erika Charola corrected many spelling mistakes of Gurindji words.

I must also thank the people and bodies that helped fund this study. This book was made possible largely through grants from the Research Fellowships of the Japan Society for the Promotion of Science for Young Scientists, the Rotary International Foundation, the Research Management Committee (UNSW), the Northern Territory History Awards and the Centre for Cross-Cultural Research (ANU). I also wish to thank Jennifer Granger of the School of History (UNSW), Julie Gorrell and Anne-Maree O'Brien of the Centre for Cross-Cultural Research (ANU), Iain McCalman, Caroline Turner and Leena Messina of the Humanities Research Centre (ANU), Janet Sincock of the North Australia Research Unit, Katherine Goodman of National Archives of Australia, Darwin, and Andrew Pitt of Northern Territory Archival Service.

Besides the Gurindji country and Dreaming, I have to acknowledge the things and places that provided me with a wonderful research environment. 'Troll' (Honda NX650) and 'Pumpkin' or 'Japarta *motika*' (Toyota Landcruiser Troopcarrier FJ45) were great vehicles and the best companions when I was lonely in the bush. 'Buffy' (Hyundai Excel) took over from these bush vehicles and has been very helpful in Canberra. Coogee beach and The Basement in Sydney, Kakadu National Park in the Northern Territory, and Mount Ainslie, Tilly's, Café Essen, Electric Shadows and Centre Cinema in Canberra provided me with ideal escapes when I got sick of studying. Music was simply essential to the research process and the completion of this thesis. Among the great albums of great musicians, my special thanks are due to Ronny Jordan's *Antidote*, Tricky's *Maxinquaye* and Erikah Badu's *Baduizm*, which I played a hundred times while driving, reading, thinking and writing.

I am greatly indebted to my family, who have been always supportive and generous about my life-making. I have never faced serious objections from them about where I go or what I do. My friends, thanks to all of you! Other than those in the Gurindji country, I especially thank Kunishiro, Wada-san, Yumi, Taguchi, Hibiyan and Chiaki in Japan; Susu, Bowhoa, Danny, Jonna, Jacob, Brandin, P-Tao, Pip, Iris, Simon, Sheron, Prang, K.K., Janine, Donald and Lisa in Sydney; Emu and Alister in Darwin; Linda, Uchida-san and Sue in Melbourne; and Chantal, Jinki, Noah, Jenny, Jane, Rani, Kalissa, Ruth, Ono-san, Maki-san, Tamura-san, Dave, Michael, Bec, Andy, Cuan, Carolyn and Julia in Canberra.

Finally, I am deeply grateful to Tadayuki Murasato, Tatsuhiro Shimada and the other members of their reading circle – my friends, teachers and nightmare. Even though my struggle in this book may not deserve your recognition, you have always been with me through the journey.

# YUKI HOKARI'S ACKNOWLEDGMENTS

In addition to my brother's acknowledgments, I would like to extend my appreciation to the following people and organisations, who have been involved in realising the publication of this book after his passing in May 2004.

My utmost appreciation goes to Professors Ann McGrath and Tessa Morris-Suzuki, who had been Mino's mentors and became the main forces behind my efforts to bring Mino's manuscript to the world. I always knew that I could count on them and that they wished as strongly as I did for this book to be published.

I also would like to acknowledge the many people who sent me inquiries about the existence of an English manuscript. Your inquiries were another reason for me not to give up.

I am deeply grateful to Sean Heffernan and Roslyn Frith for helping me obtain the Gurindji people's approval to publish the photographs in this book. I could not move forward without the Gurindji's full support, given Mino's close and respectful relationship with the community.

I thank the Australian National University Publication Subsidy Committee for their very generous contribution, as well as the Australian Academy of the Humanities and the Australian Centre for Indigenous History (Australian National University) for granting publishing subsidies. I again thank Ann McGrath for her role in the application process.

Many thanks to my friend and translator Kyoko Uchida, who

translated the first chapter of Mino's Japanese book, *Radical Oral History: Historical Practice of Indigenous Australians* (Ochanomizushobo, 2004), to serve as the Author's Preface in this book.

I was very fortunate to hand over the manuscript to publisher Phillipa McGuinness; project manager Melita Rogowsky; editors Heather Cam and Sarah Shrubb; and indexer Jon Jermey. It was such a pleasure to work with dedicated and enthusiastic professionals on this project. I would also like to acknowledge Ray Tauss, Mino's friend and now mine as well, and Kyoko Uchida for helping to proofread the text under a very tight schedule.

Last but not least, thanks go to my dearest brother Minoru, who left his manuscript in my hands with an absolute trust and patiently watched over my endeavours from the sky.

✳

Epigraph to Chapter 1 from *On the Road* by Jack Kerouac, copyright © 1955, 1957 by Jack Kerouac; renewed © 1983 by Stella Kerouac, renewed © 1985 by Stella Kerouac and Jan Kerouac. Used by permission of Viking Penguin, a division of Penguin Group (USA) Inc.

Epigraph to Chapter 2 from Hyllus Haris, 'Spiritual Song of the Aborigine' in Kevin Gilbert ed. *Inside Black Australia: An Anthology of Aboriginal Poetry*, Penguin, Ringwood, p. 60.

Epigraph to Chapter 3 from Bertrand Russell, *The ABC of Relativity*. Allen & Unwin, London, 1958. Used by permission of Taylor & Francis, United Kingdom.

Epigraph to Chapter 6 from Haruki Murakami, *The Wind-Up Bird Chronicle*, Harvill Panther, London, 1997.

Epigraph to Chapter 7 from Selwyn Hughes, 'Home on Palm' in Kevin Gilbert ed. *Inside Black Australia: An Anthology of Aboriginal Poetry*, Penguin, Ringwood, p. 154.

Epigraph to Chapter 9 from Michel de Certeau, *The Practice of Everyday Life*, trans. Steven Rendall © 1988 by the Regents of the University of California, University of California Press.

Epigraph to Chapter 10 from Sheldon Kopp, *If you see the Buddha on the Road Kill Him!*, Sheldon Press, London, 1972.

All reasonable efforts were taken to obtain permission to use copyright material reproduced in this book, but in some cases copyright holders could not be traced. The press welcomes information in this regard.

# CHAPTER 1

# WHAT AM I DOING
# IN AUSTRALIA?

*It was drizzling and mysterious at the
beginning of our journey.
I could see that it was all going to be one
big saga of the mist.*

JACK KEROUAC, 1957

## WAY TO THE GURINDJI COUNTRY

'Why am I majoring in Aboriginal history?'

'Why am I, a foreigner – a Japanese person – interested in Indigenous Australians?'

'Why, in fact, am I obsessed with the Gurindji people and their country?'

These are just some of the questions that people have repeatedly asked and implied since I began studying Indigenous Australian history in

1993. There is no simple answer to these questions, because when I look back, it was just a sequence of related incidents that led me in this direction.

When I entered university as an undergraduate in Japan, my major was economics. At that time, I had a vague aspiration of becoming an economist or businessman. If I had continued studying economics, it was likely that I may never have heard the word 'Aborigine' – let alone 'Gurindji'. However, after two years of studying economics, I got bored with it. I started reading literature in the fields of history, sociology, philosophy and anthropology. I became increasingly interested in different cultures, and particularly interested in Indigenous Australians. For some reason, I was 'captured' by Aboriginal culture, and went on to do a Master's course to study Aboriginal history.

In 1995, I came to Australia to collect historical materials for my Master's thesis. My original plan was to do intensive research in Queensland. But one of the senior academics in Japan suggested to me that I might also look at the Gurindji people in the Northern Territory. He told me about the Wave Hill walk-off and their land rights movement. At that time, I had not yet heard the name 'Gurindji'. However, I could not get an air ticket to Queensland from Japan because they were all booked out. The travel agency said I could still buy a ticket to Darwin. Believe it or not, this is how I ended up writing a Master's thesis about Gurindji history.[1]

By the time I completed my Master's thesis, I had a dream of coming to Australia to do my PhD and undertake fieldwork in Aboriginal communities. I applied for the PhD course. I was fortunate enough to receive a scholarship and acceptance to study in Australia.

*

When I first arrived in Darwin in December 1996, my plan was to send letters and facsimiles to several Aboriginal communities asking for permission to visit. For fieldworkers, asking Aboriginal communities for permission to visit is such a difficult task. In order to grant you permission, they expect that you personally know some of the community members. However, without visiting the community, how

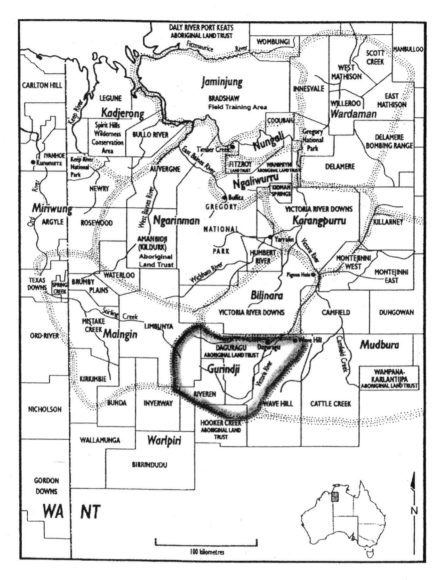

Map 1.1 Location of the Gurindji country

could one know the local people? My supervisor told me that I should be prepared for disappointment. Some other colleagues said it was a matter of luck.

I sent letters and facsimiles to ten different communities asking for permission. The result was: seven communities ignored my application, two sent me rejection messages, and only one approved my application – this was from the Gurindji country. I could not help feeling this was destiny. I applied to ten different communities but received only one positive answer, from the Gurindji people whom I had studied even while I was in Japan.

I have no way to describe my excitement as well as extreme tension while riding a motorcycle to the Gurindji country. A lot of strange concerns came to my mind: what should I say when I first meet them – 'Hello', 'G'day', or something else? What if they cannot understand my weird English accent? Are Aboriginal people 'racist' towards Asians?

On 10 January 1997, I arrived in the Gurindji country at last.

## THE GURINDJI COUNTRY

I shall now sketch some background details of the Gurindji country and the Daguragu and Kalkaringi communities within which my discussion of Gurindji history is situated. The Gurindji country is located in the upper reaches of the Victoria River. The landscape varies from hilly sandstone to grassland plains and scrubland. Although there are several large permanent waterholes which provide year-round swimming and fishing, the climate keeps a seasonal wet–dry cycle.[2] Today, the food supply comes mainly from the shop located within the community. However, the Gurindji people often go out hunting, fishing or collecting bush fruits, and the seasonal cycle determines the location of such activities.

The term 'Gurindji' normally refers to the Gurindji language and to the speakers of the language. However, according to the current view, Aboriginal people who live in Daguragu and Kalkaringi are 'all Gurindji'.[3] The Daguragu community is located within the Gurindji country at the basin of Wattie Creek, a tributary of the Victoria River, and the Kalkaringi community is about 10km south of Daguragu. The total population of the two Gurindji communities is about 600 people.

A close study of the social organisation and land ownership of Gurindji society is not the purpose of this book. Patrick McConvell and Rod Hargen have already explored these issues in the context of the Daguragu land claim.[4] However, in brief, as with most of the Aboriginal people in the Northern Territory and the Kimberley of Western Australia, the Gurindji have an eight subsection system of kinship-social categorisation: there are eight male and eight female subsections or 'skin names', and each person's 'skin' is based on a marriage rule. While there are many deviations, each subsection member is required to marry a certain subsection member. And their child's 'skin' is determined according to her/his gender and parents' subsections. Like many other Aboriginal societies, the Gurindji country contains many defined areas, and within each area there are related local descendant groups. They establish relationships along both paternal and maternal lines. The Gurindji person often calls such a defined area 'my country'.

After European colonisation, many Gurindji people worked at cattle stations as stockworkers. One of the biggest cattle stations in Australia was the Wave Hill station, located in the upper reach of the Victoria River Region, Northern Territory. The Wave Hill station was set up mostly on the Gurindji people's country.[5] In 1944, the anthropologists Ronald M. Berndt and Catherine H. Berndt visited the Wave Hill station and surveyed the living conditions of the Aboriginal workers. According to the Berndts, Aboriginal people at the Wave Hill station received, other than meat, bones and offal, 'two to three pounds of white flour, sometimes with rising (to those requesting it); one half to one pound of sugar (often less), to which was added a small handful of tea (under one ounce); and one stick of tobacco (to those requesting it)'[6] per week. Environmental damage by the introduction of cattle, relatively settled lifestyles, and the lack of young hunters and gatherers due to station work all limited their access to supplementary bush food. Only 68.4 per cent of offspring survived at that time.[7] If such colonial exploitation had lasted a few more decades, it is possible that the Gurindji people would have literally died out.

In 1966, supported by labour unions and a journalist, Frank Hardy, the Gurindji people declared a 'pastoral strike', left the Wave Hill station and established their own community at Daguragu, about 20km away from the station. They carried out a nation-wide campaign for their 'land rights' and asked the station owner to return their traditional land. In 1972, after a long struggle and negotiation, Vesteys, the owner of the station, agreed that a part of the Wave Hill station would be returned to the Gurindji people. This episode gained the public attention of contemporary Australia, and remains an event that is deeply engraved on the memories of both Aboriginal and non-Aboriginal Australians, particularly in terms of the Aboriginal land rights movement.[8]

This was roughly what I could learn about the colonial history of the Gurindji people from the already published literature. When I left for the Gurindji country, I was naive enough to expect that collecting oral histories would round out the above historical understanding; I was to collect 'useful' and 'good' oral histories as an academic historian.

*

Today, the Daguragu Community Government Council is a body representing the interests of owners and people associated with the Daguragu Aboriginal Land Trust (the area 'legally' defined as the Gurindji country). The council members, who are elected by the community members, mainly deal with funding, Community Development Employment Projects (CDEP) and other activities, which are more related to '*kartiya* [whitefella] business'. Many middle-aged and younger people today are working on CDEP, which includes road construction, making bread, arts and crafts, etc. Children attend a school located within the community.

'*Ngumpin* [Aboriginal] business' such as rituals or marriage arrangements are discussed and determined by gender-divided groups of elderly people. Like many other Aboriginal communities, the Gurindji socio-cultural space is highly gendered. Although I later found out that I was being over-sensitive, I was careful not to spend too much time with female groups – I did not want to give the impression of 'stealing women' or of 'not respecting elderly men' to my main teachers. Even though I often went hunting and fishing with the younger people or elderly women, I spent most of my time with a group of elderly males while staying in the community.

## MEETING OLD JIMMY MANGAYARRI

For a while, as I planned, I asked them questions based on my original research topic. I received answers which were similar to what I had read in other academic accounts. The people were happy to answer my questions, but they seemed to be enjoying themselves more when they taught me their language. This is worthwhile emphasising: the first thing they wanted to teach me was their language. I thought they were 'testing' me. Was I just another interviewer like they had met a hundred times before, or was I ready to be involved in 'their way' in a deeper sense? I picked up as many words as possible. People laughed at my peculiar accent and pronunciation all the time.

They also gave me one of the subsection terms or 'skin names': I became 'japarta'. People started to refer to me using kinship terms: 'I'm jampin, I call you *jaju* [grandparent]', 'I'm juluma, you're my son', 'I'm nimarra, I'm your sister', and so on. I spent most of my first field-work days learning their language, both Gurindji and Creole. My Gurindji did not improve much but I could manage to handle Northern Australian Aboriginal Creole, which is the standard language in the Gurindji and its surrounding societies today.

On 15 January 1997, I met a very old man, Jimmy Mangayarri, for the first time. Four days later, I had a long discussion with him. In fact, it was neither a discussion nor an interview, but instead it was his teachings. Those two sessions with Old Jimmy completely changed my research project – and probably my life as well. I did not have to ask Old Jimmy any questions. He had his own agenda to teach. He had a talent for analysing Australian colonial history, the origin of the European people and what is the 'right way' or 'earth law' that we should follow. He is a great historian, political analyst and moral philosopher. And, for some reason, he was eager to teach me about all his ideas.

While learning from Old Jimmy, I began to doubt if we – Gurindji people and I – really shared a single concept of 'history'. In Gurindji language, there are two words which are relevant to 'history': *larrapa* and *ngarangarni*. *Larrapa* means 'olden time' or 'early days', and *ngarangarni* means 'Dreaming stories'. What is crucial here is that you cannot say *ngarangarni* is an older time than *larrapa*. As I will discuss in the following chapters, Dreaming consists of place-oriented stories which have been 'active' throughout history. Naturally, *larrapa* and *ngarangarni* co-exist and, more importantly, interact with each other. Or it is more precise to say that *ngarangarni* is 'everywhere' and 'everywhen', which includes the space and time of *larrapa*. Therefore the study of the colonial history of the Gurindji people and their country should be a study of *larrapa*, which constantly interacts with *ngarangarni*.

In my Master's thesis, I studied the Gurindji history in an academic historical sense, but I did not know anything about the Gurindji history *in their sense*. Old Jimmy told me that my brain was sleeping, and needed training to wake it up. He was right. I did not care about my original research project any more. I decided to learn the Gurindji history and their law by following the way they wanted to teach me. After spending ten days at Daguragu, I had to go back to the university, but I promised them I would return.

## LIVING WITH THE GURINDJI PEOPLE

I sold my motorbike in Sydney and got a car licence. I went to a used 4WD car market and bought a second-hand NSW bushfire truck, an orange-coloured(!) Toyota Landcruiser Troopcarrier. After months of preparation, I left Sydney again in June 1997.

When I arrived in Daguragu on 19 June 1997, the Gurindji people warmly welcomed me, although the young people seemed to be a little disappointed by the fact that I did not ride a motorcycle any more. At the same time, they perceived me as a new resource – a troopcarrier can carry a lot of people. People started calling my car 'japarta *motika* [car]'.

I explained to them that I wanted to learn *ngumpin* [Aboriginal] law and their colonial history. However, at the same time, I minimised asking 'my questions' and tried to follow whatever they wanted to teach me. I often just repeated what my teachers said. I found that this repeating technique was the best way to encourage them to keep talking without controlling their stories. This way of listening was also useful because I could confirm what I had heard, since I sometimes misunderstood what they said.

I normally took notes while we were talking. I also often asked them for permission to record their teachings on tapes. Some people did not mind at all. Some said all right, but then became nervous about speaking. If so, I gave up recording; for me, hearing the stories was much more important than recording the stories. They told me what was secret and what was not. Some stories were not allowed to be recorded on tape, not because of who was speaking but because of the secrecy of the story. For the same reason, sometimes I was not allowed to even take notes. They instructed me to memorise it, as they do all the time. They pointed to their heads and said, 'Nomo [Don't] put down on paper, you must gotta put in your memory.' So I did.

Even though I talked a lot with many other people, I spent the most time with Jimmy Mangayarri. The people in Daguragu also regarded Old Jimmy as a good teacher for me. It is hard to explain, but after months of spending time with him, Old Jimmy became one of the very few people in the world whom I could fully trust. I cannot explain why, but beyond an undeniable cultural gap, I somehow completely trusted him. Old Jimmy asked me if I knew why I came to the Gurindji country. I said, 'I wanted to learn *ngumpin* [Aboriginal] way.' I knew I was doing research, but I also knew that, by that time, my motivation was more than simply academic. Old Jimmy had a clear answer. He said Dreaming told me to visit this country: 'He [Dreaming] bin talk'n to your memory – "Come out this country!"' I replied, 'But I don't remember …' Jimmy said my 'memory' was dead and 'he [memory] never think' so I needed training to wake it up – 'Wake 'im up. Just like you come out the bed. Get up!'[9]

In a sense, the Gurindji people's cultural/spiritual reality gradually came to dwell in my being. Let me give you another example. One night, I had a dream about two snakes dancing together. One of them held a baby. When I told this story to Peter Raymond, one of the Gurindji elders, he said I would have a baby: it was *karu* [children] Dreaming located in the Gurindji country. Old Jimmy was happy to know that my 'memory' had started working.

They told me that *karu* Dreaming would follow me all the way to Japan. It is worth emphasising: *the Gurindji Dreaming follows me all the way to Japan.* Since then, I have been more careful about contraception! What happened to me? It has been difficult for me to ignore the words from the Gurindji people. When I have a baby in the future, I am sure I will remember this *karu* Dreaming story. Of course, my cultural reality – whether Japanese, scientific, academic or 'Westernised' – will probably be different from the Gurindji people's. I also know I am not into so-called New Age culture at all. However, through my fieldwork, I found the 'reality' of Dreaming gradually affected my life and being. I am sure many fieldworkers have had similar experiences. The problem is, such experiences are seemingly 'supernatural' so you are not supposed to discuss them in a secular-academic context.

I am not saying here that I became spiritually Aboriginal. I know, and everyone in the Gurindji country knows, that I am not a Gurindji, but a person from Japan. However, I learned from the Gurindji people that Dreaming could be cross-cultural. In other words, Dreaming is not necessarily ethnocentric.

\*

While staying in Daguragu, I was also eager to participate in and learn their *business* [ceremonies], even though I knew I had to keep most of what I learned secret. This was because I found that learning their *business* was one of the most direct ways to know their law, or philosophy/cosmology. The Gurindji elders were pleased by the fact that I was serious about their *business*. We sang songs and danced all night from dusk till dawn. At daybreak, we stopped singing and celebrated each other as a 'winner'. I was exhausted, but I loved this moment. My body also learned something essential about *ngumpin* way.

One day, the Gurindji elders were talking about attending a very big *business* in Docker River, about 200km west of Uluru [Ayers Rock], or 1200km away from Daguragu. Warlpiri, Luritja, Pintupi, Pitjant-jatjara, Yankunytjatjara people, as well as Gurindji, Ngarinman and Mudburra people were all invited to hold this big ceremony. I was truly excited about this ceremonial journey. The Gurindji teachers told me how serious and big this ceremony would be. I was honoured that they allowed me to join.

We left Daguragu on 27 October 1997. The trip to the Docker River community was a series of disasters. I could not even count how many times we became bogged and had to dig holes. Cars broke down. Water ran out. I was seriously worried about perishing somewhere in the desert. Everybody was exhausted, but we still sang Dreaming songs while driving.

When we arrived in the Docker River community on 1 November, I was introduced as a person belonging to the Gurindji mob. People expected me to behave as a member of the Gurindji. They taught me about what this ceremony was, but they did not allow me either to be just an observer or to join the non-Gurindji side. In the ceremony, I performed my obligation as a part of the Gurindji. After participating in the ceremonies for three days, we left there on 4 November. I will never forget this great ceremonial journey with the Gurindji people.

I left the Gurindji country on 1 January 1998. Before leaving the community, Billy Bunter, a very strong 'law man' in Daguragu, said to me, 'You are one of us, you can come back any time.' Mick Rangiari, one of the 'bosses' of the Daguragu community, gave his kind regards to my family. Jimmy Mangayarri said, 'Don't forget what I bin tell you.'

## CROSS-CULTURAL POSITIONING

In order to answer the question 'Why am I majoring in Aboriginal history?', I would like to claim that my Japanese cultural background will allow me to make a unique contribution to the field of Aboriginal studies. However, before doing this, I want to make clear that there are some pitfalls to avoid when asserting this point.

One such pitfall is claiming 'objectivity', based on the fact that I am not an Australian. For example, Bain Attwood adopted this strategy. He claimed he detached himself from political issues related to Aboriginal history because he was a New Zealander.[10] If this is the case, I should be 'more objective' than him because I am not even a 'white' person. However, what is problematic here is academic historians' obsession with their 'objectivity'; the desire to take a politically neutral stance.[11] As Ann McGrath argues – and Attwood himself also admits – the practice of history itself is already involved with politics.[12] As I will discuss soon, my Japanese background may take me to a different political positioning with Indigenous or non-Indigenous Australians, but I do not intend to assert that I am taking a neutral political stance.

Another pitfall appears even more appealing: I may claim that aspects of my Japanese cultural-historical background such as Zen Buddhism, a community-based social environment, or Japan's continuous effort to integrate Eastern and Western values, will bring new perspectives for understanding Aboriginal culture and their history. However, such a notion of 'I, the Japanese' is rather problematic. Minoru Hokari as a 31-year-old middle-class Japanese male is certainly a 'condition' of my work. However, if this condition forces me to present or theorise Aboriginal/Gurindji history from a 'Japanese perspective', this is nothing but 'Japanese nativism', or replacing 'theory from the West' with 'theory from Japan'.[13] This does not solve any problems related to the representations of Aboriginal history by non-Aboriginal historians.

Rejecting naive 'objectivism' as well as essentialistic 'nativism', I would like to set my study in a more relational (i.e. cross-cultural) perspective. This work is the product of the Gurindji people's interaction with a Japanese person. I believe this 'relationship' itself is the very condition of this book. From the very beginning of my fieldwork, the Gurindji people saw me as a 'non-Aboriginal' as well as a 'non-white' person. They often asked me if I was a 'China-man', or if not, where the hell I came from. In general everyday context, I was categorised as *kartiya*. However, if you ask them what *kartiya* means, they will instantly answer 'whitefella'. The Gurindji language has only two words for the general categorisation of people – *kartiya* [whites] and *ngumpin* [Aboriginal]. Because I was obviously not *ngumpin*, I naturally fell into the category of *kartiya* – namely, 'non-Aboriginal'.

Nevertheless, my cultural positioning in the Daguragu community was not the same as that of whites. For example, they sometimes asked me what 'Japanese Dreaming' is like. As far as I know, the Gurindji people never ask this question of whites. Accordingly, they called me '*Japanee* [Japanese] *ngumpin*' when I talked about Japanese (relatively traditional) culture to them. They see Europeans as having no Dreaming.[14] However, there is a general understanding among the Gurindji people that Japanese, Chinese, Indians, 'Africans' and many other non-European people in the world all have their Dreaming or 'law'. When I told them that Japanese 'law' became more Westernised, they sympathised with me and said, '*Kartiya* way everywhere.' My Asian background certainly created a particular dynamic between the Gurindji people and me. Here is another example: one day, a young man approached me and asked if I knew Pauline Hanson.[15] He explained that she does not like 'my mob' and 'your mob'. Then, he suggested that I sing sorcery songs with him to kill Hanson!

It is entirely fair to say that all fieldworkers establish their distinctive personal relationships with local people according to their distinctive personal backgrounds. In my case, being Japanese was one of the essential factors in determining our relationship. As a result of that relationship, I did not (have to) phrase the questions of colonial invasion as: 'What did *we* do to your people and country?' Instead, our relationship implied that my question was: 'What did *they* do to your people and country?' I was not part of the colonised, but I was not part of the colonisers either.

Furthermore, it also became a source of pride for them that a person from overseas visited the Gurindji country to learn the *ngumpin* way. The Gurindji elders often introduced me to the people from other communities by saying, 'He nomo [not] from Sydney, nomo Melbourne. Him from Japan, oversea!' At the same time, my privileged position as an 'international student' also determined their request of me: that I circulate their stories not only in Australia, but also in Japan and many other countries all over the world. These are the conditions which, without a doubt, shaped the structure and nature of this book.

## WRITING A BOOK

While preparing and structuring my writings, I found I needed to follow up several small questions to crystallise the issues and make my arguments clearer. It was also suggested that I make a legal agreement regarding copyright with the community members. Of course, I also knew that learning the *ngumpin* way and their history is neverending work. I may be able to collect enough information to complete a book, but that does not represent at all the end of my journey to the Gurindji way of historical practice.

I arrived in the Daguragu community on 31 December 1998, almost exactly one year since I had left there last time. I received a warm welcome from the Gurindji people again. When I met Old Jimmy, he said to me, 'I bin thinkin' longa you!'

Again I asked questions which I had brought from Sydney, but I learned more new stories from them as well. I also made an agreement with the Daguragu Community Government Council to share the copyright of the primary information – fieldnotes, tapes and photos – of my research. Helen Morris, one of the council members, complained that many researchers came there to study, but all the products had gone to Canberra. Accordingly, I added one more clause in our agreement saying I would submit my published works to the community.

I would like to emphasise that during my fieldwork no Gurindji person ever asked me the question, 'Why are you studying Gurindji history?' Instead, their question was:

'Why do *kartiya* [non-Aboriginals] never learn from us?'
'Why do they never listen to our stories?'

After my second fieldwork trip, I also began to realise the Gurindji people's purpose in teaching me their law and history. They often told me that non-Aboriginal people should know their stories. Old Jimmy said as follows:

> When you go back to your place, don't forget that you look story longa your book [fieldnotes] … Maybe your boss look that book (and says) 'Oh, he got good story … On the history, now that book.' They look, they gonna follow the book. What you bin learn 'em on this country, on the history, they gotta follow that law. That's the way.

They knew I was from a different country called Japan. They understood that their stories would be carried not only around Australia, but also overseas. They seemed to be proud of this. The Gurindji people also clearly understand their current political situation, a recurrence of Australian racism.[16] After telling me what 'Captain Cook' had done in their country, Mick Rangiari showed his anger towards the governmental policy: 'Government want us back to that time, live in humpy, nomo [no more] house, nomo *motika* [car] … Government never listen, government try to change the law, hard for *mibala* [us].' He also told me what I have to do: 'Send books, spread out story all around. Send this cassette [tape recordings] your people. Let them know … Spread out Gurindji *jaru* [stories]!'

Why am I majoring in Aboriginal studies? One answer is that this Japanese person who used to study economics was coincidentally interested in Australian Aboriginal culture and coincidentally involved with the Gurindji people and their history. An alternative story is that Dreaming brought me to the Gurindji country to receive training from the Gurindji people in order to bring their teachings to a wider audience. I must struggle throughout this book between these two different modes of explaining the world. Keeping their requests in mind, I wound up my third fieldwork trip and left Daguragu on 20 March 1999.

In Canberra, Greg Dening once advised me not to write a thesis for three examiners, but to write a book to change the world.[17] This may be what the Gurindji elders expect me to do. All I know is that the Gurindji people spent a lot of time with me – and this is not because they were dedicated to my academic career. They perceived me to be a person who could bring their stories to a wider audience.

So here you are …

# CHAPTER 2

# MAINTAINING HISTORY

*I awakened here when the earth was new*
*There was emu, wombat, kangaroo*
*No other man of a different hue*
*I am this land*
*And this land is me*
HYLLUS HARIS 1988

Where does 'history' come from? We know, by definition, that history comes from the past. But *how* does it come to us? To put it another way, how do we *experience* the past? History always realises itself in the *present*, because without human efforts to perform the events and experiences of the past, the past never becomes a history. History has been explored, crafted, expressed and maintained constantly by people all round the world within the sphere of the present. Therefore, the ways of maintaining history directly influence the shape of the past that we experience in the present.

In many 'Western' and 'Westernised' societies, history-maintenance has been largely dominated and 'authenticated' by professional academic historians. Of course, for example, historical monuments are crafted by artists and museums are mostly managed by governments. However, in terms of identifying the 'historical truth', we normally rely on professional historians' work conducted in archives and libraries. In this way of shaping the past as an 'authentic' history, a handful of professional historians are the mediators who connect the past and present, which are otherwise *supposedly* distanced and disconnected.

While learning history from the Gurindji people, I realised that they maintain histories in a remarkably different manner from what I *thought* history-maintenance ought to be.

## BODY FOR PAYING ATTENTION TO THE WORLD

The Gurindji people, especially the elders, often sit on the ground and do nothing for a long time. I *thought* they were doing nothing. If there is no ceremony or urgent meeting, they will often spend all day apparently doing nothing. You may wake up early in the morning and sit down in the men's cultural area (men's boughshade) if you are a man. Women have women's boughshade. If you are hungry, you have breakfast at smoko time. You eat your tucker under the tree next to the shop and stay there for a while. You may go back to the men's or women's boughshade and, if you like, play cards with other people. Otherwise, you probably just sit there until you get hungry again.

What are the elders doing while sitting on the ground and being still? It took me a while to realise that they were actually seeing, listening and feeling. If you want to know what is happening in this world, you should stay still and pay attention to the world. Be aware of what is happening around you. Do not make your own 'noise', which often fogs your senses.

The Gurindji elders did not teach me in the way I wrote above. Instead, when I sat with them they told me what they saw, heard and felt. They told me, for example, that you could see the thick cloud over the hill so it would rain soon, you could hear fighting happening on the other side of the community, maybe grog or jealous business, or you could feel the warm wind from the north, that's why it's very hot these days. If dogs started barking at each other, they pointed to the dogs and told me they were fighting or playing. You see an aeroplane coming in this direction, so it may be a mail plane or flying doctor plane.

Of course, I could see and hear as they did, but I did not *pay attention* to such things. In the community, I certainly paid attention to the people who told me the stories, but I could not pay enough attention to the many other things around me. In fact, I am not only like this in the community. I am often preoccupied by my own work, thoughts or schedule, so sitting down and being still meant doing nothing to me.

The idea I learned was: do not use your body and senses to look for something. Instead, something will come to you if you are quiet enough to take notice. Keeping your body still and using your senses is the way to know the world. The Gurindji elders pay attention to the clouds, the fight, the wind, the dogs or the aeroplanes because this is the way to know the world around you. They even pay attention to the voice of Dreaming, which, unfortunately, may not be easy for many people to follow because of the cultural 'gap'. I usually try to understand the world by asking and searching. However, Gurindji people demonstrated to me how to know the world by simply being still and paying attention.[1] The art of knowing is not always the way of searching, but often the way of paying attention.

In fact, this way of using your senses applies not only when you are sitting, but also while you are moving your body. Paying attention to the world is even more acute while moving around the country. Furthermore, this does not just apply to the elders. Gurindji people – young or old, female or male – listen and see very carefully, and tell each other what is happening around them while they are moving. For instance, you see birds are flying over there, the bushfire down south, crocodiles have moved to the other side of the river, many donkeys are here and braying too loudly, or the fire site is there, so someone must have been there recently. They see and listen, then report and share their findings with each other.

You move your body not only for hunting or visiting other people, but also for knowing what is happening around you. Therefore, you do not always make your own noise. I am using the word 'noise' here as the preoccupation with your own thoughts, which fog your senses. My attention was often so lost and scattered that I could not receive as much information from the world as the Gurindji people did.

Your body is the essential medium through which you know the world. It does not matter if you are sitting, standing or moving. Pay more attention to the world around you and use your senses to receive information from the world.

## BODY FOR PRACTISING HISTORY

Paying attention is also essential when the Gurindji people practise their history. Paying attention to the world means not only knowing what is happening, but also remembering what happened here and there. The Gurindji people do not search for history as most academic historians do. Instead, they *pay attention* to their history. History often comes to you if you are alert enough to notice it. While you are sitting or moving, you can see, listen, feel or even touch the history around yourself, but only if you are sensitive and knowledgable enough to notice it.

For instance, you drive a car to visit your family in another community and see a hill, and you remember (or you hear the elders' teachings or discussion) that old people were killed there by *kartiya* [whitefella] in the early days. While hunting, you remember (or are told) not to go into that cave because dead people's bones and spirits are in there. You are fishing in a waterhole and you remember (or are told) that this old man's father dived underwater here and asked the rainbow snake to make a big rain. That's how old Wave Hill station was washed away. You see drunken people fighting each other and you remember (and discuss) how and why grog was introduced to the Gurindji country. When someone 'steals' an old man's promised wife, the elders are grumbling that *ngumpin* [Aboriginal] law was 'more hard' when they were young. History should be listened to, seen and felt around oneself in everyday life. History is something your body can sense, remember and practise.

However, if you are too busy doing other things, or if you do not have much time to sit still and wait, the elders often do not mind telling you the history in response to your questions. I tried to avoid this way of learning history, but I have to admit that I sometimes asked my questions of elders because my schedule was restricted. After all, everybody knew that I was a visitor. I am not a Gurindji, but a person who visited there to learn their history. The Gurindji people kindly understood and accepted my 'researcher-like' attitude.

When I say 'taking notice of the history around yourself', I am not mystifying or romanticising the Gurindji way of historical practice. I am simply emphasising that, for the Gurindji people, history is not a subject that you 'choose' to learn. Instead, *history is happening everywhere in everyday life.* The body is also essential in order to express history. Storytelling is often communicated by your body actions. Body (action) is part of human memories of the past. How the *kartiya* shot the Aboriginal people, how the Aboriginal people speared the kangaroo before using rifles, how the people used to be chained at the police station.

These stories were all performed through miming the physical actions. In addition, the Gurindji people often draw diagrams on the ground to explain their history. They also use stones, trees, seeds, fish, kangaroos, rivers, hills, billabongs, rain, clouds, sun, hands, heads, faces, spears, boomerangs, nulla-nulla [digging or fighting sticks], hats, cars, rifles and many other objects to express their history. For the Gurindji people, all bodies, objects and landscapes contain memories. Therefore, historical practice includes not only words, but also visual expression.

The body is essential for practising Gurindji history. Whoever you may be as an individual, you see the history. You listen to the history. Your body senses and feels the history. You remember history by listening, seeing and sharing. And you practise history by remembering and performing. You use your body by listening, seeing, visiting, performing, sharing, sitting, moving and interacting. The Gurindji historians demonstrated to me that historical practice is a bodily work. It is a lived experience.

*

Some may say I am exaggerating the difference between 'Western' academic and the Gurindji people's historical practices. At the same time, others may say the difference is so great that we cannot share a single concept of 'history'.

I believe that it is important to acknowledge the 'gap' between the academic mode of history and the Gurindji people's historical practice. We should not ignore this gap and *pretend* that we can all share 'history' without much trouble. However, acknowledging the gap should not be the end of the story but a starting point to *communicate across the gap*. Even though the Gurindji people's body/place-oriented historical practice is quite a contrast to academic historical disciplines, academic historians also live in their everyday lives away from their academic consciousness. It is not too difficult to realise that we all do experience history in our bodies and places without the academic discipline in our everyday lives. In other words, what Gurindji historians are doing in their country is not necessarily unfamiliar for the rest of the people. The gap is unavoidably there, but we can still understand and communicate with each other once academic historians become humble enough to accept that they cannot dominate 'history' all over the world.

## WHAT IS IN THE WORLD?

According to the Gurindji people, the world is full of life. In fact, it is not easy to find non-living beings in this world. Deborah B. Rose explains this idea by saying:

> For many Aboriginal people, everything in the world is alive:
> animals, trees, rains, sun, moon, some rocks and hills, and
> people are all conscious. So too are other beings such as the
> Rainbow Snake, the Hairy People and the Stumpy Men. All

have a right to exist, all have their own places of belonging, all have their own Law and culture.[2]

My experience in the Gurindji country was similar to what Rose describes. There are many living beings, especially in the bush. Apart from plants and animals, there are, for example, *kaya* [ghosts] living in the cave that come out at night and kill you and steal the meat from your campsite. *Mungamunga* in the bush and *kurrukang* in the water are both beautiful women who seduce men and sleep with them. *Munpa* [bush blackfella] are dangerous people. They live in the bush and envy the Aboriginal people living in the community. Bush blackfella often drive a black car and come to the community to steal food and women. Dead people's spirits are often around too. They may help and protect you, but you should be careful, because they can also be *kaya*. Dreaming or ancestral beings are all alive in the world too. They include stones, hills, rivers, waterholes and rainbows as well as animals, insects and plants.

What is probably more important is that the earth itself is alive too. Jimmy Mangayarri told me this. He picked up a handful of sand and taught me that you may think this *janyja* [soil] was just soil, but this was a 'man'. He also said the earth tells you the 'right way'. Furthermore, one of Old Jimmy's favourite sayings was, 'Don't matter what it is, everything come out longa this earth.'[3] You may find similar explanations in other ethnographies. For example, an Aboriginal person in the Kimberley told Erich Kolig that the ground is like 'a huge battery' that maintains life. You can 're-charge' this battery by practising rituals.[4] The world is full of life. Moreover, every living being comes from the earth, which is also alive. In this sense, one may say the world is alive.

However, what is really meant by 'the world is alive'? How is it possible? Up to this point, we understand that the world is alive, but we have not learned how and why. These questions cannot be answered without understanding the creation and maintenance of this world in Gurindji cosmology.

## DREAMING (1): ORIGIN OF THE WORLD

When Old Jimmy says that everything comes from the earth, he means that everything was created and has been maintained by the earth. I understood this 'earth' as the most general or abstract idea of what we normally refer to as Dreaming. There are plenty of anthropological works arguing about 'What is Dreaming?' There is no way I can summarise them or participate in these debates. Instead, here I want to present what I learned largely from the most important teacher for me, Jimmy Mangayarri.

The earth – or, in a sense, 'place' – is neither a conceptual nor a non-organic space in which every being exists and lives. Instead, place is the origin, cause and reason of every life and its existence. To describe this, Old Jimmy often used the following five different words: 'earth', 'Dreaming', 'law', 'right way' and 'history'.

At first glance, these words seem to explain the sequence of the world's creation. A naive understanding of Old Jimmy's teaching is that the earth was there first. Then Dreaming came out to shape the place and other beings. Dreaming beings came out of the earth, travelled to other countries and made everything. Creatures are not just plants, animals and people; the landscape itself is also a product of Dreaming. Dreaming also made the 'law' for this created world so that we can maintain the world by following and practising the law. Instead of 'law', Old Jimmy sometimes used the phrase 'right way' to refer to the Dreaming 'track' and to ethical behaviour. Eventually, this became the history of the maintained world.

However, Old Jimmy's teaching is not really as simple as this, because earth, Dreaming, law, 'right way' and history are also interchangeable with one another. For instance, when Dreaming beings shaped a hill and made law, the hill became the law itself. In general, the landscape is not just the product of Dreaming, but is itself Dreaming. In the same way, Dreaming did not just create the law – Dreaming *is* the law. Since Dreaming itself is law, a place becomes the law as well.

This concept of 'law' is of fundamental importance when one discusses moral philosophy. Billy Bunter, another elder of Daguragu, often told me that, 'Our law is this hill, that river, (so that) nobody can change the law.' Law does not only come from the earth; law also is the earth. Law is tangible, visible and physical.

However, once again, what is the relationship between these three terms? How could it be possible that earth, Dreaming and law are identical? At this point, I would like to remind you of another of Old Jimmy's terms: 'right way'. Using this phrase, Old Jimmy teaches us that there is an issue of morality. As I will discuss at length in next chapter, 'right way' is a geographical Dreaming track *as well as* ethical behaviour. It is important to understand that the 'right way' does not include the physical/metaphysical separation. 'Right way' is a geographical landscape as well as human (and non-human) behaviour. Morality is spatial as well as behavioural. The earth, Dreaming and law are identical because all of these have the same essential quality, namely, the 'right way' or the morality of the world.

Accordingly, another question arises: why is the Dreaming landscape moral? What is ethical activity? Or more generally, what does 'morality' mean? These new questions shift our attention from the origin of the world to the way of maintaining the world.

## DREAMING (2): HISTORY OF MAINTAINING THE WORLD

Dreaming stories tell you not only about the origin of the world, but also about how the world has been maintained. The world has been moral because Dreaming came out of the earth not only for creating but also for maintaining the world.

Now it has become clearer why the earth or Dreaming is 'law'. This is because Dreaming teaches us how to look after this created world. The Gurindji people have been a part of moral history because they have been participating in sustaining the world by following the Dreaming, or the 'right way'. However, needless to say, maintaining the world is not like maintaining a car. You are a part of the world while you are not a part of your car. The world is not an object to be maintained. Instead, people can exist because the world is alive and keeps its morality, and the world exists because people are alive and keep their morality: the world maintains you as you maintain the world.

Here, I am using the term 'morality' in the sense of an attitude to the world as well as the visible evidence of the maintained world. Moral behaviour is an attitude which contributes to sustaining the world. Ritual practice is a typical example. Visiting your country and communicating with your country or ancestral beings is also an important practice for maintaining the world.

At the same time, you should take notice of physical evidence – visible memories – that show that the world is maintaining its morality. That hill is there, and this river is here. This Dreaming rock is here and that Dreaming waterhole is still there. Bush tucker is always around the country. The rainbow snake is active in making big rains during the seasonal cycle. These are all visible memories of the world's creation as well as evidence that the morality of Dreaming has been maintained. In fact, such memories themselves are visible morality because if these objects and landscape are broken, the world loses its morality. The 'right way' or law is moral. In the same way, the land is moral, and Dreaming is moral. You may still ask, 'Morality for what purpose?' The answer is, however, now clear: for maintaining the living world, a part of which is the people themselves.

This is the 'history' of the moral world. This is history because this is how the world has been maintained. Landscape is history because it contains visible memories and evidence that tell you that the world has been maintained. The Gurindji people are also part of moral history because they hold their memories of the world's creation, and thus they are the evidence that the world has been maintained.

I would like to note that history is not just a story of the past. The earth is always there. That hill has been there and should always be there. Dreaming is always active, and therefore this world should always be maintained. Therefore Dreaming is not just a story of the past; it contains the present and the *potential* future at the same time. That hill was there, is there and should be there all the time. So were/are/should be Dreaming, earth, law, 'right way' and history. Dreaming is a story of any time. More precisely, it *should be* in any time.

Earth, Dreaming, 'right way' and law are the origin of the world and the history of maintaining the world. Dreaming is the moral history. As long as the world is alive, moral history is happening there. Land is the history. People are the history. You can see, listen, touch and feel the history through your physical interaction with memories of places. In other words, history can always occur everywhere as long as both place and people are part of it.

## MOBILITY: RELATIONSHIP BETWEEN BODY AND THE WORLD

I need to shift focus once more. I have discussed the meaning and function of the body and the world, but I have not explored the relationship between them. Since people are a part of the living world, the relation between a person and the world is not like subject and object. If so, then what is it like?

I will explore two key issues: mobility and knowledge. At first glance, these seem to be totally different issues – movement is a physical matter and knowledge is a metaphysical issue. However, in my understanding, the relationship between mobility and epistemology is fundamental to exploring the conditions of Gurindji historical practice. In my understanding of Gurindji philosophy, the relationship between their movement and their epistemology is a clue to answering the question: 'How is "self" related to the world?'

When I was at Daguragu, I was amazed by how frequently people moved. Some people were away for a couple of weeks visiting their relatives; some had gone to Darwin and nobody knew if they would ever come back. Visiting other communities for ceremony is as usual as doing ceremony in your own community. Even staying in the community, people love to go bush – hunting, fishing, swimming or even just moving around their country.

A simple explanation of Aboriginal mobility is commonly given: Aboriginal people are 'nomadic'. Anthropologists used to explain Aboriginal mobility by economic necessity.[5] A hunting and gathering economy is possible only by constantly moving your camping sites. However, contemporary Aboriginal mobility cannot be explained in this way, since today you can access enough food within the community. Today, most of the food eaten is from the shop located within the community. The Gurindji people often go hunting, fishing and gathering, but normally this is not because they are hungry.

In fact, I do not need to discuss 'why they move', as the answers are often very clear: because the Gurindji people like hunting, because they like bush tucker, because there is a ceremony in another community, because a relative is sick in Darwin, because they want to drink in town, because they get bored being in the community, and so on. Our question 'Why are they nomadic?' cannot be answered only by asking 'Why do they move?' Instead, the real question should be '*How do they move?*'

## WHERE IS HOME? WHAT IS HOME?

For a while, I thought the Gurindji people liked travelling, just as many settlers do. I also thought the key to answering 'How do they move?' would be the way they travel. It is always exciting to get out of your home and travel around the world. I expected Aboriginal people would appreciate the value of travelling because they are 'nomadic'. I was influenced by Bruce Chatwin's popular book *Songlines* (1987), a typical example of a book exploring this idea. Chatwin sees the 'nomadic' lifestyle as the origin of his (settlers') desire for travelling.[6] It is possible that this explanation is at least partly true. For example, our trip to Docker River for a ceremony was so special that the Gurindji people talked about this event repeatedly and remember it as a great journey. Such a trip is a special occasion for them. However, I would like to explore the more common practice of everyday mobility in the Gurindji country. In this sense, I realised that their movement is normally not travel at all. Their mobility is not for getting out of their home but for *living in their home.*

For the Gurindji people, 'home' is not a small box called a 'house' – which they call 'camp' in Creole. I found that the Gurindji people use their house almost like a storeroom. They keep their rifle and perhaps a few other valuable things in the house, but they spend most of their time outside. They cook, eat, watch TV, play cards, and even often sleep outside their houses. Continuing with this analogy, the outside of a house within the community is a kind of 'living room' in which you can eat, play, talk and sleep. Since the community has been well developed in the last couple of decades, this 'living room' is now full of utilities. Technically, you can survive by staying in this outdoor living room without moving to any other places.

If a house is a storeroom and the community is a living room, what is 'home' for the Gurindji people? By home, I mean a place where one lives with one's family – a place offering security and happiness. At this stage, my answer is that their home is their country itself. There are so many other 'rooms' you should visit and stay in, such as 'fishing rooms', 'bush plum rooms' or 'ceremonial rooms'. There are also 'sacred rooms' which you should go to and stay in only with an old person who knows how to behave, and there are 'kaya [ghosts] rooms' which you should never visit or stay in.

Therefore, the Gurindji people naturally move around their country because they do not want to stay only in the storeroom or living room all the time. Furthermore, for some people, the community is not even a part of their country. Staying there for them is like visiting neighbours or relatives, because their 'home' or country is away from the community. Even if visiting one's relative's countries or a town like Katherine means leaving your home, it still cannot be called 'travel'. These trips are more or less like visiting your neighbour or going shopping. 'Travel' happens only when you go to a place far away, such as Docker River or Adelaide, which you rarely visit and where you have few relatives. To sum up, for the Gurindji people, 'nomadic' life does not mean a travelling lifestyle or life without a home, but it means *life in a massive home.*

Here, for the time being, the answer is given: the Gurindji people move around a lot not because they are travellers by nature, but because their home is much bigger than settlers' small boxes or houses. Furthermore, we also should not forget that the world is alive and full of life in the Gurindji country. Therefore, their home is not only huge; it is also a shared space. That being said, the relationship between you and your home cannot be like that between owners and their private property. The world and people maintain each other. You have the obligation of maintaining your living country as your country has the obligation of looking after you. When you move around your country, whatever your purposes are, you should always be aware that you are surrounded by your home, which is full of life. You are not the owner of your home, but a part of it.

Therefore, although I do not object to the usage of the word 'nomadism' when referring to Aboriginal mobility, it should be used in the broader sense of the term. Aboriginal nomadism never means an everyday-travelling lifestyle; it means a life of communicating with the country, part of which is people themselves. This is the key to understanding the meaning of the Gurindji people's movement, because 'Why are they "nomadic"'?' can be answered only if we understand 'How do they maintain their country?' What does movement mean for the relationship between people and their country? In order to explore this question, I would like to return to our focus on Dreaming once again. This time, the focus is 'Dreaming and mobility'.

## DREAMING (3): ETHICS OF SPATIAL MOVEMENT

Morality in the Gurindji cosmology is related to the way the world is maintained. Ritual practice and visiting one's country and communicating with ancestral beings are fundamental activities enacted to sustain the world. This is moral behaviour. I would like to emphasise here that such moral behaviour is not possible without movement. In short, mobility is simply essential for people, as well as for the Dreaming, in order to maintain the world. I would like to discuss the meaning of movement in relation to three key themes: origin, history and morality.

Dreaming created this world by moving around the country. Therefore, movement occurred at the first stage of creation. It may be interesting to compare this cosmology to the Bible – the Christian understanding of the creation of the world. It is well known that in John 1 it says:

> In the beginning was the Word, and the Word was with God,
> and the Word was God. He was with God in the beginning.

Through him all things were made; without him nothing was made that has been made.[7]

Let me use these phrases to explore my understanding of the Gurindji cosmology:

> In the beginning was the movement, and the movement
> was with the Dreaming, and the movement was Dreaming.
> Movement was with Dreaming in the beginning. Through the
> movement all things were made; without movement nothing
> was made that has been made.

While the Christian God created the world by word, Dreaming created the world by movement.

This origin of the world also became the history of the world. The world has been maintained because Dreaming beings have been active in sacred sites as well as Dreaming tracks. Dreaming has been active all the time. Dreaming tracks that connect sacred sites are not 'roads' that Dreaming beings sometimes travel, but more like a 'river' or stream through which Dreaming beings continuously move. Therefore, the history of the maintained world can also mean the history of maintained mobility. The world is alive because Dreaming beings are always active and mobile.

As the Dreaming has maintained people through its movement, so do people maintain their Dreaming through their movement. In ritual, they follow the Dreaming track through their songs, dances and drawings. Songs, dances, paintings or objects following the movement of Dreaming and 're-charge' the power of Dreaming and its mobility. Such movements are ethical because they contribute to maintaining the world, its power and its morality. One should maintain the world through one's 'ethical movement' as Dreaming does. These ethics of spatial movement occur not only in ritual practice, but are applied in everyday activities as well. In everyday practice, you may not physically follow the Dreaming track, but it is essential to move around the country in order to relate and connect yourself to places. Your country or home is alive. It needs your care as you need its care. Going fishing and singing out for the country is a typical mutual relationship between people and their country: people look after the country by visiting and communicating with it and the country looks after the people by giving them plenty of fish. When visiting somewhere, people often sing songs that are related to the country. While moving, people pay attention to the world.

It is your movement that connects you to the world and its moral history. Movement is the origin of the world, the history of the world, and the morality of the world. After all, it does not always matter what the purpose of one's movement is. Rather, the process (that is, movement itself) is a necessary part of maintaining the Dreaming and the law, and is itself a reason for being 'nomadic'. Movement is the essence of life, world and history, and of the relationship between the world and your being.

Without ethical movement, there is no maintenance of the world. People and Dreaming sustain the world together through their ethical movement. Having got to this point, let us move on to a new question: how are these ethics of movement reflected in the Gurindji knowledge system? In other words, what is the relationship between the Gurindji people's 'nomadic' lifestyle and their epistemology?

## A WEB OF CONNECTION WITHOUT A CENTRE

The idea that mobility is the essence of maintaining the world also means that you do not have a 'central place' in the world. One of the reasons you have to move around the country is that Dreaming sites are scattered all over the country. As anthropological works show, there is no 'central sacred site' through which you can maintain the whole country. And there is no 'central ceremonial place' where you can 're-charge' the entire world. T.G.H. Strehlow explains that since the major totemic sites were 'linked according to the nature of their totems with the totemic sites of other subgroups and even of other tribes, not one of them was fitted in any sense to act as a sort of central "capital" site for a whole tribal subgroup or a whole tribe'.[8] Therefore, people and ceremonies should be shared and exchanged between different places, communities and countries.

In general, a sacred site or a community cannot claim itself as the centre of the world. Sacred sites are the points where people's and Dreaming beings' movements are connected. Dreaming tracks are the lines which connect the sites and people rather than divide them. Therefore movement is a fundamental function, since the Gurindji cosmology is based on networking among many sites, countries and people without the concept of the 'centre'. The world is maintained through the web of connection between Dreaming beings, people and their countries and ceremonies.

This view of Gurindji cosmology leads us to the unique positioning of 'self' in the world. In short, 'self' becomes remarkably relationalised. This happens on at least three levels. First of all, 'self' as a living human cannot be the centre of the world. The Dreaming or ancestral beings are as alive as living human beings. Humans cannot exist if the Dreaming dies, because humans are a part of this living world that is sustained by the Dreaming. Humans not only maintain the world but are also maintained by the world. In other words, your existence relies on Dreaming activities, and vice versa. Therefore, humans are not the central source of agency in the world. Instead, human activities are relationalised by Dreaming activities.[9]

Second, 'self' as a part of the country is not the centre of the world. Dreaming cannot be alive without maintaining its sacred sites and tracks, which are strongly connected with other people and their countries; the existence of you and your country is guaranteed only by interaction with other people and their countries. Naturally, your 'self' as well as your country cannot claim to be the centre, but they become parts of the web of connection. Therefore you cannot maintain your country by yourself, but only by connection with other people and their countries.

Third, your personal 'self' cannot be the centre of your community. There is no one in the community who can be the 'central figure' of the community. It is true that the older and more knowledgable you are, the more people respect your opinion. There are words such as 'boss', 'big man' or '*kanparijang* [leading/older person]' which may indicate authority in the community. However, I found that such a 'boss' does not have much 'right' or 'power' to make decisions without consulting other community members. Furthermore, even though it seems male elders tend to control many of the parts of a community's decision making, women do have their own social life. As men have men's *business*, women have women's *business*. In addition, there are joint male–female ceremonies which are possible only if the two sexes co-operate with each other. Children and young people have their own social life as well. It seems that there is general agreement that the seniors maintain authority over the juniors, and the elders often try to 'control' them. However, it often does not work. It is common practice among young people to run away to the bush or a town (mobility!) when a ceremony starts. There is no one person, nor any institution, which can control the whole community by her/his/their/its own will. Decision making is the process of negotiation with one another to build a 'connection' among the people in the community.

To sum up, there is no being which can be the centre of the living world. And there is no country which can be the centre of all countries. Moreover, there is no person who can be the centre of a country or community either. In other words, 'self' finds its position in the web of connection: the connection with other beings, other countries and other community members.[10]

## AN OPEN AND FLEXIBLE SYSTEM OF KNOWLEDGE

As 'self' is relationalised through the web of connection, so knowledge is also relationalised. There is no person, as well as no place, that generates exclusive knowledge, spreading it out, like radiation, from one place to all the other places. Instead, in this information system, knowledge is created anywhere and mobility brings it everywhere in all directions.

At the same time, however, one should not overlook the relational authenticity of storytellings. Stories have their 'belonging': belonging to certain person/s and belonging to certain place/s. Some people and places may generate more stories than others. A person who has more knowledge and connection to other people and places may assert more authenticity over more stories than others. In addition, places such as towns, communities, ceremonial sites or hunting-fishing points attract people (and Dreaming beings) and thus create a lot of stories to be carried and shared. It is, in a sense, like the internet: some sites hold more information and attract more attention than others, but in the end, there is no 'central site'. The knowledge or stories are exchanged and shared through the web of connection.

The information system is based on people's mobility and connection to each other and their countries. This system creates a particular manner of maintaining people's collective knowledge. Because there is no authentic centre that guarantees the validity of information, knowledge naturally acquires many variations through the process of networking.

In the Gurindji country, two or more contradictory stories tend to co-exist. People often do not even regard it as a contradiction. As I will demonstrate in the following chapters, the Gurindji people's historical knowledge accepts many different versions of events. Information running through the web of connection is rarely judged according to whether it is right or wrong. Multiple variations of information are produced, pooled and maintained as a bundle of possibilities without urgent judgement. On one level, it is true that the Gurindji knowledge system is closed, because there are many aspects of secrecy. However, on another level, the Gurindji way of maintaining knowledge can be called highly open. It is an open system because wherever and to whomever stories belong, they are pooled, and multiple variations are preferred. This mode of knowledge system is not only open; it is also flexible. It is a flexible system because they choose a story from the pooled possibilities according to the context of their storytellings. Knowledge or pooled stories are always chosen and used according to the context of the story being told.

## TEMPORALITY AND THE GURINDJI EPISTEMOLOGY

I would like to further explore the relationship between mobility and epistemology from another angle: the temporal aspects of this relationship. The importance of place in the Gurindji cosmology should not be underestimated. However, it is remiss to deny the concept of 'time' in their epistemology. Although the intricate relationship between history and place (time and space) will be discussed in following chapters, I would like to briefly explore three concepts (or functions) of temporality – those of 'right time', 'enduring time' and 'spontaneity' – in Gurindji cultural and social practices.

First of all, it cannot be overestimated that the seasonal sense of 'time' is fundamental to hunting and gathering activities. To be successful, you always need to know the 'right time' to hunt, fish and gather. The Gurindji people always pay attention to their country, noticing if the bush plum is ripe, if bush turkeys are round and fat. When you notice rain comes, you know lots of fish will come back to the river. Of course, their pooled knowledge also tells them the 'right time' to hunt what, and where to go and how. The idea of 'right time' in right place is crucial for mobility in hunting and gathering. The 'right time' for their ceremony is also a major concern among the Gurindji people. This is not only the seasonal timing of conducting the ceremony. In a ceremony there is a 'right time' to start singing, and to start dancing, and also a 'right time' to stop the ceremony. Thus the concept of 'right time' is essential for both their hunting and their ceremonial activities. The Gurindji temporality needs a concept of 'right time' to perform a right action. The sense and the knowledge of 'right time' have always been integral to the Gurindji epistemology.

Second, in order to maintain their information system, it is important to spend an enormous amount of time discussing, learning, teaching and sharing. The open and flexible system of knowledge can function well only if people do not rush to make a decision. It was amazing to know how long people could sit down, discuss and negotiate an issue in order to explore every possibility of their decisions. For example, the rumour that the Gurindji people were invited for the big *business* in Docker River had been talked about in the community for a long time. When I heard the story for the first time they were talking as if this ceremonial trip would happen the next week. However, whenever I asked them when the departure was to be, they told me 'maybe next week'. And there had been discussion for a long time about which route to take, who was to go and what would be done there, etc. One day, people from Yarralin visited and joined this discussion. On another day, there was discussion with Lajamanu people. The Daguragu people also went to Yarralin and Lajamanu to discuss this journey. When they finally decided to leave for Docker River, it had been nearly two months since I had first heard the rumour of this journey for ceremony. In order to keep the knowledge system functioning well, you should take as much time as you need. I do not think there is a concept of 'wasting time' in decision making.

In this sense, the Gurindji knowledge system can be called 'process-oriented' rather than 'outcome-oriented'. Knowledge procedure is as important as the product. People's mobility must be promoted, and then new stories must be exchanged again and again and again. Information should be pooled more and more and more. Discussion and negotiation goes on and on and on. This process of maintaining their knowledge requires 'enduring time'.

Third, I also need to emphasise the importance of 'spontaneity' in the Gurindji temporal structure. Once a decision has been made, action follows immediately. I was often shocked by how quickly the Gurindji people made themselves ready, once they had decided to make a move. Hunting happens when they decide to go. People often came to my house and asked if I would like to go hunting with them. When I asked them 'when?', the answer was normally 'now'. There is no delay. In fact, people often told me that they would take me to a certain place 'tomorrow' or 'next week'. However, my excitement was often dashed to find them the next morning saying 'Oh, maybe tomorrow/next week.' I finally got used to this manner of either immediate action or not knowing when it would be.

This 'spontaneity' does not only happen in hunting activities. In many other cases, the time they decide to do something is the time they actually make a move. The time they decide to go swimming is the time they are leaving for a billabong. The time they decide to go to the town is the time they find a lift. As you may guess, such immediate action occurred when we started our ceremonial journey to Docker River as well. To be honest, I still do not know how the 'right time' to move was determined. After waiting for two months for the Docker River trip to happen, I became suspicious about the journey itself. I thought it would never happen. However, when it happened, it happened ridiculously quickly. When they finally decided to leave the community, we were driving cars towards the south by the evening of the same day!

## WHAT IS THE GURINDJI PEOPLE'S HISTORICAL PRACTICE?

Let us now return to our original topic: the conditions of maintaining history. I have already explored this question in terms of the Gurindji people's physical practice (body and history) and the idea of a maintained world (Dreaming and history). Here, I would like to explore the meaning of (1) movement, (2) an open and flexible system of knowledge, and (3) the three temporal dimensions, in the Gurindji people's historical practice.

History is *happening* all over the country, so mobility is essential to physically access the places and to pay attention to history. Furthermore, mobility creates the unique relationship between 'self' and the world. You find 'self' in relation to the web of connection: connection with other beings, other countries and other community members. Naturally, historical practice becomes relationalised into the web of connection as well. You are not the central or control agent of a practising history. Nor can you practise the history by yourself. Instead, your historical practice must 'connect' to places, Dreaming, countries and people. History happens when you visit the hill which contains the memory of people killed by Europeans. History happens when you see the young people using a rifle instead of a spear while hunting. History happens when you realise that the rainbow snake recently rose up again and made floods around the country. Historical practice can be possible only through the interaction between the living world and yourself: history happens in-between body and place.

The Gurindji people maintain their historical knowledge based on its multiplicity. It is natural and preferable to maintain many different versions of a certain event. On one level, one can say that different variations of histories are pooled among the people in the same way that a warehouse maintains its stock. A storyteller chooses a story from the pooled knowledge according to the context of where, what, and who she/he is relating it to and what she/he is trying to express. However, on another level, you can also say that every historical narrative is a new version of the event because your positioning in the networking world is never the same. You are part of the web of connection, and your mobility always brings you to a new position in this web. Therefore, places and your body connect with each other and create histories differently in particular contexts. This process means that history is always situated in time and space. Thus the Gurindji way of historical practice reflects their open and flexible system on two different levels: (1) pooled and maintained historical knowledge, and (2) situationalised and contextualised historical knowledge.

We need to observe that the above two aspects of historical knowledge are related to their temporal structure. First, the Gurindji way of historical practice requires a sense of 'right time' and 'spontaneity'. Historical knowledge is always relationalised and situationalised. Therefore history only happens 'spontaneously' at the 'right time' in the 'right place'. Every historical narrative is a product of a certain connection among the storyteller, listener, other beings or objects and places, so that a particular opportunity does not happen twice. You cannot postpone this opportunity for sharing the history with particular people and particular objects in a particular place. History happens 'spontaneously' when the 'right time' comes.

Second, you also need 'enduring time' in order to maintain historical knowledge. Since Gurindji history is not documentary cultural practice, you need the repetition of storytelling in order to share, remember and maintain historical knowledge. In the same way, places need to be visited repeatedly to maintain the history. In short, historical knowledge can be pooled and maintained only by a never-ending repetition of storytellings and visiting places.

✳

To sum up, Gurindji history does not have a standard or official text-book which anyone can access equally at any time or in any place. Instead, Gurindji history *happens* to particular people, in particular places, at specific times. At the same time, this situated history occurs repeatedly for anyone, anywhere, at any time. In other words, historical knowledge has been created and maintained through the web of connection among the people, Dreaming beings and their countries.

The findings of my study do not represent an exception to the conditions of the Gurindji way of historical practice. This book is based on the Gurindji people's pooled and maintained historical knowledge. At the same time, it is the product of my personal commitment to certain community members in particular places at specific times. There is no other way of practising, learning and sharing the Gurindji people's history.

# CHAPTER 3

# PLACE-ORIENTED HISTORY

*It is important to remember that space-time is
not supposed to be Euclidean. As far as the geodesics
are concerned, this has the effect that space-time
is like a hilly countryside.*
BERTRAND RUSSELL 1958

Indigenous Australians' cultures are so strongly related to their land that numerous attempts have been made by scholars to understand the Aboriginal meaning of landscape, or Dreaming geography. In the anthropology of Australian Aboriginal societies, land relationships have been at the centre of many debates.[1] One of the features of recent arguments about Aboriginal land relations is discussion of the colonial landscape.[2] These works help us understand the influence of colonisation on the Aboriginal landscape. However, my question in this chapter is not about how colonisation *influenced* the Aboriginal landscape, but rather how the Aboriginal landscape *negotiated with* colonisation.

## TIME AND SPACE, HISTORY AND LANDSCAPE

Indigenous Australians' understanding of time and space is discussed at length in Tony Swain's controversial book *A Place for Strangers* (1993).[3] Through a comparative study of Aboriginal concepts of being across the Australian continent, Swain denies the existence of a concept of 'time' in precolonial Aboriginal societies. As an alternative, he emphasises the ontological importance of place or space in 'original' Aboriginal worldviews. Swain also claims that the concept of time and history gradually infiltrated into Aboriginal worldviews through contact with external peoples, such as the Melanesians, Indonesians and Europeans. His argument is highly problematic due to his assumption of a 'precolonial' or 'original' Aboriginal ontology. Furthermore, Swain's notions of time and history are narrowly defined and based on Western conceptions of these terms. Accordingly, his denial of time and history in precolonial Aboriginal ontology is difficult to accept.[4]

Despite these problems, my understanding of the Gurindji ontology corresponds with Swain's emphasis on the importance of place in Aboriginal being. John Rudder, for example, uses terms such as 'temporal location' or 'temporal space' to describe the Yolngu concept of time.[5] Howard Morphy also points out the 'subordination of time to space' in the Aboriginal Dreaming landscape.[6]

These arguments may lead us into two different approaches to the subject of colonial history and Aboriginal landscape. First, they arouse our interest in the historical change in Aboriginal ontology, or their concepts of time and space. The Aboriginal mode of being is more grounded in spatial dimensions than in temporal dimensions. Therefore Martin Heidegger's ontology, which assumes time to be the distinctive ontological function that can represent European modes of being, cannot represent Aboriginal modes of being.[7] On the ontological level, Australian colonisation can be regarded as a conflict between space-oriented modes of being and time-oriented modes of being. The second approach is to set Australian colonial history within an Aboriginal landscape. If, as Morphy says, time is subordinated to space, it is possible that history is subordinated to place in Aboriginal cosmology. Instead of studying how colonial history changed Aboriginal cosmology, one may be motivated to study how colonial history was included in Aboriginal cosmology.

With these points in mind, we may apply two different approaches to the relationship between colonial history and Aboriginal landscape. The first approach can be called the 'history of landscape', whereby the Aboriginal view of landscape may have been altered through colonial history. Through the colonial conflict of different cultural concepts of time and space, Aboriginal landscape may have changed from a space-oriented view to a time-oriented view. For example, it is reasonable to assume that the physical transformation of the landscape, especially environmental changes, may affect the space-oriented Aboriginal cosmology. Due to the intrusion of settlers and their industry, landscapes were visually altered over the years. Aboriginal people may have had to confront unexpected and uncontrollable changes to their view of landscape, which they could not accept without acknowledging or adopting a Western linear temporal structure or time-oriented history. There should be studies of the historical change in the Aboriginal view of landscape. The 'colonial history of Aboriginal landscape' is a positive approach to exploring the question of history and landscape.

I would now like to introduce another approach into my discussion. This second approach can be referred to as the 'landscape of history'. If the Aboriginal time–space concept is more or less space-oriented, the colonial history may be interpreted by the Aboriginal landscape. Morphy suggests that the Aboriginal ancestral past is reproduced in their Dreaming landscape.[8] In the same way, the colonial past may also be reproduced in the Aboriginal landscape.

However, this assumption must first confront the fundamental differences between Dreaming story and colonial invasion history: while Dreaming is sacred, stories of European invasion are not held to be sacred in Aboriginal cosmology and geography. That being said, what is the nature of Aboriginal narratives of their colonial histories? How can Aboriginal cosmology accept colonial history as a part of the landscape? Do Dreaming stories and colonial stories occur in different dimensions in Aboriginal cosmology?

## LANDSCAPE AND MORALITY

To answer the questions above, it is worthwhile looking into the recent discussion devoted to the subject of 'myth as history, history as myth'.[9] Although the aims and conclusions of these works are not consistent, their common theme is the intricate relationship between history and myth within Aboriginal narratives.[10] One of the most famous examples of Aboriginal colonial stories is probably the history of Captain Cook.[11] It is common knowledge in the Victoria River district that Captain Cook came to Darwin and invaded Aboriginal land. Deborah B. Rose argues that although Captain Cook never personally appeared in the area, the story accurately represents the local understandings of the immorality of colonial invasion and colonial law. White people's law, which allows them to go into another people's country, to start shooting people and stealing their land, represents a total lack of morality.[12] For Aboriginal people of many places in Australia, moral law comes from Dreaming geography. Land is the origin and evidence of the existing world. Invading another people's land and killing Indigenous people is fundamentally immoral.

There is a strong contrast between Aboriginal law with morality and European law without morality. From this Captain Cook history, one may infer that Aboriginal people make clear distinctions between Aboriginal law and European law in terms of its moral value. Aboriginal stories of the European intrusion into the Australian continent are immoral histories. Consequently, most colonial stories are not Dreaming stories.[13]

It is academics, not Indigenous Australians themselves, who categorise both Aboriginal colonial histories and their Dreaming stories as 'myths'. For Aboriginal people, it is not a question of a story being a myth or history, because these stories are all 'real'. Instead, there is a strict difference between sacred (Dreaming) and immoral (colonial) stories. As I discussed above, it must be understood that Dreaming stories and European invasion histories are not the same types of stories. If so, how can Dreaming stories interact with colonial history? Is it possible to consider the Aboriginal Dreaming landscape and invasion history within the same dimensions?

In searching for a key to this problem, let us consider how, or to what extent, Aboriginal people put these stories into different categories. In fact, we can see that Aboriginal people consider colonial histories within the same framework of thought as Dreaming stories when they examine and assess the moral ground of European law. Through the Captain Cook history, Aboriginal historians make a comparative study of two different laws. While Dreaming and colonial history are different types of stories, we can also say that both stories are situated within a common 'moral dimension'. In the process of their examination, Aboriginal Dreaming stories (Aboriginal law) and their stories of European colonisation (European law) both fall within one dimension in terms of moral philosophy.

Aboriginal Dreaming cosmology is characterised by place-oriented morality. In contrast, Captain Cook can never be Dreaming since his law is immoral. Consequently, Captain Cook cannot be placed within the Dreaming landscape. Dreaming stories and European invasion histories form different categories for Aboriginal people. However, we may also say that both the Dreaming and colonial stories are situated in the same horizon in terms of 'law': Aboriginal law has morality, but Captain Cook law does not. Nevertheless both are still regarded as laws.

Here again, I remind you of our original question: what is the relationship between colonial history and the Aboriginal landscape? Do colonial histories have spatial or geographical locations in the Aboriginal landscape? Can the place-oriented Aboriginal cosmology assimilate (supposedly) time-oriented colonial history? The key to answering this question is not that Dreaming stories and the colonial narratives of Aboriginal people are both 'mythological'. This does not reflect Aboriginal views. For the Aboriginal people, the key issue is most probably the *spatial dimension of morality*. If one can *see* the moral value within the landscape, it may be possible to find the 'location' of colonial immorality in the same landscape. Are there any relationships between colonial history and the Aboriginal landscape? If so, how are they connected? An Aboriginal historian must be the one to answer these questions.

## 'FOLLOW THE RIGHT WAY'

Following my introduction to Jimmy Mangayarri, he was eager to teach me about the 'right way'. He often said to me, 'You must follow the right way.' Naturally, whenever I had a chance to talk with him, I focused on knowing what the 'right way' was. However, understanding the 'right way' was not an easy task, because it was not clear to me if the 'right way' is a geographical track or a moral rule. One of our first conversations was as follows:

> *Mino (M)*: So, old man, you tell me the right way. What is the right way?
> *Old Jimmy (J)*: You look round. Sun go down that way (west), sun get up that way (east), this is the right way.

He also drew three straight lines from the west to the east on the ground. Figure 3.1 represents the Dreaming tracks of the Gurindji people and their neighbours' cultural geography. Old Jimmy explained that the emu, corella and *Jurntakal* travelled from the west sea to the east sea. Of the three, the most important Dreaming in this discussion is *Jurntakal*, a very powerful and dangerous snake. The general idea of *Jurntakal* is that it is a snake; its species is normally not specified. It is known to have originated from the sea near Wyndham (Western Australia) and then travelled to the east. There are many secret sites related to *Jurntakal*. Most *Jurntakal* sites are dangerous places that should be treated carefully. I heard many stories of people dying because of their mistreatment of *Jurntakal* Dreaming sites.[14]

Old Jimmy often drew only a single line and explained it was *Jurntakal*. I would like to emphasise that wherever he sat and whichever direction he faced, Old Jimmy drew a line from the west to the east, and then told me this was the 'right way'. To confirm this, I always brought a compass to check the directions of his sand drawings, and there were no deviations. Therefore, for the moment, we may conclude that the 'right way' is a geographical track of *Jurntakal* Dreaming. The 'right way' is not an ideological idea, but a track which has a spatial direction within a particular geography.

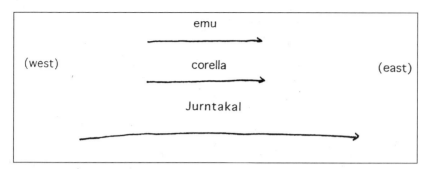

Figure 3.1 Three Dreaming tracks

However, the question remains: why is *Jurntakal* Dreaming track the 'right' way? We know this geographical track is a 'way', but we do not know how this track or 'spatial direction' can be *right*. Old Jimmy told me that *Jurntakal* rose from the earth, and through his travelling he shaped landscapes and created the people and law of each country:

> *Jurntakal* knows a lot. *Jurntakal* can tell you the right way. *Jurntakal* is the boss of people. He is the only one boss. You cannot run over the law. Law from him. He made all law, people, everything.

He also told me that the *Jurntakal* law is the earth law. *Jurntakal* rose from the earth, and furthermore, Old Jimmy said the earth itself is alive:

> *Yunmi* [we] come from this dirt. Earth is alive just like you and me. Everything don't matter what it is, everything is from this earth, dirt. You born in the ground. Earth know … You don't know the earth, earth tell you, that's why you born.

One may interpret Old Jimmy's teaching in this way: in this living and conscious earth, motion occurred from within the earth to the surface, and across the surface. *Jurntakal* is right because he rose from the earth and gave people the law. According to Old Jimmy's philosophy, this single line representing the 'movement from west to east' (Figure

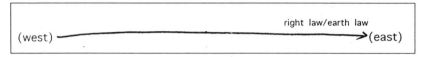

Figure 3.2 Right way/Earth law

3.2) opens up the ontological and moral dimensions of the world. This movement is the fundamental moment that is shaping the world.

I said 'moment', but this moment, in fact, has endured: the creation of the world is not just the event which happened in the past but is also contemporary, because *Jurntakal*'s (and many other Dreaming beings') movements are continuous. The movement of Dreaming is the ontological origin and the creator of the beings in the world, as well as the original morality that sustains and maintains the existing world.

From Old Jimmy's perspective, spatial direction/movement and morality/law are undifferentiated. The earth, *Jurntakal* or his movement from west to east are all at once the historical, ontological and moral origin of beings in the world. We exist, live and die under the earth law. *Jurntakal* always shows us the 'right way' because his law comes from the earth through his great travels. Therefore, the 'right way' includes a geographical Dreaming track, *as well as* ethical behaviour. In Old Jimmy's philosophy, the 'right way' does not involve a separation of the physical and metaphysical. 'Right way' includes the geographical landscape *as well as* earth law. The earth, Dreaming and law are inseparable from one another.

In Old Jimmy's sacred geography, *Jurntakal* is the one who made the law, living beings and the world itself. Everything comes from *Jurntakal*'s movement. As I mentioned in the previous chapter, you can find similar expressions from other Aboriginal people as well. In addition to the Aboriginal expression of the earth as 'a huge battery',[15] for instance, Hobbles Danayarri of Yarralin told Rose, 'Everything come up out of ground – Language, people, emu, kangaroo, grass. That's Law.'[16] Rose explains that 'in many parts of Australia, the ultimate origin of the life of country is the earth itself'.[17] In Old Jimmy's view, the *Jurntakal* track is the 'right way' because through his travels, he has been making law or 'everything' that is coming from the earth.

On the way to the Gurindji country, 1997

Jimmy Mangayarri, 1997

Japarta *motika*, 1997

Peter Raymond, 1997

*Karu* Dreaming Hill, 1997

On the way to Docker River, 1997

Old Jimmy
showing the
'right way',
1999

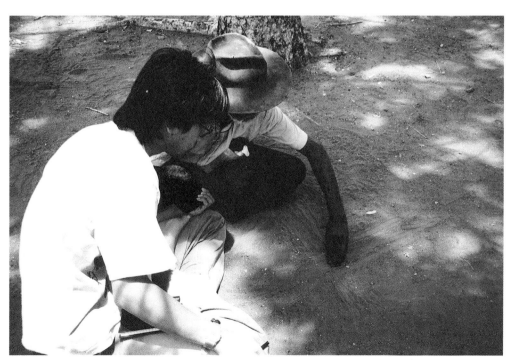

Old Jimmy drawing on the sand, 1999

Spears from the Top End, 1997

Blackfella Knob from Daguragu, 1997

George Sambo pointing at Seale Gorge, 2000

Old Jimmy demonstrating how *ngumpin* were chained, 2000

Ronnie Wave
Hill, 1999

Wave Hill Junction, 1999

Daguragu's fashion scene, 1997

Teddy Crew, 1997

Stanly Sambo, 2000

Banjo Ryan, 1997. Photo courtesy of Mayumi Uchida

Lipananyku, 1997

Rainstones, 1997

Seven Mile Waterhole, 1997

Alex Moray, 1936(?), photo courtesy of Vern O'Brien

Mick Rangiari, 1997, photo courtesy of Mayumi Uchida

*Partiki* tree in the Daguragu township, 1997

Violet Donald, 1997

Gough Whitlam and Vincent Lingiari, 1975, photo courtesy of Darrell Lewis

Ruins of the stone wall at Jimparrak, 1997

Victor Vincent visting Jimparrak 1997

Harry George sitting at the memorial stone, 1997

Presentation at Daguragu, 2000

Billy Bunter, 1997

Presentation at the council meeting, 2000

Old Jimmy and Mino, 2000, photo courtesy of Marina Pacific

## HOW DO YOU FOLLOW THE RIGHT WAY?

However, another question to solve is: what does he mean that we must 'follow' the 'right way'? So far, we understand the 'right way' as a spatial and geographical track. Therefore, following the 'right way' may mean to physically follow the *Jurntakal* track of the Dreaming geography. In a ritual sense, this explanation may be correct. Nevertheless, this is not always what Old Jimmy means by 'follow the right way'. Rather, in many cases, his use of the word 'following' refers to our moral behaviour. In this sense, the 'right way' comes to mean the moral behaviour rather than the geographical track. According to Old Jimmy, *Jurntakal* teaches the 'right way' through dreams:

> *J*: When I sleep, I never forget this. He [*Jurntakal*] tell me and I can speak with him. Just like a telephone.
> *M*: You talk with *Jurntakal*?
> *J*: Yes, just like telephone, that is just like a dream.
> *M*: He tells you right way?
> *J*: Yes, he teach you the right way. You wake up, you had dream, just like a telephone. You might study at school. You might write a paper, teacher tell you. Just like this. Same way.
> *M*: So, can I have a right way? He tells me the right way?
> *J*: Yes, that's why I tell you. Do the right thing. You study at school, high school. Just like this, you learn right way.

As we use a telephone, *Jurntakal* uses a dream to tell him the 'right way'. He also said you needed 'training' to talk with *Jurntakal*, which was like learning at a school. In this explanation, it seems that 'way' means people's behaviour rather than a geographical track. He often said to me, 'Do the right thing.' From this viewpoint, one may conclude that Old Jimmy uses the word 'way' in two different senses: the 'way' as in the geographical track of *Jurntakal* Dreaming, and the 'way' as in the moral rule of the earth law.

However, Old Jimmy also told me another story which made me realise that the situation is even more complex than stated above. Old Jimmy sometimes called the earth law 'high school' when he emphasised the educational aspect of Aboriginal law. Using sand drawing, Old Jimmy explained that there are differences between European school education and the 'Aboriginal school' or their way of training:

Old Jimmy drew two lines from the west to the east. He explained line (A) is European schooling, and line (B) is Aboriginal schooling. He said he belonged to line (B), an Aboriginal school, or as he calls it, a 'big high school'. He told me that the European school is 'only the half way'. Old Jimmy taught me why a European school is 'only the half way' in several different aspects. This can be summarised into three main reasons:

1: A European school is based on books, but an Aboriginal school is based on the earth.
2: A European school requires only a decade to complete but an Aboriginal school takes a lifetime to complete.
3: An Aboriginal school is *physically* bigger than a European school.

First of all, a European school is based on books and pencils. These have, according to Old Jimmy, nothing to do with the earth law. He said, 'My book is on this earth ... I never use pencil. I got more experience on this earth.' Even though you may be able to read and write, you are only 'half way' without knowing the earth law. For Old Jimmy, a European school is a place to learn how to read and write, which may be useful skills but are never as valuable as knowing the earth law. Without learning the earth law, education is incomplete.

This view brings him to his second reason: a European school finishes too early. From Old Jimmy's point of view, European education

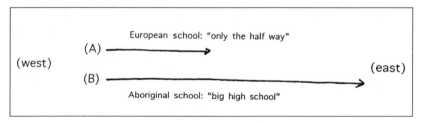

Figure 3.3 Aboriginal school, European school

starts when a child reaches the age of five, and most pupils finish school by 15–17 years of age. If one compares this period to the process of being a fully initiated man in Aboriginal society, Aboriginal school is a lifetime of education.[18] Billy Bunter, a middle-aged community member, told me that he still had 'thirty, forty years to go. For old people, I'm still child. Old people, they know every song and dance. I am blind.' From this perspective, it is reasonable to say that an Aboriginal school is a 'big school' and the European school is only a 'halfway school'.

Furthermore, according to Old Jimmy, an Aboriginal school is bigger than a European school not only because of the education period, but also in terms of its physical size. Old Jimmy said an Aboriginal school is much bigger than a European school because an Aboriginal school – *Jurntakal* track – is from the western sea to the eastern sea. Since Aboriginal law is the earth law, an Aboriginal 'school' itself is also the earth or Dreaming landscapes of their land. From Old Jimmy's point of view, the geographical Dreaming track *is* the Aboriginal school. In comparison to the physical length of the *Jurntakal* track, it is logical that a European schoolhouse is a lot smaller than an Aboriginal school. For Old Jimmy, geography (place) and education (morality) are not discrete concepts.

I would like to provide another example of the spatial dimension of morality. Old Jimmy drew a line from west to east, and said, 'We longa [belong to] this high rise ... this is the good way.' Then he also drew other lines, one from south to north, and the other from north to south, and said, 'This way is down ... Go down, no good that way ... You go this way, you drown (losing the right way).'

The way to the north as well as to the south is 'bad way', or as he also said, 'bad move'. If you follow that way, you lose the right way. On another occasion, he drew Figure 3.5 and told me the way from the north to the south is to 'break the law'. If you break the law, you may follow the way (A) or the way (B). You do not know which way to go.

Old Jimmy also explained that the right law is like a twig. If you break it you can never join it together again:

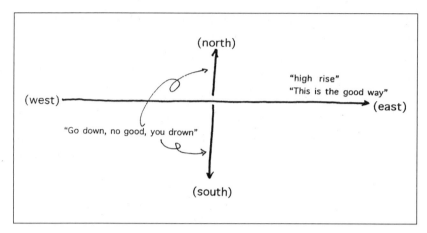

Figure 3.4 Good way, bad way

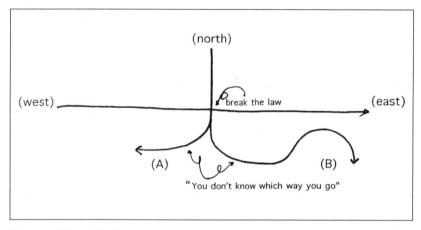

Figure 3.5 'Break the law'

> *J*: See this (a twig), only one way. When you broke it, can you
> join again?
> *M*: No, no.
> *J*: See, you throw away. You never do this. You must keep
> our way, never broke. If you broke the law, what can you do?
> That's why you do the right way to go.

Once you break the law, you can never follow the right way, you lose it.
Using a twig to represent the earth law (because a twig comes from the

earth), Old Jimmy explained that you should not break the law. The landscape itself represents the nature of Aboriginal law as well. Billy Bunter of Daguragu often told me that Aboriginal law is 'that hill and this river', so you cannot move that hill to another place. This means you cannot change the law. A small portion of nature (a twig) or the landscape (hill and river) represent Aboriginal law.

I would like to summarise his basic idea of the 'right way': from Old Jimmy's perspective, spatial direction and morality are undifferentiated. The earth, *Jurntakal* or his movement from west to east shows us the 'right way'. The 'right way' includes a geographical Dreaming track *as well as* moral behaviour. In Old Jimmy's philosophy, the 'right way' does not involve a dichotomisation of the physical and metaphysical. The 'right way' is spatial as well as behavioural; landscape includes a moral dimension.

## WHICH WAY DID CAPTAIN COOK COME?

During my stay in Daguragu, Old Jimmy often taught me the nature of European people, their law, and colonisation. Old Jimmy analysed the nature of colonisation from a spatial and a moral perspective. He also used his method of sand drawing to analyse Australian colonialism. Let us learn how Old Jimmy, as a historian, analyses Australian colonial history.

When I asked Old Jimmy from which direction the English came, he drew a line from north to south, and said, '*Kartiya* [the English] bin come from here [the north] … He cut 'em cross (the right way) … He broke the law.' For Old Jimmy, the concept of morality–immorality is related to a spatial direction.

Captain Cook came to Darwin and started to invade Aboriginal land. Captain Cook arrived in Darwin harbour and proceeded towards to the south. In his advance, Captain Cook cut across the *Jurntakal* Dreaming track. Captain Cook came from the wrong direction and moved in the wrong direction, and in doing so, he broke the 'right way' or the earth law. Here, colonisers' spatial movement accurately represents the immorality of Australian colonialism.

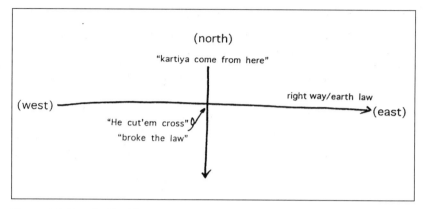

Figure 3.6 Captain Cook's movement

It seems that for Old Jimmy, directions, either north or south, are not important. The significant point is that England is not located on the 'right way'; the English came to Australia and cut across the 'right way'; they broke the earth law.

In Figure 3.7, Old Jimmy drew a circle (A) indicating England: 'Maybe England here.' He also drew another circle on the 'right way'

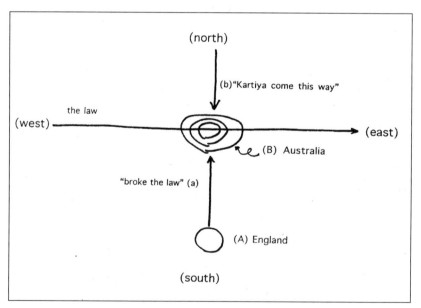

Fgure 3.7 Location of 'England'

or the 'earth law' and said, 'This island for *yunmi* [us].' While he drew a line (a) from south/England (A) to north/Australia (B) and said English people had broken the earth law, he also drew another line (b) from north to south and told me the English came this way. Here, spatial direction clearly implies morality.

The colonisers' behaviour and movement are both perceived as immoral and contradictory to the earth law. There is no separation between spatial and behavioural morality in Old Jimmy's analysis. Thus, the conditions of colonialism are interpreted through the colonisers' spatial direction and movement. Old Jimmy repeatedly criticised the colonisers' immoral attitude:

> *Kartiya* [the European] never understand. He maybe think
> *ngumpin* [Aboriginal people] stupid. He think he can do
> whatever he like. *Kuya, wankaj* [like this, very bad] ... *Kartiya*
> never ask people. *Kartiya* must ask people ... you know, all this
> idea from fuck'n Captain Cook ...

Aboriginal people never went to England, but Captain Cook came to Australia without permission. White people stole Aboriginal women without permission. In Old Jimmy's view, the core of the immorality of Australian colonisation is that Europeans never asked for permission to enter Aboriginal land. He even suggests an acceptable mode of co-habitation:

> Why he never say: 'Oh, come on mate, you and me live
> together. You and me living together, mates together ... Mate
> together. Live together. One *mangari* [food]. One table. Cart
> up wood together. No more fighting one another ...' But
> you never do that. You decided to clean the people out from
> their own country. *Ngumpin* [Aboriginal] never went and
> kill you there longa England. He never made a big war longa
> you there, finish you there. No! You did the wrong thing,
> finishing up *ngumpin*. Like that now, no good that game.
> Well, you made it very hard.[19]

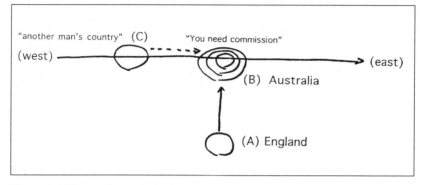

Figure 3.8 'You need permission.'

Old Jimmy explains this in the sand drawing, Figure 3.8.

Old Jimmy said that circle (C) is 'another man's country', and explained that whenever they come to our country, 'you need commission [permission]', which Captain Cook or the English never sought. 'Another man's country' is not necessarily located on the *Jurntakal* track in the geographical sense. As long as people maintain the morality, their land and behaviour are accepted as following the 'right way' in Old Jimmy's moral geography. In contrast, an immoral land (England) is located outside the line because their law does not come from the earth.

In the same manner, immoral attitudes should not be positioned on the 'right way' either. This is not just about European intrusion into the Aboriginal countries. Old Jimmy also criticises the fact that *kartiya* have even stolen the earth; Old Jimmy does not approve of the mining industry. However, he also said you needed at least the permission of the local people if you really want to do it: 'He [Europeans] ask 'em

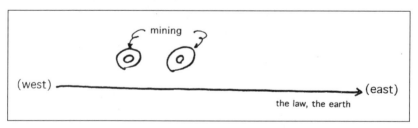

Figure 3.9 Moral geography of mining

boss of this country … Maybe he say yes, maybe say no … They can't do what they like.' To explain this to me, he also showed the moral geography of mining by drawing two circles outside the 'right way'.

He said as follows:

> You got a mining, gold mining. Dig 'im, dig 'im the earth. He took that earth. He got money the people on this earth. What did you live on earth? What did you make? Here is this earth. That's why. You dig 'im, just like stealing. He took earth, just like this. You got earth, mining took earth.

Through the above figures, Old Jimmy has made a clear distinction between moral and immoral disposition in his sand drawings, which represent the landscape of his country. His country as well as 'another man's country' that is ethically acceptable is located on the 'right way' or the earth law. In contrast, an immoral country (England) and immoral attitude (mining) are located outside the line because their law does not come from the earth. The localities and attitudes of different people have their position in Old Jimmy's moral geography.

## OLD JIMMY'S MORAL MAP OF THE WORLD NATIONS

It should be noted that for Old Jimmy, and also for other Aboriginal people in the Victoria River district, 'England' and the 'English' represent an immoral locality and people. That being said, if you are 'good *kartiya*', you are not from England. Therefore, we should understand Old Jimmy's definition of English as the immoral colonisers who invaded the Australian continent, and England as the geographical origin of these colonisers. Old Jimmy explains this view as follows. Drawing (A) he explained as follows:

> *J*: Other thing I tell you. (Aboriginal) People there.
> – *drawing a big circle* –
> This one, this one, this one, this one, this one, this one, this one.

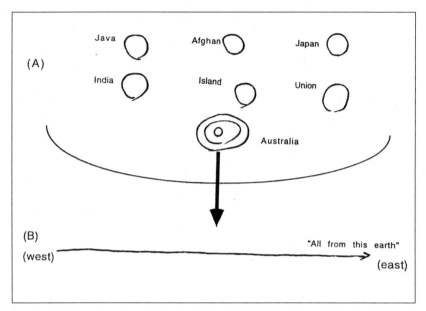

Figure 3.10 Moral map of the world

*– drawing six small circles –*
This is Japan, this is Afghan, this Java, this is India, this is
(labour) union mob, this is (another) island.[20]
*– erasing the drawing (A) and drawing one line (B) from west to east –*
All from this earth (B). You are in the one law. But we don't
know England. We don't know what made England.
*– scooping sand –*
You come out on this earth. You come from earth.
M: *Yunmi* [you and me] came from earth?
J: Yes, *yunmi* came from earth but English is not from earth.
We don't know him. I don't know him. We don't know what
made him.
M: But you explained, this one, this one, this one, this one, but
all come from the earth?
J: Yes, don't matter what land, it's same earth. You got
different fruit and that land you gotta different fruit and
different land, different land, different land. But we are on the
same earth. You understand now. Different fruit, different

fruit, different fruit, different fruit, different fruit, but we are
(all) on one earth.

In Figure 3.10, it is clear that the earth, or the line from west to east, represents morality. Even though one might be living in a different country or island, all people are 'on the one earth law'. The exception is England, because from Old Jimmy's viewpoint, England, or the place of Captain Cook's law, cannot represent the earth law.

In contrast, the '(labour) union' is regarded as a country and, even though most union members are European in Australia, they are from the earth law. As I will discuss in Chapter 5, the labour union is highly regarded as 'good *kartiya*' among the Aboriginal people in the Victoria River district. This is because of their strong support for the Gurindji walk-off at Wave Hill station in 1966. The union members supported Indigenous Australians and fought against colonisers' dispossession of Aboriginal land. Therefore, it is logical for Old Jimmy that the union members did not come from immoral England but from the moral earth:

> Union mob and Captain Cook different country ... He [union
> members] help people. Put land back ... Tommy Vincent,[21]
> union mob all right law ... English man nomo [never] longa
> *yunmi* [us].

Every moral person comes from the earth, but an immoral person must have come from England because his/her law is different and wrong. Old Jimmy also said to me, 'English *kartiya* (is) different (from) other person *kartiya*.' Therefore, for example, even though 'Japan' is regarded as another moral land in Old Jimmy's sand drawing, we should understand that the Japanese who were oppressive and exploitative colonialists could be regarded as English.

## PLACE-ORIENTED HISTORY

Old Jimmy knows and can draw spatial directions of morality. Through this process, colonialism is interpreted and assessed through his sand drawings, which are metaphysical *as well as* geographical. By considering the geographical direction of morality that has been created by the great transcontinental travel of *Jurntakal* Dreaming, Old Jimmy found the immoral directions on the same geography. Using the image of moral–immoral geography, he succeeded in analysing and 'visualising' the history of Australian colonisation in the Dreaming landscape; the colonial history is transformed into the Aboriginal landscape.

Old Jimmy demonstrated to me that Aboriginal history is within the moral–immoral landscape. As we have seen, a distinguishing characteristic of Old Jimmy's ideas is that he has a sense of 'locality' within the moral geography; he can find a spatial place, direction and movement for different people, countries and attitudes. Through this process, historical events are interpreted, assessed and allocated certain geographical locations and directions in his metaphysical and geographical landscape. I submit Old Jimmy's analysis of Australian colonisation as one of the original and unique examples of place-oriented history practised by the Aboriginal historians.

However, it should be noted that my discussion in this chapter does not intend to generalise Aboriginal perspectives on Australian colonial history; instead it introduces a distinctive historical analysis made by an Aboriginal historian, namely Jimmy Mangayarri of Daguragu. It should also be emphasised that during my fieldwork, Old Jimmy was the only person who used sand drawings to explain Australian colonial history. Most of his methods of analysis and expression are attributed to his personal talent. As each academic historian has her/his own distinct approach, different Aboriginal historians have different forms of analysis. Even though Old Jimmy's storytelling is highly original, his expression is widely accepted and appreciated among local people. I often heard people say to Old Jimmy, 'That's very good story, *marluka* [old man].' Therefore, Old Jimmy's originality is within the Gurindji mode of historical practice.

As an Aboriginal historian and a moral philosopher, Old Jimmy's consideration was not a 'history of landscape' but a 'landscape of history'. Morphy's argument about the 'subordination of time to space' may be applied to the Gurindji perspective of colonial history as well. From Old Jimmy's viewpoint, histories are more space-oriented events than time-oriented events. Colonial events are understood through spatial directions of morality in the Gurindji cultural geography. The colonial past is integrated into the landscape; history becomes landscape. Or in a stricter sense, for the Gurindji historians, *history is landscape*.

I also want to briefly discuss the issue of the Gurindji sense of spatial direction. Broadly speaking, I found that the Gurindji people have a keen sense of geographical direction and location. For example, a standard greeting, '*Wanji-kawu?*' in Gurindji means 'Which way are you going?' They first ask a person their direction and locality. Moreover, when driving and asking them to tell me the way, instead of saying 'turn right (or left)', they normally replied 'turn north (or south, east, west)'. People were also eager to know 'which way' my country (Japan) was. In addition, whenever any person, not only Old Jimmy, drew a map of certain places on the earth, geographical directions were always accurate. For place-oriented culture, a spatial and geographical sense of direction may be significant aspects at both physical and metaphysical levels.

It is also worth noting that Old Jimmy never draws maps on paper or canvas. One reason may be that the Daguragu community itself is not productive in the arts and that Old Jimmy is not very interested in paintings. However, I want to make it clear that Old Jimmy once told me that paper is not from the earth:

> See, you got map like this.
> – *pointing to my fieldnote* –
> But we put on the earth … We see the country. We nomo
> [never] use paper. This is the way. You see the difference. You
> use paper, but we put on the earth.

If you draw a map on a paper, the drawing will lose direction, because on paper, north is not always pointing to the geographical north. A map on paper lacks spatial direction.

This brings Old Jimmy to another analogy: European law lacks morality because their law is written on paper. Paper represents European law. Europeans write a law on paper, and then whenever they do not like their law, they just throw the paper away and write a new law on another paper. 'Kartiya [European] law change every year.' But Aboriginal law never changes because their law is the earth law. 'On the earth, never change … (law) still there.'

He also explained that *kartiya* law is like a fly, because, like the insect, it changes direction all the time. European law written on paper lacks spatial direction, and thus lacks morality. Because it is written on paper, you can change the law whenever you want to do so. As a result, *kartiya* law cannot set a fixed direction and morality. Australian settlers' society has sometimes terribly abused Aboriginal people and at other times supported them. Thus, Old Jimmy's analysis of European law accurately reflects Australian policy towards Aboriginal people, which constantly changes direction.

## WHERE DID THE ENGLISH LAW COME FROM?

Before finishing this chapter, it may be worth mentioning that Old Jimmy once told me that he does not know the immoral source of *kartiya* or Captain Cook's law. I asked Old Jimmy, if the Europeans did not come from the moral earth, where did they come from? When I asked this question, his answer was, 'I don't know':

> *M*: Do you know what is *kartiya* [the European]? Where is *kartiya* from?
> *J*: I don't know what *kartiya* believe. We don't know (their) earth. We don't know nothing.
> *M*: You don't know nothing …
> *J*: We don't know nothing.
> *M*: Nothing about *kartiya*?
> *J*: I don't know why, what breed.
> *M*: You don't know what breed *kartiya*.
> *J*: Hmmm.

*M*: What do you reckon? Do you have any idea? What do you reckon? You don't know or …

*J*: I don't know nothing.

*M*: No idea …

*J*: Because we don't know all this idea.

*M*: You don't know all this idea. I see, I see.

Old Jimmy knows that England was never located within the moral geography, and the English colonisers came to Australia from an immoral direction. However, he also said, 'I don't know why, what breed (*kartiya* and their law).' Since Old Jimmy already confirmed that their immorality never came from the earth law, there exist two possibilities: either *kartiya* law is not from the earth, or the English earth is different from the other countries' earth. However, instead of answering this, he often said, 'I don't know.' Therefore, I came to understand that his answer 'I don't know' is already the answer: as long as it does not come from this moral earth, there will never be a clue to revealing their origin. This is because, as Old Jimmy often said, 'Don't matter what it is, everything must come from the earth.' If not, it is too alien to consider.

However, this was not the end of the story. Spending more time with Old Jimmy, I began to realise that Old Jimmy's 'I don't know' was actually the expression he used to emphasise how alien and immoral *kartiya* law is. To tell the truth, I later found out that Old Jimmy, as well as other Gurindji elders, actually had their historical knowledge as well as analysis to answer the question 'Where did the *kartiya* and their law come from?' This was revealed to me about two months after I had the above conversation. I discuss this issue in the next chapter.

# CHAPTER 4

# JACKY PANTAMARRA

Most studies based on Aboriginal oral histories cover the period from their historical origin – Dreaming, where storytellers were born, or where their (grand)parents were born – to their colonial experiences. However, to my knowledge, there has been little attention given to the Aboriginal analysis and knowledge of European history. I suspect this is because academic historians tend to think that even though Indigenous Australians hold historical knowledge of their origin as well as of their colonial pasts, they do not know much about the history of Europe. However, the Gurindji historians elucidate their analysis of the historical and ontological origin of European colonialists.

'Where did the Europeans come from?'
'Why did they colonise Australia?'
'What was the (im)moral foundation of their law?'

These questions have been examined by Gurindji historians through their cultural mode of practice, which I would like to call the 'methodology of Dreaming'. In this chapter, I seek to demonstrate the validity of Aboriginal analysis of European history.

## AN ENGLISHMAN IN AUSTRALIA BEFORE CAPTAIN COOK?

One may be surprised if I were to say that there was an Englishman who landed in Australia and encountered Aboriginal people *before* Captain Cook arrived. I am not talking about Macassans or Dutch explorers who visited the northern coast of Australia from the 18th century onwards. He was from England. His name was Keen Lewis, but he was more commonly known by his Aboriginal name of 'Jacky Pantamarra'. When I heard this story from Jimmy Mangayarri, Thomas Mungka and Tommy Wajabungu, I could not help trying to confirm many times if this Englishman really came to Australia 'before Captain Cook'.

Following is the first session with Old Jimmy and Thomas about Jacky Pantamarra:

> *Jimmy (J)*: Australia, that why he start off. This Keen Lewis, Keen Lewis.
> *Minoru (M)*: Keen Lewis?
> *J*: Keen Lewis.
> *M*: What's that? Keen Lewis?
> *J*: That fella bin come on this Australia-na.
> *M*: *Yuwayi* [Yes].
> *J*: Keen Lewis.
> *M*: Keen Lewis.
> *J*: Yeah, *kartiya* call 'im Keen Lewis we call 'im Jacky Pantamarra.
> *M*: You call Jacky Pantamarra?
> *J*: Yeah, that the fella-na. That fella bin come longa this country. And he claim (Australia) belonga him … He come up this country. Why he never pay 'im people [ask permission to Aboriginal people]?
> […]
> *M*: So, what time [when] he come here?
> *J*: Oh, he bin come longa this country, where come out this country, what the *ngumpin* belonga this country, and him bin come longa this country, might be from somewhere about

England. English, England. Come to Australia, *ngumpin* country. Why he never pay 'em people?

*M*: Never pay 'em people.

*J*: Never pay 'em.

*M*: Jacky Pantamarra never pay 'em.

*J*: Never pay 'em. What *yunmi* come longa this country, what *yunmi* claim on. (Jacky Pantamarra) claim(ed) on this my country (as his own land). Keen Lewis-na. Keen Lewis, Jacky Pantamarra. Yeah.

*M*: Jacky Pantamarra, *yuwayi*. So, he is the first *kartiya* to come here?

*Thomas (T)*: Yeah.

*J*: First *kartiya*-na.

*T*: First *kartiya*.

[...]

*J*: Captain Cook come out on this country, alright, (then) he start shoot 'em people.

*M*: How about Keen Lewis? Captain Cook, same?

*J*: Well, he come out, he is the first one. Keen Lewis is the first one.

*M*: Keen Lewis is the first one, *yuwayi*.

*J*: Captain Cook after.

*M*: Captain Cook, after, *yuwayi* ... Oh! So, Keen Lewis come here first, after that, Captain Cook come here, and start kill 'em people?

*J*: He shoot 'em people-na.

*M*: Shoot 'em people, *yuwayi*.

*J*: You know he bin here, he never like me. Even you, English never like you.

I had to learn about this mysterious figure of Jacky Pantamarra. Who was Jacky Pantamarra? What did he do in England and Australia? Furthermore, how can we share the history of Jacky Pantamarra with the Gurindji people? These are the questions to be explored in this chapter.

Although many Gurindji elders know Jacky Pantamarra as the first European who came to Australia, very few people can actually talk about him. Many of them often said Captain Cook was the first *kartiya* who came to Australia. However, when I asked about Jacky Pantamarra, they admitted he came to Australia before Captain Cook, but then they pointed to Old Jimmy and said, 'Ask that *marluka* [old man], he know 'im more.' In addition, people regarded Old Jimmy as my main teacher. Therefore, I learned most stories of Jacky Pantamarra from Old Jimmy. It should be noted that my discussion of Jacky Pantamarra is based mainly, but not exclusively, on Jimmy Mangayarri's historical analysis.

Jacky Pantamarra has several unique characteristics as well as a geographical and genealogical background. I would like to introduce Old Jimmy's teachings about several distinctive aspects of Jacky Pantamarra. For a while, I will minimise my own analysis of these stories. However, I also have to categorise, summarise and add some information in order to let readers comprehend the stories more easily. In addition, since Old Jimmy briefly told this story of Jacky Pantamarra to Deborah B. Rose in the 1980s as well, I will add her version when necessary. I do acknowledge that my manipulation by categorising and summarising Old Jimmy's narrative may twist his original ideas and our conversation, but this risk has to be taken otherwise readers may not grasp the picture of Jacky Pantamarra.

### JACKY PANTAMARRA WAS BRED FROM A 'MONKEY'

One of the most interesting stories for me was that an ancestor of Jacky Pantamarra was a monster-like animal which had four or five arms (or legs). Old Jimmy explained that through 'some sort of breed', Jacky Pantamarra came out from this animal called a 'monkey':

> *J*: He [Jacky Pantamarra] come out this country. And breed 'em, breed 'em, breed 'em, breed 'em. Some sort of breed. Gotta, might be two arm here, two arm here …
> – *pointing to his body –*

You kinda breed.

*M*: *Yuwayi*, you breed 'em, breed 'em, breed 'em.

*J*: Gotta two arm, four arm all together. That's why he use breed.

*M*: He breed 'em here, he breed 'em here.

*J*: Yeah, he breed all this country-na. Breed 'em children long time-na. You can see what he do, see what he, he gotta, he gotta sort of, monkey, you know that monkey?

*M*: Monkey? Yeah. Monkey, he shoot 'em monkey, too?

*J*: That's way he breed. That's the white men breed.

*M*: Oh, that's the way that white man breed. Monkey, *yuwayi*. So, Jacky Pantamarra breed 'em monkey.

*J*: Some sort of man longa next one. Might be follow five fuck'n leg or four leg or a lot some, him breed, some, some or big head and small body ... [everything] sort of a, sort of animal breed.

It must be noted that Old Jimmy probably has never seen a monkey. For him a 'monkey' is a mysterious animal which could have four arms or four/five legs. This monkey or 'sort of animal' bred itself many times until Jacky Pantamarra evolved in England. Later, Jacky Pantamarra also bred many *kartiya* even in 'this country', or Australia. In this dialogue, I could not figure out the relationship between Jacky Pantamarra and monkeys. Readers may have recognised that some of my comments such as 'He [Jacky Pantamarra] shoot 'em monkey', or 'Jacky Pantamarra breed 'em monkey' overstepped and did not follow Old Jimmy's story. However, the following story describes this relationship more clearly:

*M*: Jacky Pantamarra breed 'em monkey, or monkey breed 'em Jacky Pantamarra?

*J*: Might be he breed 'em out of the monkey-na.

*M*: *Yuwayi*.

*J*: Monkey, you can see all this bloody English people up the monkey ... take that monkey.

*M*: Take that monkey. English people take that monkey.

*J*: Yeah. Now every show you. See that monkey. Well that must be mate.

*M*: So monkey must be …

*J*: Same breed.

*M*: Same breed, might be mate.

*J*: That way, mate.

This story confirmed for me that Jacky Pantamarra came out *from* a monkey. Old Jimmy explained both monkey and Jacky Pantamarra are the same blood and 'mate'. Therefore, it is clear that English people have some genealogical relationship to a monkey. This brings us to the next point: Jacky Pantamarra came out of monkeys and then he became the first English person or 'white man'. Jacky Pantamarra is the first English person who came to Australia. However, in fact, he is also the origin of all English people and their history:

*J*: Ah, him from England.

*M*: From England.

*J*: See, you know what … That's why he breed *kartiya* [whites].

*M*: That's why he breed the *kartiya*.

*J*: By that one-na. Jacky Pantamarra.

*M*: Jacky Pantamarra.

*J*: That's why you now you go. You know he make that human all way … *kartiya*-na. See, that the way the *kartiya*, you see that in history belonga the *kartiya*, it's Jacky Pantamarra. That one bin born longa country.

In the above discussion, it is clear that Old Jimmy said Jacky Pantamarra bred *kartiya*. This is a 'history belonga *kartiya*'. The story of Jacky Pantamarra represents the history of Europeans. Old Jimmy also told Deborah B. Rose that Jacky Pantamarra later established London.[1] Furthermore, it is important to know that Jacky Pantamarra wrote many books:

*M*: Is Keen Lewis finish [dead], or still alive?

*J*: Ha?

*M*: Is Keen Lewis, Jacky Pantamarra.

*J*: He finish.

*M*: He finish, yeah.

*J*: ... You know him book. Still I got 'em the book, like this. Turn on another book. All that.

*M*: He wrote a book?

*J*: He gotta a lotta book.

*M*: Oh, Jacky Pantamarra, he got a lot of books?

*J*: *Yuwayi*. Make it, make it ...

Jacky Pantamarra made many books. But why? The following is Old Jimmy's answer:

*J*: England him born there. He born and ... this old Jacky Pantamarra. That's why he had on the book-na. Allat [everything] put 'em down on the book.

*M*: All put 'em down on the book. What sort of? He made 'im book?

*J*: You must got book, you know. You know, some sort of book him made, teach 'em (white) fellas, allat, teach 'em up. Did he get bad, did he get ... and allat, allat [all] silly idea.

*M*: All the silly idea, *yuwayi*.

*J*: That's all (from) Jacky Pantamarra.

By now, it became clear that Jacky Pantamarra created books which contain 'all silly ideas', and he taught these ideas to *kartiya* – his descendants. What are these 'silly ideas' which Jacky Pantamarra produced, wrote, taught and spread among *kartiya*?

## JACKY PANTAMARRA LET CAPTAIN COOK
## COLONISE AUSTRALIA

Among 'all silly ideas' Jacky Pantamarra created, one of the silliest was probably the idea of colonisation. This idea is related to Jacky Pantamarra's development of the tools for colonisation. At first, Jacky Pantamarra had no tools, only a shanghai [slingshot]:

> *J*: That's why him bin breed breed. He had no anything one
> … that Pantamarra. He had no rifle, he had a bit live on longa
> … you know that shanghai?
> *M*: Shanghai.
> *J*: Well you see, well, kids call 'em shanghai. Kill 'em *julak*
> [birds], he put the stone, he kill 'em. Like that
> – *showing how to use shanghai* –
> *M*: So Jacky Pantamarra never use rifle.
> *J*: No.
> *M*: He uses this, what 'em call?
> *J*: Shanghai.
> *M*: Shanghai, *yuwayi*.
> *J*: He gotta some … You put 'im like that … hit the man.
> *M*: Oh, yes, oh yes. So he use 'em this shanghai, and kill the
> animal and kill the man, too.
> *J*: Yeah. He kill 'em man, too. He kill 'em man, too. Like what
> his Pantamarra way living.
> *M*: That Jacky Pantamarra way of living.

It is worthwhile emphasising that using the shanghai, Jacky Pantamarra killed animals as well as human beings. This was the 'Jacky Pantamarra way (of) living'. Old Jimmy also said that Jacky Pantamarra used a bow and an arrow. Figure 4.1 is the sand drawing he used to explain what a bow looked like.

The fact that Jacky Pantamarra did not use a rifle but used a shanghai and bow is worth considering. In fact, Old Jimmy told Rose that Jacky Pantamarra apparently visited America to learn new technologies and then invented the rifle.[2] After inventing these tools, Jacky

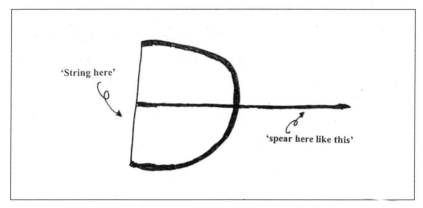

Figure 4.1 Jacky Pantamarra's bow

Pantamarra initiated the colonisation of Australia. Jacky Pantamarra eventually came to Australia and claimed it as his own country. He did not ask permission from the local Aboriginal people. Instead, he commanded Captain Cook to colonise the land by killing the Indigenous people:

> *J*: That the one. (Jacky Pantamarra thought) he is the boss of
> this country. That he reckon he is the boss. What he done? He
> never pay me. See? He never pay 'em *ngumpin*. And he all up
> put people the Captain Cook.
> *M*: He put the Captain Cook.
> *J*: Captain Cook come out this country, Australia. He start
> shoot 'em. Shoot 'em allat people.

Old Jimmy's historical analysis tells us that Jacky Pantamarra and Captain Cook are from the same family in England. Their relationship seems like that of a strategist and a militarist. Jacky Pantamarra claimed he was the boss of Australia and sent Captain Cook to invade and shoot the local people. Old Jimmy accused both Jacky Pantamarra and Captain Cook of starting the Australian colonisation.

## JACKY PANTAMARRA'S WAY OF LIVING

Old Jimmy explained that Jacky Pantamarra killed animals, got their skin and then earned money. These animals included goannas, kangaroos, lizards and dogs:

> *J*: ... He [Jacky Pantamarra] had might be make out of the goanna, kangaroo, some lizard, all 'em skin. That's why he make the money.
> *M*: Oh, then you make 'em money. He get 'em skin ...
> *J*: Skin, from dogs. See, that why what 'bout *kartiya* bin come longa this country ... dog, and give it the policeman. Well, that's all, that get all the money. See, that all for money.

It seems that Jacky Pantamarra was probably a dingo and crocodile hunter and that was how he earned money. In another story about Jacky Pantamarra's personal life, Old Jimmy often emphasised that Jacky Pantamarra killed his wife. Old Jimmy saw it in the newspapers when he was a little child:

> *M*: Jacky Pantamarra, Keen Lewis. Cheeky [dangerous] person, cheeky one.
> *J*: Cheeky one. And you see on the newspaper.
> *M*: You see on the newspaper?
> *J*: Jacky Pantamarra get his wife, ... fuck'n hand like that. Fuck'n make 'em ...
> – *making a gesture of hitting a woman's head* –
> *M*: Kill 'im?
> *T*: Yeah, it's true.
> *M*: Really? He kill 'im wife?
> *J*: Yeah, yeah. (I) see 'im, band 'im. That's way he do.
> *M*: That's way he do. *Nyampawu* [why]?
> *J*: I don't know *nyampawu*. You did see that book on newspaper on this country-na.
> [...]
> *J*: Yeah. That why what happen, you know ... he bust his wife.

Pull 'em from hair, get fuck'n beat stick on it.
*M*: Kill 'em.
*J*: That why.

While showing me how Jacky Pantamarra hit and killed his wife, Old Jimmy explained that he saw such a photo (or drawing?) in the newspapers. He did not know why Jacky Pantamarra beat and killed his wife. However, on another occasion, he told me such wife beating was common among *kartiya*:

> *M*: You see, Jacky Pantamarra? You see him, or hear …
> *J*: No. I see him when I was little boy. I see him on the newspaper.
> *M*: Oh, when you were little boy, you see 'im on the newspaper?
> *J*: Yeah, I bin see. Well, … see that one, I see 'im on the newspaper, he beat 'em that woman belonga him, pull 'em the hair, get his hand *karnti* [stick].
> *– gesturing like hitting a woman's head with a stick in his hand –*
> That what all *kartiya* bin do-na.
> M: Some early days …
> *J*: Early days, that's what that all the history.

Old Jimmy told me such wife beating had been 'what all *kartiya* bin do'. I understood that Old Jimmy blamed Jacky Pantamarra for the origin of wife beating and domestic violence against women in general.

Furthermore, Old Jimmy claimed that white men's practice of sexual relations with Aboriginal women was Jacky Pantamarra's idea:

> *J*: You got all idea from this old Jacky Pantamarra. Well (when) he was passed away, he had all his idea before he passed away. And he breed 'em, breed 'em, breed 'em, breed 'em all, all […] all English *kartiya*, he made 'em marry with black woman-na.
> *M*: English *kartiya* married with black women?

*J*: Yeah. black women, and breed all *yellowfella* [an Aboriginal person who has a non-Aboriginal parent].

*M*: Breed the *yellowfella*.

*J*: Well that's all that idea you had Jacky Pantamarra.

*M*: All belonga Jacky Pantamarra.

*J*: All idea longa him.

## ALL BAD IDEAS COME FROM JACKY PANTAMARRA

The historical role of Jacky Pantamarra has become clearer: the first English/European person is the origin of all bad ideas. For another example, Old Jimmy told me that Jacky Pantamarra also brought alcohol to Australia and he started the alcohol problem among Aboriginal people:

> All this bad idea is longa Keen Lewis [Jacky Pantamarra].
> He breed 'em all bad idea. Keen Lewis bring grog [alcohol]
> longa this earth ... Drink grog make 'em fight everywhere, no
> good all together ... Before Keen Lewis, we live good time.
> No grog, no fighting that time ... People live on proper food.
> Bush fruits, kangaroo. We never eat 'em *buluki* [cattle], horse.
> We eat 'em kangaroo, fruits ... Today, we eat 'em *kartiya* food.

All negative practices such as murder, wife beating, drinking alcohol and colonisation started because of Jacky Pantamarra's ideas.

Stories of Jacky Pantamarra convinced me that the English people are a distinct people who followed on from Jacky Pantamarra, whose origin was not a moral Dreaming but 'some sort of animal' called 'monkey'. English people are morally wrong because they were taught by Jacky Pantamarra's book which was full of 'silly ideas'. Old Jimmy said, 'All these bad idea longa Keen Lewis book':

> *J*: Because (of) this one [Jacky Pantamarra], English different
> longa *yunmi* [us].
> *M*: *Yuwayi*, English different longa *yunmi*, *yuwayi*.

*J*: Different to anybody.

*M*: Different to anybody. *Yuwayi.*

*J*: He breed by Jacky Pantamarra.

*M*: He is bred by Jacky Pantamarra …

*J*: Well, he [the English] get all idea out of the Jacky Pantamarra.

## WAYS OF SHARING THE DIFFERENCE

Old Jimmy's historical narratives may perplex academic historians and many non-Gurindji readers, who cannot simply accept or agree with his analysis. Jacky Pantamarra is definitely part of the historical knowledge of the people of Daguragu and other communities around the Victoria River district. However, the stories of Jacky Pantamarra are so mysterious that it is hard to believe such a person existed. At first glance, it seems to be impossible for non-Gurindji settlers to share the history of Jacky Pantamarra with the Gurindji people. If so, shall we ignore this story by saying, 'This is the wrong history'?

What I emphatically reject is the polemic notions that 'We know the right history' and 'They are telling the wrong history'. Instead of making an easy judgement, I call for carefully and patiently paying attention to what Gurindji historians tell us. This is because we do not know about the Gurindji mode of historical practice. It is increasingly common for academic historians to use Aboriginal oral histories in order to bring Indigenous voices into their narratives. However, I doubt that enough attempts have been made to set Aboriginal oral accounts within the culturally distinctive structure of their storytellings.

The point I want to make here is quite simple: Aboriginal oral history should be used as a supplementary source for the 'academic mode of history', but also needs to be acknowledged and understood in the context of Aboriginal cultural modes of historical practice. On the other hand, we also need to beware of over-emphasising the difference between academic and Indigenous modes of history. This might entrap us into cultural separatism. We might listen to Old Jimmy's stories, but if that is all we do, our conclusion will be: 'Aboriginal histories totally contradict academic "historicity", so there is no way to share history between academic and Aboriginal historians. I am happy to respect their beliefs, but they have nothing to do with mine.' Therefore, academic historians may categorise the story of Jacky Pantamarra as a 'myth' rather than a 'history', and claim that histories should be analysed by historians, while myths are of interest to anthropologists. Shall we forward this story to anthropologists by saying, 'Here is an Aboriginal myth for you'?

It is outside the scope of this book to discuss the problem of academic 'division of labour' in detail. However, I would like to make it clear once again that for Old Jimmy, as well as for most of the Gurindji people, there is no such distinction between 'myths' and 'history'. As far as I have learned, both Dreaming stories and colonial stories are real. If one still insists on making a division between the anthropologists and the historians, I believe the study of Dreaming stories may be for anthropologists and the study of colonial stories should be for historians.

After all, the purpose of this book is to learn historical analysis from Aboriginal historians and to reflect upon communication between Western-academic and Indigenous-Gurindji modes of historical practice. I believe this is the appropriate way of struggling towards a historical 'reality' and 'truthfulness' which we – Aboriginal and non-Aboriginal people – may be able to share.

## KARTIYA FROM MONKEYS, NGUMPIN FROM DREAMING

Let us return to the historical analysis of Jacky Pantamarra. First, it is reasonable to assume that Old Jimmy, and some other Gurindji people, are probably familiar with the basic idea of evolutionary theory.[3] Considering the story about Jacky Pantamarra 'coming out of a monkey', we can assume that some settlers – perhaps school teachers – told the Gurindji people that human beings evolved from primates. Gurindji historians accepted this as the basis for understanding the origin of Europeans.

It is significant that the Gurindji historians did not apply evolutionary theory to themselves, but only to European colonisers. Gurindji people are confident of their own origin. They have been created and maintained through the law of Dreaming. The Dreaming is the origin of their being. What they did not know was the historical and ontological origin of *kartiya*. Their analysis concluded that *ngumpin* originated from Dreaming, but *kartiya* originated from 'monkeys'.

This idea of the genealogical difference between Aboriginal people and the European colonialists reinforces the belief that *kartiya* lack morality but *ngumpin* have ethical origins. In Gurindji cosmology, colonisers cannot come from the Dreaming since they lack morality, which Dreaming always holds. Old Jimmy thinks everything is from the earth except *kartiya* and their law. Everything coming from the earth must have a certain morality which is founded by Dreaming. There is no 'monkey Dreaming' in the Gurindji sacred geography. *Kartiya* whose origin is a 'monkey' cannot have Dreaming, morality, or the earth law. One should not picture the monkey as the animal that we know when considering Old Jimmy's image of a 'monkey', since he probably has never seen this animal. For Old Jimmy, a monkey is a mysterious creature which has four or five legs. Old Jimmy's idea that Jacky Pantamarra came out of a monster-like animal called 'monkey' supports the reasoning that *kartiya* are an immoral people. *Kartiya* are not from Dreaming, but were bred from a monkey.

## STORIES FROM THE TOP END?

The story of Jacky Pantamarra corresponds not only to evolutionary theory, but also to many other aspects of colonialists' activities in the early stages of Australian colonisation.

For example, Old Jimmy tells us that Jacky Pantamarra started the idea of *kartiya* men stealing *ngumpin* women. This story corresponds to the history of sexual relations between *kartiya* stockworkers and *ngumpin* women in the Victoria River district and other regions.[4] Furthermore, we learned that Jacky Pantamarra killed animals (goannas, lizards or dogs), got their skins and sold them.

This story not only has a connection to the dingo hunters' activities in the Victoria River district, but probably also has connections to Macassan activity on the north Australian shores before European colonisation, as well as to crocodile hunters in the Top End of Australia in the early 20th century.[5]

It is evident that the Gurindji people have retained their communication with northern Aboriginal people through their kinship and ceremonial networks. Before the Gurindji walk-off movement started in 1966, most of the Aboriginal people in the Victoria River district worked at cattle stations. Since there was not much work during the wet season, Aboriginal workers left stations and went 'walkabout'. This walkabout season was important for maintaining activities such as hunting and ceremonies. This period gave Aboriginal people a chance to communicate with other groups living in other places. As Lyn Riddett says, it was the opportunity for them to meet other Aboriginal people and discuss the daily life of cattle stations.[6] It is not difficult to imagine that they exchanged stories of settlers' activities and discussed the nature of *kartiya*, their law, country and origins.

One should not underestimate Aboriginal information networks. For example, as Ronald and Catherine Berndt point out in their fieldwork at Wave Hill station in 1944, almost all the Aborigines had at least one close relative in another area, such as Mistake Creek, Limbunya or various stations on Victoria River Downs (VRD).[7] Rose also emphasises that during this ceremonial season information was exchanged intensively, and that these Aboriginal information networks criss-cross the continent and are probably thousands of years old.[8] These ceremonial and kinship chains of communication from the Gurindji country easily reach the Top End countries as well as the southern desert countries. When I was at Daguragu, the Gurindji people received bamboo spears from Timber Creek and Yarralin communities. I learned that these spears were made in the Top End and brought down through the Daly River country. While most of these spears would go further south to the desert countries, the Gurindji people also had boomerangs and shields which came from southern Warlpiri country, in order to trade each other's products.

These trade routes were information routes as well. Through these ceremonial and kinship networks, the Aboriginal people in Victoria River district may have received 'early days' stories about Macassans and Dutch ships on the northern Australian coast, crocodile and buffalo hunters of the early 20th century, and episodes of early explorers in different areas. Through the networks, many of these stories may have evolved and developed into different versions. Accordingly, the history that *kartiya* explorers arrived in north Australia before the English started their colonisation of Australia – that is, 'before Captain Cook' – could also be a source of Jacky Pantamarra stories.[9]

This possibility also brings us to speculate about where the name 'Jacky Pantamarra' comes from. For example, even though I admit my guess is not based on linguistic analysis, the name 'Pantamarra' makes us suspect that it may come from the word 'Balanda', which means 'Europeans/whites' in Indonesian as well as in some Aboriginal languages in Arnhem Land.[10] Furthermore, it is worth considering why the first *kartiya* was called 'Jacky'. In the same way that 'Paddy' denotes Irishness, 'Jacky' or 'Jacky Jacky' generally denotes Aboriginality in colonial Australian societies. For example, an Aboriginal man, Galmahra, who guided Edward Kennedy's expedition, and William Westwood, who blackened his face to escape detection, were both called 'Jacky Jacky'.[11] It is safe to say that the word 'Jacky' has been used as a stereotyped and discriminatory term for Aboriginal males among settlers. By calling the first *kartiya* 'Jacky', Aboriginal people in the Victoria River district may have returned this term to the colonial settlers with great sarcasm.[12]

The first *kartiya* who came out from England had a European name: Keen Lewis.[13] However, Aboriginal people created his *ngumpin* name, 'Jacky Pantamarra'. 'Pantamarra' may have come from the story that there were *kartiya* who came to northern Australia before Captain Cook, and the word 'Jacky' may have been given to this first European because of its discriminatory connotations.

## MAKING OF THE EUROPEANS

It is also interesting to compare the stories of Jacky Pantamarra and Captain Cook in order to understand the Gurindji way of constructing European/English history.

There are different roles for Jacky Pantamarra and Captain Cook: Jacky Pantamarra as a planner, Captain Cook as an invader. Even though people told me that Jacky Pantamarra was the first Englishman who came to Australia, most of the detailed invasion stories are attributed to Captain Cook rather than Jacky Pantamarra. It is clear that Jacky Pantamarra's main role is more like that of a *founder* of all 'silly ideas'. Jacky Pantamarra was the one who bred all bad ideas and wrote the book [law].

When the Gurindji people construct the colonial past, it is natural that they wonder about the unethical grounds of Captain Cook's attitude towards Indigenous Australians. Why did Captain Cook come to Australia without asking the Aboriginal people? Why is Captain Cook's law so unethical? Where did this law originally come from? *Kartiya* law cannot be from Dreaming. If so, what bred such silly ideas? Or, more generally, what was the origin of the European colonisers? In order to understand Captain Cook's and the settlers' unethical attitudes, Aboriginal people need to analyse the origin of European law, their frame of mind, and the origin of European people. In this sense, the Gurindji way of applying evolutionary theory is remarkably successful. By adopting the European-oriented theory, but turning it around in a carnivalesque way, the Gurindji people have found the historical and ontological origin of colonial Europeans and their law.

*

The Gurindji historians' analysis of European history clearly reflects their own experience of the colonial past.

Many of today's Gurindji elders spent much of their lives in cattle stations. It requires further discussion to determine if Aboriginal stockworkers were simply exploited by settlers' enterprise, or whether they were proud of being stockmen and enjoyed their work.[14] However, it is clear that there was physical separation between Aboriginal workers and European workers on cattle stations. My previous work suggested that the Gurindji people's life on the Wave Hill station was a typical example of colonial separatism. I studied three different aspects of physical separation at Wave Hill station. First, in stockwork, the higher positions (such as manager and head stockman) were dominated by European workers and the lower positions (such as stockmen and unskilled labour) were for Aboriginal workers. Second, in the daily life at the homestead, the living area was physically separated so that Europeans rarely visited Aboriginal camps. Third, in the rainy season, this separation was even wider, since most Aborigines left the cattle stations and went for their 'walkabout'.[15] It is debatable whether these physical separations made Aboriginal people comfortable or uncomfortable in their cattle station life, but they probably affected the Aboriginal analysis of Europeans.

Bain Attwood's *The Making of the Aborigines* (1989) gives us a Foucauldian insight into this racial separatism. Attwood argues that the notion of the 'Aborigine' is a historical invention of the dominant culture, of the white-Australian consciousness. Australian settlers observed, studied and exercised authority over Indigenous Australians.[16] The idea of this physical separation in the cattle station was clearly based on the Eurocentric sense of superiority. It is not too difficult to imagine that the settlers' racial separatism led the Aboriginal people to construct an Aboriginal mode of separatism as a counter-action. This was the 'making of the Europeans' which had been happening within the Aboriginal counter-colonial practice. The Gurindji people observed, studied and analysed the origin and nature of the colonialists and their land. In the same way that settlers' culture constructed the notion of 'Aborigines', Aboriginal people constructed the notion of immoral 'English' people. When the Gurindji people faced Eurocentric separatism, they accepted the racial separatism without adopting Eurocentrism.

'Aboriginal separatism' claims that Indigenous Australians are different from settlers; they are of different origin, use different tools, and have different law. However, in their understanding, Aboriginal people are never inferior to settlers. On the contrary, by analysing the nature of Jacky Pantamarra, a founding figure of European colonisers and their law, the Gurindji people believe in *ngumpin* law as a moral law and despise *kartiya* law – Jacky Pantamarra's book – which contained pernicious ideas that allowed them to invade Australia.

It is ironic that while European societies regarded Australia as a 'convict country', Indigenous Australians understood England as an 'immoral country'. In the same way as 'Aborigine' was the invention of settlers' thought and practice, '*kartiya*' was the invention of Gurindji thought and practice; these identities are the dual product of Australian colonialism.

## METHODOLOGY OF DREAMING

Since Old Jimmy admits that Jacky Pantamarra has already passed away, it is clear that Jacky Pantamarra is a story about the past. However, it is clearly problematic from a Western-academic historical perspective to accept the 'fact' that Jacky Pantamarra is thought to have lived for an unusually long period of time. How could it be possible for one person to evolve from a monkey, breed Europeans as a progenitor, develop technologies from the bow to the rifle, encourage Captain Cook to colonise Australia, and then appear at the time of Old Jimmy's boyhood?

From these stories, one general point becomes clear: Jacky Pantamarra can appear at any time in the past. To understand this temporal nature of Jacky Pantamarra, it is worthwhile comparing it with the concept of time in Aboriginal Dreaming. Dreaming is not based on the linear concept of time. Rather, Dreaming events have been occurring all the time. Stanner's famous definition of the temporal structure of Dreaming is 'everywhen'.[17] A.P. Elkin explains that for Aboriginal people the 'past [...] is present, here and now'.[18] Rose says, 'Dreamings all exist all the time', and thus Dreaming is 'a synchronous set of events, those things which endure'.[19] Tony Swain denies any temporal concept in Dreaming, and suggests calling it 'abiding events'.[20]

The history of Jacky Pantamarra shares a similar temporal structure to Dreaming. Jacky Pantamarra is not confined to a particular temporal point. Jacky Pantamarra is the origin of Europeans, yet in the same way as Dreamings (the origin of Aboriginal people), Jacky Pantamarra also manifests and acts in any past time. Jacky Pantamarra was an 'abiding person' who 'endured' 'everywhen'. The Gurindji historians applied the Dreaming temporal structure in order to inquire into the origin of the European colonialists.

However, even though the way Gurindji people analyse the origin of Europeans reflects the structure of Dreaming cosmology, it must be noted that Jacky Pantamarra is never part of their Dreaming. First of all, Jacky Pantamarra was a person who is already dead. Jacky Pantamarra does not exist in the present. He has 'abided' in every moment of the past, but he existed *only* in the past. In short, while Dreaming is an eternal event which is happening all the time, Jacky Pantamarra never exists in the present or the future. I understand this as the Gurindji historians' desire: Australian 'colonialism' was – or should be – over by now. Colonial law should not 'endure' any more.

A similar point was made by Hobbles Danayarri in Rose's study:

> I'm speaking about now. We're friends together because we own Australia, every one of us no matter who – white and black. We (can) come together, join in ... That will be all right. That will make it better from that big trouble. You know before, Captain Cook made a lot of cruel, you know. Now these days, these days we'll be friendly, we'll be love each other, we'll be mates. That'll be better. Better than making that trouble. Now we'll come and join in, no matter who ...[21]

＊

The other reason that Jacky Pantamarra is not part of Dreaming is because he does not have a place within the sacred geography. Dreaming must have its sacred and moral geography. Dreaming is comprised of spatial or geographic events rather than just temporal or historical events. Dreaming stories always have a connection with certain places or landscapes. Rose explains that Dreaming is 'marked most powerfully by synchrony, and it, too, is located in real named space'.[22] The Aboriginal mode of history has its ground in the spatial dimensions rather than the temporal dimensions: time is subordinated to space in Aboriginal cosmology.

Jacky Pantamarra lacks ontological ground in the sacred geography of Dreaming. Jacky Pantamarra's geographical origin is explained as 'England'. The Gurindji people do not accept 'England' as a part of the sacred geography because the English and their law lack morality. For Aboriginal people in the Victoria River district, 'England' is an island for immoral colonialists. In this sense, the immoral country called England is a product of Aboriginal thought and their analysis of Australian colonisation.

However, this does not necessarily mean their understanding of the past is wrong. What I seek to do here is not to disprove the historical factuality of the Gurindji's understanding of England, but to explore their way of constructing the Gurindji 'reality' of England in order to share the historical 'truthfulness' with them. Jacky Pantamarra, the origin of *kartiya*, is not a Dreaming being. The ontological ground of Jacky Pantamarra (or the English/Europeans) does not have roots in the Dreaming geography. Instead, Jacky Pantamarra is the first European who came out of a 'monkey' in England and spread all bad ideas there. This cursed country of 'England' is geographically *as well as* morally distant from the Aboriginal countries where the Gurindji people's Dreaming is generated.

In the same way that the ontological and geographical origin of *kartiya* is located in the immoral country called England, the nature of their colonial law is to be found in Jacky Pantamarra's teachings, especially his books. This perspective corresponds to the Gurindji moral philosophy.

It is not only Old Jimmy who makes a clear distinction between *ngumpin* law and *kartiya* law; it is also many other Gurindji elders. They often point out that *kartiya* law is immoral because it is not from the earth but is 'written' on paper. In Chapter 2 I mentioned Old Jimmy's idea of paper law and earth law as well as Billy Bunter's explanation of Aboriginal law as a river and a hill. A further example came from Jock Smiler of Yarralin, who demonstrated to me how *ngumpin* law and *kartiya* law are different. Jock dropped a piece of paper, which was carried away by the wind. He told me this was *kartiya* law. White people write their law on paper, but you never know which way the paper goes. Then he dropped a stone, which fell straight down to the ground. He said this was Aboriginal law: '*ngumpin* law (is) stone law. Never change, stop here.'

It would not be a coincidence that Jacky Pantamarra taught his 'silly ideas' to his descendants by writing books. It is clear that Jacky Pantamarra's teachings or *kartiya* law did not originate from the moral earth. I found it meaningless to ask which took precedence: Jacky Pantamarra's teachings were immoral because they were written, and they were written because they were immoral. Likewise, *kartiya* came from England because they were immoral, and *kartiya* were immoral because they came from England.

The Gurindji historians' analysis of Jacky Pantamarra is bound up with their analysis of *kartiya*, the 'English' or European colonialists. The history of Jacky Pantamarra contributes to the idea of the fundamental differences between Aboriginal people and colonial settlers. It is also worth noting that Jacky Pantamarra used a shanghai, bow and arrow, and rifle; he never used Aboriginal tools such as a boomerang, spear and shield. The story of Jacky Pantamarra makes a clear distinction between the history of European tools and the history of those of Indigenous Australians. In general, I found the Gurindji people usually emphasised the difference between *ngumpin* and *kartiya* rather than their similarity. Even though they admit *ngumpin* and *kartiya* are both 'human being', their analysis of settlers mostly explains the difference between the two 'races'; the fundamental differences of their origin, place, past and present.

✳

Gurindji people maintain their own mode of analysing colonial history. Faced with the colonisation of their countries, Gurindji people have been practising their investigation of the nature of colonialism, the ontological origin of Europeans as well as their law. As the academic way of constructing the past reflects the contemporary Western system of knowledge, the Gurindji approach to the past is also situated within their system of knowledge and its practice. The 'methodology of Dreaming' provides the theoretical tools the Gurindji historians use to explore the history of *kartiya*.

Since the 1970s, academic historians have challenged 'The Great Australian Silence' and made efforts towards introducing a historical perspective into Aboriginal studies.[23] It is indisputable that the historical dynamic approach towards Aboriginal societies has succeeded in opening up a new field that is distinguished from static anthropological analysis. However, academic historians now face an even more fundamental methodogical question: why do we apply the Western concept of 'history' to the Aboriginal past? Academic historians have begun to doubt the validity of historical analysis of Aboriginal pasts.[24]

Ann McGrath argues that some scholars today tend to avoid discussing Aboriginal experiences of history, and 'focus purely on critical studies of European representations of Aborigines, sometimes assuming that this topic relieves them of any obligation to include or co-operate with Aboriginal authors'.[25] This approach reveals the continuing nature of colonialism. Furthermore, as McGrath points out, 'a retreat to studying "our representations of them" can exaggerate the boundaries between "us" and "them", thus leading to a form of intellectual apartheid'.[26] Being self-critical is essential within the dominant post-colonial paradigm, but should not be the final goal of our interrogation of colonialism. It is also crucial to seek ways of communication across different modes of historical practice, not only in a theoretical sense, but also in an empirical – or, rather, 'experiential' – sense.

Western-academic historians may need to be a little more humble. We do not, cannot and should not dominate the production of historical knowledge. Instead of forcing our historical practice on Aboriginal pasts, we must learn the Aboriginal way of constructing the past, and then seek ways of interacting with their mode of history. I believe that this is the only way to open up democratic communication between the different approaches towards the past.

# CHAPTER 5

# WAVE HILL STATION

## 'BIGGEST MISTAKE'

The Gurindji historians explore the question of where, how and why the colonial encounter happened. It was a 'shoot 'em time'; many *ngumpin* were shot by *kartiya*.

Captain Cook came to Australia. According to Jimmy Mangayarri, Captain Cook came to Darwin and said, '(This is) good country, put the place [colony] in there.' The first station was established at Port Darwin, then Captain Cook came down to the south, to places such as Timber Creek station, and later, the Gurindji country. He said, 'Oh, he [Aboriginal people] gotta good country, (let's) make 'm station there.' Captain Cook started shooting *ngumpin* in order to steal Aboriginal people's countries and set up cattle stations.

Mick Rangiari's story started with Captain Cook coming to Sydney Harbour: Captain Cook first came to Sydney. At that time, he looked around the beach but he did not see anyone. When he came back from England, Captain Cook brought many people with him and arrived at La Perouse and set up the first settlement. When they first saw Aboriginal people there, *kartiya* thought they were 'monkeys'. Captain

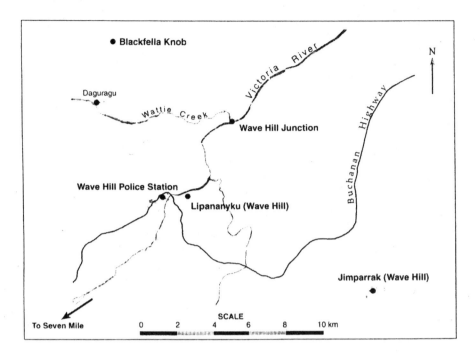

Map 5.1 Around the Gurindji country

Cook's mob went back to their camp and got guns and bullets to start shooting *ngumpin* in order to 'clear up' and 'kill 'em people for no reason'. Mick and other Gurindji historians often use body actions for this part of the story. They use their arms and faces to represent a rifle at the ready, and demonstrate shooting by mimicking the sound of gunfire: 'duuuuuun, duuuuuun'. Captain Cook brought more people from England and 'spread from Sydney' all over Australia. Later, not Captain Cook himself, but his followers came to the Gurindji country and 'claim(ed) a bit of station'.

Another Gurindji elder, Dandy Danbayarri of Kalkaringi, said Captain Cook first came from 'Big England' to Sydney by boat. He then came to the Gurindji country by horse in order to 'shoot 'em up *ngumpin*'. Ronnie Wave Hill of Kalkaringi was not sure if Captain Cook first came to Darwin or Sydney, but he was convinced that Captain Cook came to the Gurindji country. George Karlipirri of Daguragu also said that Captain Cook appeared in the Gurindji country.

Strictly speaking, every Gurindji person narrates slightly different versions of Captain Cook's story. It is part of the nature of the Gurindji ways of historical practice that even though there are contradictions between the stories, different variations of historical knowledge co-exist. However, even though people have different ideas about which part of Australia Captain Cook came to, no one ever told me that Captain Cook had been a good person. Captain Cook is the evil figure of the *kartiya* who came to *ngumpin* countries (Australia) and 'shoot 'em Aboriginal people'. Probably no one from the Gurindji country would disagree with what Mick Rangiari calls this tragic beginning of colonisation – 'biggest mistake'. Old Jimmy asked, 'Why they [settlers] never said "(Let's) live together"?'[1] I believe that many academic historians would readily share this idea of the 'biggest mistake' with the Gurindji historians.

*

A story of Captain Cook was not normally narrated as an independent story by Gurindji historians, but was often used as a 'gateway' to enter different aspects of their colonial experiences. For example, Captain Cook's activities in Australia are deeply related to the origin of the *kartiya*, Jacky Pantamarra's thought and practice. Stories of Captain Cook were also used to refer to the nature of European pastoralists, especially Vesteys. Jimmy Mangayarri has a clear idea that the 'Vestey mob' were the people who followed the law of Jacky Pantamarra and Captain Cook. Vesteys men were the same people as Captain Cook. Vestey men and Captain Cook were both from England and 'live on English way … live on Jacky Pantamarra's book'. They had stolen *ngumpin* country by shooting people. 'Vestey men put the (European) people everywhere. That's why Captain Cook come here and shoot the people [*ngumpin*].' Captain Cook's journey to the Gurindji country is related to the history of people being shot by *kartiya* and the establishment of cattle stations by Vesteys.

From an academic historical perspective, it was not the Vesteys, but Nathaniel Buchanan and his family, who established the first Wave Hill station, in the early 1880s.[2] Vesteys took over the property in the 1910s.[3] However, according to the Gurindji historians, the

Vestey mob established cattle stations all over the place by following Captain Cook's journey, which included the first Wave Hill station at Lipananyku. Therefore, it seems that 'Vestey time' started from the very beginning of the colonisation of their country.

## 'SHOOT 'EM TIME'

In 'early days', *ngumpin* got shot and killed by *kartiya* all over the country. According to Roger Yiriwa of Daguragu, *kartiya* thought *ngumpin* were 'devils'. *Kartiya* started shooting Aboriginal people, not only men but also 'mother, piccaninny [child]'. 'Whiteman don't like Aborigines. People got shot by whiteman, from every country, shoot 'em Aborigines, early days.' Mick Rangiari's agitation is even clearer: '*Kartiya* hunting, not for *buluki* [cattle], not for kangaroo, but shoot 'em Aboriginal people. Clear up!' Stanly Sambo said it was a 'shoot 'em time'.

Why did settlers kill Aboriginal people? There are many ways to answer this question: because *kartiya* followed Jacky Pantamarra's book or Captain Cook's law, because *kartiya* wanted to 'clear up' *ngumpin* in order to use the land for their own purposes – 'shoot 'em people just for land' – or because they thought Aboriginal people were 'monkeys' or 'devils'. Mick Rangiari also suggested that *kartiya* killed *ngumpin* 'for no reason'.

Another interesting answer was given by Old Jimmy. According to Old Jimmy, one of the reasons that *kartiya* shot *ngumpin* was that *ngumpin* stole *buluki* [cattle] from the station: '*Ngumpin* bin steal 'em *buluki*. That's why *kartiya* bin cheeky [dangerous, aggressive], shoot 'em *ngumpin*.' Moreover, *ngumpin* knew the cattle belonged to *kartiya*. *Buluki* is 'nothing belonga [not part of] Dreaming'. I asked Old Jimmy why *ngumpin* stole *buluki*. I was expecting answers such as 'because bush tucker was eaten by cattle' or 'because we did not like *kartiya* bringing strange animals'. However, his answer was different: because beef was 'good *ngarin* [yummy meat]'! In fact, Old Jimmy's analysis is different from the academic historians' argument. I will return to this point later.

## BLACKFELLA KNOB AND SEALE GORGE CAVE

The place to which they often referred me as an example of such killing episodes was Blackfella Knob, located 3km north of Daguragu. It seems that Blackfella Knob forms a symbolic memory of Aboriginal massacres in the Gurindji country.[4] Why did they particularly pick Blackfella Knob as an example? I think it was partly because one can see the hill from the Daguragu township. Gurindji historians often pointed to Blackfella Knob, and told me the tragic stories from 'early days'. Landscape is often important evidence of history as well as a motivation for storytellings.

The other reason why the Gurindji elders repeatedly mention Blackfella Knob is probably because the mass killing that occurred there was so traumatic for the people that it became a symbolic event in their historical narratives. In telling the story of Blackfella Knob, I found that the Gurindji historians are in fact telling the history of the first contact which *happened everywhere*.

However, at the same time, even though the Gurindji people told me many times about the mass killing at Blackfella Knob, they did not tell me detailed stories. This could be because they did not have any more detailed stories than the ones I learned, but maybe it was because they did not want to talk about it in too much detail. In the same manner, even though they pointed to the hill in the distance for me, I found that they were reluctant to go close to the hill.

According to Harry George of Daguragu, it was 'before Vestey time' that Captain Cook came to the country and 'shoot 'em *ngumpin*'. Aboriginal people were on the top of Blackfella Knob spearing *kartiya* and running away from their shooting. *Kartiya* kept circling the base of the hill and shooting *ngumpin*, 'little baby, woman, everybody (got shot)'. 'Big mob' got shot and killed, but Ronnie Wave Hill said some young people managed to run away from the shooting.

The Gurindji history does not explain who were the people who killed 'big mob *ngumpin*'. The nearest cattle station to Blackfella Knob was Wave Hill, and the nearest police station was at Bow Hill, and later Wave Hill.[5] It could have been Vesteys men, police trackers, or maybe even Aboriginal trackers. After telling the story of the mass killing at Blackfella Knob, Tommy Wajabungu told me that Bow Hill police station was established 'on the dead man's bone'. It was not clear to me if he meant this in relation to the Blackfella Knob story, or in a more abstract sense, corresponding to 'shoot 'em time' in general.

Dead people's bones were carried by *ngumpin* survivors to Seale Gorge Cave. The Gurindji people often told me about the bones in the cave after telling the stories of 'shoot 'em time' or mass killing at Blackfella Knob. Seale Gorge Cave is an important site for the Gurindji people today. To my knowledge, this is not simply because Seale Gorge is a sacred Dreaming site, but also because it is a dead people's place. *Ngumpin* who were killed by *kartiya* became *kaya* [ghost] and live in the cave – even today.

When I went to Seale Gorge to fish with three other Gurindji men, they told me not to walk too far away. They were concerned that I did not go too close to the cave without preparation. Peter Raymond told me one would get sick if one went too close to the site. George Sambo also explained to me that people had to let *kaya* know first before entering the cave. He said singing out would have to be done in 'our language [Gurindji]'. Therefore, you should go there only with knowledgable old men. After telling me the story of Captain Cook, Blackfella Knob, and later the dead people's bones in Seale Gorge Cave, Harry George said to me, 'I'll take you (to the cave) sometime.' Some other old men were also talking about taking me to Seale Gorge Cave, but they did not. I do not really know why they did not take me to the site. It could be because they thought I was not ready to visit the site yet, or they did not really want to approach the place of *kaya*, or maybe they simply could not find an opportunity to do so.

The relationship between place and memory which is the crucial aspect of the Gurindji way of historical practice is not always facilitated through the physical connection of visiting the site. On the contrary, I found that being told *not to visit* could also explain a lot about their history. In other words, the Gurindji people also practise history through connecting with the place *by not visiting*. I did not insist that they take me to the place. Someday, they may take me to the cave and start telling more about 'shoot 'em time'. You never know. You just never know.

*

Regarding the story of 'shoot 'em time', even older Gurindji elders such as Roger Yiriwa or Mick Rangiari said they did not experience it but learned about it from old people – the exception is the oldest man in Daguragu, Jimmy Mangayarri. To my knowledge, he is the last survivor in the Daguragu community who experienced the 'shoot 'em time'. At the Bow Hill police station, there was a big bloodwood tree to which Aboriginal people used to be chained and tied up by police trackers. By opening both his arms, Old Jimmy demonstrated to me how people were chained: 'chain here [the wrist of his right arm], chain here [left] ... (and *kartiya*) shoot 'em'. He also demonstrated how *ngumpin* were hanged on the tree.

Old Jimmy rarely spoke of his personal life experience, but one time he told me the story of his mother and granny [maternal grandmother] being killed by *kartiya* in front of him. When he was a little boy, *kartiya* told his mother to stop her son [Jimmy] crying, but she could not. *Kartiya* kicked his mother's *pinji* [kidney] and she died.[6] His *granny* also got shot by *kartiya* and her body was burned at the riverbank by *kartiya* to destroy the evidence.

Old Jimmy often said to me, 'I bin see 'em through my eye!'; 'I never forget. I saw it through my eye ... in my memory.' 'Shoot 'em time' was part of his life experience.

## 'NO MORE SHOOTING, WORK FOR *KARTIYA*'

The Gurindji people did not remember, did not care, or did not tell me exactly how the first Wave Hill station at Lipananyku (Old Wave Hill station) was established. However, people often told me how the first *ngumpin* started working for *kartiya* at Lipananyku. Ronnie Wave Hill seemed to have a special kind of authority over this story.[7] Therefore, I mainly use his storytellings, along with alternative versions from other Gurindji historians.

Old Wave Hill station received a letter from the Darwin government. It said, 'Don't shoot 'em (Aboriginal people). You can't shoot 'em nomo [any more]', 'Nomo [Don't] shoot 'em. Give 'em job.' Therefore, the station *kartiya* decided to take some young Aboriginal men into the station. Roy Yunga explained that the *kartiya* went to the west of Wave Hill and found *ngumpin* holding a corroboree. The *kartiya* tried to catch some young boys but ended up shooting them and kidnapped only women. According to Ronnie Wave Hill, the *kartiya* finally found one Aboriginal boy. This *ngumpin* boy – his skin name (subsection name) was japarta – was caught and taken to Lipananyku by *kartiya*. He became the first *ngumpin* to be '*walyak* [inside] longa *kartiya*'. He gradually learned English.[8]

*Kartiya*'s attempt to bring some *ngumpin* into the station continued. Later, the *kartiya* found two little boys fishing at the Wave Hill junction. The *kartiya* quietly approached them, and said, 'Hey, come in! Come this way!' When these *ngumpin* saw the *kartiya*, they got terribly frightened about being shot, but the *kartiya* were already too close for them to run away. *Kartiya* took these two *ngumpin* to Lipananyku. The *ngumpin* thought they would be killed there, but instead, the *kartiya* gave them beef, flour and tea, as well as clothing. These two *ngumpin* boys stayed there with *kartiya* and started to learn English.

Later (a few years later?), the *kartiya* ordered them to go back to the bush and explain to the other *ngumpin* that *kartiya* would not shoot them any more but wanted *ngumpin* work for them: 'OK, youbala [you fellows] go, find 'em more people. Bring 'em in.'

When these two boys went back to their families, the families were surprised to find out that these boys had survived and grown into 'big boys'. Since they wore clothes, they looked a bit like *kartiya*. The two *ngumpin* explained to them, 'They can't kill *ngumpin* … When we take (you) back (to the station), (whitefella) make you worker. They can't kill you.'

Accordingly, a lot of *ngumpin* came down to Lipananyku. A *kartiya* put marks on a wooden stick with a knife in order to count the number. The *kartiya* said, 'Oh, that's enough.' Then they held a big meeting. The two *ngumpin* and one *kartiya* explained, 'Don't frighten.

*Kartiya* don't shoot 'em.' *Ngumpin* said, 'Oh, that's good!' The *kartiya* said, 'Nomo fight, (you) work here.' *Kartiya* gave them *mangarri* [food], and the next morning the *kartiya* took them to the store and gave them clothing. This was how the Gurindji people started to work for *kartiya* at Old Wave Hill station.

## CONFLICTS AND FIGHTS

I did not learn much about the stories of *ngumpin* attacking *kartiya* from the Gurindji historians. Ann McGrath described a clash that occurred between Captain Major and Tiger Goddard at Wave Hill station in 1935.[9] The Wave Hill Police Journal held a report from 1956 that alleged some Aboriginal stockmen refused to work at Wave Hill station.[10] Another story I found in archival documents was about an Aboriginal man who 'struck' a manager of Wave Hill, 'Mr. Willock':

> The manager informed me [a director of the Native Affairs
> branch] that earlier in the year (1947) four natives from their
> No. 2 Camp left and said they were just like white men and
> could leave the job when they felt like it … Later (July or
> August) the manager was informed by his overseer that the
> natives were not going to work and their spokesman was
> interviewed by the manager who alleges that when their
> discussion was over a native named JERRY passed the remark
> 'We are just as good as you … whites'. The manager turned
> and asked him to repeat it and the native struck him. A fight
> ensued and eventually the native gave up. Other native[s] came
> down from the camp with their spears and the white staff also
> gathered round. It is difficult to get a coherent story other
> than there was a lot of shouting and yelling on both sides but
> as far as I can ascertain the only people using physical violence
> were the manager and the native Jerry. The result was that all
> natives except seven have returned to work and these seven are
> just sitting around the camp.[11]

This report affected me in two ways. First, I was excited to know that even in the 1940s, some of the Gurindji people had already given a demonstration of stopping and leaving stockwork to demand the right of mobility as well as the recognition of their importance as stock-workers. It is also noteworthy that the event happened in the year following the Pilbara walk-off. This naturally raised questions: was there any connection between this event and the Pilbara walk-off, and the later Wave Hill 'strike'?

However, I also felt disappointed that the Gurindji people did not remember much about this story. I was not told this story before I found this report. After finding this episode at the National Archives of Australia, I asked people in Daguragu about it, but I later realised that they have not clearly held onto this story even though *ngumpin* Jerry as well as *kartiya* manager Willock were in their memory. I had to conclude that the story was not very important for the Gurindji historians. From the Gurindji historical perspective, this event was probably not successful enough, not adventurous enough, and not violent enough to remember as a part of their 'early days' history.

Although some incidents were reported,[12] there have been very few stories of *ngumpin* attacking *kartiya* in the Gurindji country both in oral and documentary accounts. It is quite a contrast to the stories that Deborah Bird Rose as well as Peter and Jay Read explored in the northern part of the Victoria River district.[13] It seems there were many more Aboriginal physical attacks against settlers in the northern areas than in the Gurindji country.

## MYSTERY OF 'LEICHHARDT' KILLED AT WATTIE CREEK

There was only one story I was told of where *ngumpin* murdered *kartiya* in the Gurindji country. However, due to lack of information, I must admit that I have no way of exploring this story beyond simply presenting what I learned: according to Old Jimmy, a *kartiya* named 'Leichhardt' travelled through the country in order to shoot *ngumpin*. Two *ngumpin* attacked and speared him at Wattie Creek. They cut his stomach and filled it with stones, and then threw him into the river.

This story probably makes readers think of the famous explorer Ludwig Leichhardt, who disappeared during his expedition, an attempted east–west crossing of the continent, in 1848.[14] However, how much should I speculate about this story? From an academic historical perspective, there is no substantial evidence that the murdered *kartiya* was Leichhardt. From a Gurindji perspective, this was just another story of how one bad *kartiya* was killed by *ngumpin*. From a cross-cultural perspective, I can neither trace how the name 'Leichhardt' was remembered by the Gurindji people nor explore the historical reality and truthfulness of 'Leichhardt' or '*kartiya* killed at Wattie Creek'. I can only speculate and suggest that the Gurindji people *needed to remember* at least one story of rebellion in the Gurindji country.

## MYSTERY OF THE REBEL, 'MAJOR'

In fact, there is a more complicated story told by the Gurindji historians. It was about a *ngumpin* called 'Major' who killed many *kartiya* during his journey from the Northern Territory to Western Australia. The story was not located in the Gurindji country, but some elders passionately told me about this episode. I wondered why. After sharing the story I learned from the Gurindji elders, I would like to discuss the importance of a history which is *not located* in the Gurindji country.

Mick Rangiari once told me 'Major' might have come from somewhere in Queensland, but later the elders seemed to agree that he was a Jingili man. The Gurindji elders did not explain much to me about Major's background, but the story started when he had shot one *lubra* [Aboriginal woman] and two *kartiya*.

Major was a stockworker, and his wife did domestic work. They both worked for *kartiya* at a stockyard in Pigeon Hole (Montejini station).[15] However, 'Young *kartiya* did silly thing.' This *kartiya* took Major's wife to his camp and slept with her: '*Kartiya* bin take 'm *lubra* belonga him [Major]', '*Kartiya* got 'em *ngumpin* woman!' The next morning, Major picked up a rifle and bullet and shot his wife, who was washing clothes and plates at the river. Two *kartiya* there tried to run away from Major's shooting, but he eventually shot and killed both of them.

According to Old Jimmy, Major later moved to the hill near Mistake Creek station. Major lived there for a while and shot and killed many *kartiya* there. Old Jimmy justified his activity by saying, '*Kartiya* shoot 'em (Aboriginal) people, (so that) he take 'em over, clean *kartiya*.' However, other *ngumpin* did not help him because they were too frightened. Major had to fight against *kartiya* by himself. Later, Major moved his camp to Texas Down and then to Nine Mile Creek. There he was finally shot by an Aboriginal police tracker. Before being shot and killed by police trackers, Major said, 'Oh, youbala [you fellows] got me, OK, youbala can shoot me.' He lifted up his hands – Old Jimmy showed me this through his actions – and then they shot him to death.

Mick Rangiari gave me more detail about Major's itinerary: when he killed a *lubra* and two *kartiya*, he went to Mt Sanford (VRD) to find a job, pretending he had done nothing. Then Major moved to Limbunya station, but he was by himself and *ngumpin* there did not want to mix with him. Major tried to talk to them but no one helped him. He kept travelling through Inverway to Mistake Creek station. There he shot and killed a couple of *kartiya* travellers. By that time policemen were investigating and looking for him. Major moved to Nine Mile Creek. After a gunfight at the hill near Nine Mile Creek, he ran away to Ord River station but policemen still chased him. There he shot and killed two more *kartiya* and ran away to the hill near Mistake Creek. Major killed some more *kartiya* policemen on the hill, but an Aboriginal tracker finally shot him. Before he died, Major said, 'I bin try help everybody (*ngumpin*). I bin shoot 'em whitefella. You silly my people shoot me.'

It is also important to note that both Old Jimmy and Mick Rangiari, as well as George Karlipirri, said it was Tinker, George's father, who finally shot and killed Major. Tinker was a police tracker. I asked them a naive question about why *ngumpin* worked for *kartiya* policemen. Old Jimmy said, 'Oh, because *ngumpin* bin frighten. *Kartiya* fright 'em him. (*Kartiya* said,) "If you don't help me, I shoot you!"' Roy Yunga's father was a police tracker as well. He also said his father had to shoot *ngumpin*; otherwise *kartiya* would have shot him.

When I heard this history, I was truly amazed by their very detailed storytelling about Major despite the fact that the episode was not related to the Gurindji country. And later, in Canberra, I was once again amazed, and also perplexed, because the story I had learned obviously had direct and indirect connections with several incidents where Aboriginal people killed settlers – these happened in several different places around (but not in) the Gurindji country.

Let me start with Bruce Shaw's study. Using Aboriginal and European oral accounts as well as contemporary newspapers, Shaw explores the story of 'Major', who killed at least three Europeans near Texas Downs and Blackfellow Creek in 1908.[16] Major originally came from Wadaman country, and he was brought to east Kimberley as a boy by a European named Jack Kelly.[17] His second wife, who followed him from his first murder until he was shot dead, was called 'Knowla', which was probably her skin name.[18] Major killed a European named Scotty McDonald at Texas Downs station, and then disappeared into the hills. Later he killed two more Europeans, at the Blackfellow Creek outstation in Lissadell.[19] He ran away and travelled and lived in hilly places over countries such as Argyle, Mistake Creek, Nine Mile, Turkey Creek, etc. Major and his companions also harassed white travellers and stockmen. According to Aboriginal oral accounts, Major killed about twenty Europeans, mostly around Mistake Creek country.[20] He seemed to intend to return to his Wadaman people via Wave Hill and Darwin, and had a premonition about his death.[21] He was chased by white and Aboriginal police trackers and was finally shot and killed at Nine Mile Creek.[22] This was the story of Major's death told by Jack Sullivan: '… he [Major] could no longer load his gun. He lifted up his hand: "You got me", and they walked up and did him in. They shot him little by little …'[23]

Second, there is Peter and Jay Read's study of 'Major'. In 1895, two Europeans named John Mulligan and George Liger were speared by Aboriginal guerrillas at Jasper Gorge, the rugged country of the Victoria River basin. The attack was done by Ngarinman, Ngaliwurru and Wadaman people and the name of one of the attackers was 'Major'. The 'revenge massacre' took place later, at Gordon Creek. The Reads cross-examined the story from both documentary and oral sources.[24]

Third, there is Rose's study of 'Alligator Tommy'. Rose also narrates the story based on both oral and documentary accounts. Alligator Tommy was from the Alligator River area in Arnhem Land. Tommy worked at VRD as well as in the Darwin area.[25] In January 1905, Alligator Tommy and a *lubra* [Aboriginal woman] called Nowra and three Europeans – Harry Edwards, Richard Frost and Henry Benning – were at Long Leach (Pigeon Hole). Presumably, Nowra was Tommy's wife, but she was 'taken' by *kartiya*. When Edwards and Frost threatened Tommy with a gun, he responded by shooting Frost, Edwards and Nowra. Benning ran away and later became a witness at the trial.[26] An Aboriginal account claims that Tommy shot 'a mob of white men',[27] and also that Nowra was pregnant by a 'yellow fellow [mixed descent]'.[28] Alligator Tommy was arrested near Darwin and sentenced to death. He escaped from gaol once but was re-arrested and hanged at Fannie Bay gaol in December 1905.[29] I would like to add one more oral account of this incident. Ruby Roney, who was born in New South Wales in 1892 and went to the Territory in 1904, gave an oral account of this episode which she heard while she was at Delamere station, which was located in Wadaman country. I omit her detailed story since it is almost identical to Rose's except for the name of the Aboriginal killer: Ruby said his name was 'Major'.[30]

While trying to give a clearer picture of the Alligator Tommy incident from documentary and oral sources, Rose confesses, 'the stories of Alligator Tommy are a jigsaw puzzle from hell'.[31] However, my hell seems to be even worse.

## HISTORICAL REALITY OF GURINDJI'S MAJOR

Figure 5.1 depicts a comparison of several elements in these four different but possibly connected stories, and a map of geographical locations of the incidents.

| | SHAW | READ | ROSE | GURINDJI |
|---|---|---|---|---|
| Name of killer/s | Major | Major and others | Alligator Tommy ('Major' by Roney) | Major |
| Country of killer/s | Wadaman, later in east Kimberley | Wadaman, Ngarinman, Ngaliwurru | Alligator River (Arnhem Land), later in VRD | Jingili, later travelled to WA |
| The killed or injured | Three or more Europeans | Two Europeans | One Aboriginal woman and two Europeans, or 'a mob of white men' | One Aboriginal woman and two Europeans, then later many Europeans |
| Place of killer's attack | Texas Downs, Blackfellows Creek (WA) | Jasper Gorge (VRD) | Pigeon Hole (VRD) | Pigeon Hole or Montejini, later Mistake Creek and WA |
| Place of killer's death | Shot at Nine Mile (WA) | N/A | Hanged in Darwin | Shot at Nine Mile (WA) |
| Year | 1908 | 1895 | 1905 | N/A |
| Note | Major's second wife's name was Knowla | 'Revenge massacre' happened at Gordon Creek | Killed Aboriginal woman's (skin) name was Nowra | |

Figure 5.1 Four stories of Major

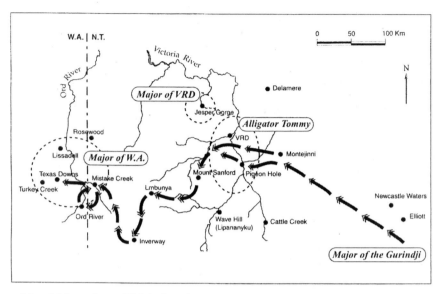

Map 5.2 Locations of 'Major' stories

My purpose here is neither to prove how much of the Gurindji story of 'Major' was based on historical 'facts', nor to explore how imaginative their story was. Instead, I aim to struggle with and think through the historical reality and truthfulness of the Gurindji version of Major's story.

First, it is not difficult to notice that the earlier part of the Gurindji's account of Major (Major of the Gurindji) is almost identical to the incident of 'Alligator Tommy', and that the latter part is closer to Shaw's story of Major (Major of WA). In particular, Old Jimmy's story of Major's dying speech – 'You got me', and lifting his hands to receive gunshots – is surprisingly similar to Jack Sullivan's version. The story of Major of WA was certainly carried to the Gurindji country through the Aboriginal information network.

'Major' was such a common name among Aboriginal people in the area that it is hard to judge, for example, whether Major in Read's account (Major of VRD) and Major of WA are in fact the same person. We can only tell that both Majors could have been from Wadaman country. It is also possible that Ruby Roney mis-remembered the name 'Alligator Tommy' as 'Major', because she could also have heard the story of Major of VRD and/or Major of WA. Such a coincidence is also found in the Aboriginal woman's name in these stories. Alligator Tommy's wife and a wife of Major of WA were both remembered by their skin name of Knowla/Nowra.

From a Western-academic perspective, it is reasonable to assume that the Gurindji historians have combined all these stories into one big historical narrative of Major's long heroic yet tragic journey. However, instead of asking the academic-oriented question 'How did different histories became one big myth?', I want to explore the importance of the *locality* of Major's journey in the Gurindji cultural geography, which I believe is a more truthful approach to the Gurindji people's historical practice.

We should not ignore the Gurindji claims that Major originally came from Jingili country – located further east of Mudburra country. This is uniquely the Gurindji's perspective, since other accounts indicate that Major was from either Wadaman, Arnhem Land or Queensland. Why did Major in the Gurindji story come from Jingili country? I believe that the idea of 'Major from the east' was crucial for the Gurindji people. The Gurindji historians located Major's historical appearance not only in Pigeon Hole, Limbunya, Inverway, Mistake Creek and Texas Downs, but also in Jingili country and Montejini station. There were no significant cattle stations in the south of the Gurindji country. Therefore, in the Gurindji historical practice, Major's itinerary of 'clear up *kartiya*' covers most of the cattle stations around the Gurindji country (Wave Hill).

I need to remind you here that the Gurindji people did not give me any stories of significant rebellion against *kartiya* within the Gurindji country. Although there are oral and documentary accounts of cattle killings, I could not find a substantial documentary source which clearly shows Aboriginal murder of settlers in the area of Wave Hill station. I suspect this was because the Gurindji country was flatter in comparison to the mountainous northern countries. It was probably too difficult to attack *kartiya* effectively in the Gurindji country. If one wanted to be a member of the resistance, one would have moved up to the northern sandstone area of Bilinara or Ngarinman countries.[32]

The Gurindji people in the Wave Hill area were mainly descendants of those who did not/could not efficiently and violently resist the *kartiya* in their country. I believe this geographical condition is strongly related to the Gurindji analysis of Major's legend. In their historical practice, Major was a hero who killed *kartiya everywhere*. He perhaps did not come to Wave Hill because there was no hideout in the Gurindji country. I also want to emphasise that the Gurindji historians told me that *ngumpin* did not help Major, and the Gurindji man Tinker actually killed Major, and Major said, 'I bin try help everybody. I bin shoot 'em whitefella. You silly my people shoot me.' Even though their country was *kartiya*-friendly – that is, they had no choice but to be obedient to *kartiya* – I felt that the Gurindji people had a 'sense of guilt' that they did not fight against *kartiya* aggressively enough in the early days. I wonder if this guilty feeling was one of the conditions of the initiative the Gurindji showed in their later action. The 'resistance' by the Gurindji people was more organised and well prepared, but happened much later, in 1966.

## 'EARTH PUNISH *KARTIYA*, TOO'

The countries further west of Daguragu, where the Limbunya and Mistake Creek stations are, are well known, and to some extent notorious, as being areas holding very dangerous *mangaya* [Dreaming sites]. Limbunya is Jimmy Mangayarri's country. Old Jimmy warned me that I should never walk around there by myself: 'Limbunya, plenty *mangaya*. You can't walk around. Very dangerous, proper dangerous'; 'This place [Daguragu], you can walk around anywhere. But that way [Limbunya], very dangerous.'

Mistake Creek station is also the location of several very powerful *mangaya*. While I was in Daguragu, a Gurindji man came back from Mistake Creek station. He was working as a stockman there but got sick and came back to Daguragu. Investigations started among the elders, and they soon found out that he had discarded the *Jurntakal* dreaming by digging a Dreaming waterhole. People whose *kuning* [Dreaming totem] were *Jurntakal* helped him through the ceremony to recover from the sickness. However, he passed away at the Darwin hospital about a month later.[33] This tragedy reminded me of Old Jimmy's teaching: 'Earth is man. He watch 'em you. Earth punish you ... Earth can punish you any time.'

Old Jimmy emphasised that the Dreaming can punish *kartiya* as well. Earth is alive, earth is powerful. If we – it does not matter if 'we' are *kartiya* or *ngumpin* – mistreat the earth, the earth punishes us. We have to look after the earth as the earth looks after us:

> *Kartiya* don't know. He reckon ground. He don't know what's
> in there. He just go anywhere. He think he do good thing, but
> he do bad thing ... You don't know Boss [Dreaming] there.
> He might kill you ... *Wangaj* [bad], very dangerous ... Maybe
> *mangaya* look (at you). *Mangaya*, he kill 'em.

It is crucial to notice that Old Jimmy's teachings explain that the Dreaming has been interacting not exclusively with Aboriginal people, but also with non-Aboriginal people. In the same way as the *karu* [children] Dreaming followed me all the way to Japan, the Dreaming punishes you whoever you are, if you profane *mangaya*.

Old Jimmy worked at Limbunya station as a stockworker during the 'Vestey time'. One day, a *kartiya* dug into the ground near his house at Limbunya station (for burying the petrol tank underground?). However, by digging the ground, he profaned *mangaya* without knowing it. The next morning when he woke up, he saw many *pirlki* [maggots] coming out of ground. This *kartiya* got sick and died. Soon after his death, a fire rose from the ground and burnt his house as well as his body. This episode seems to be related to the fire that burnt down the Limbunya mechanic store in 1961. According to the police report, a person called Anthony John Perry was burnt and killed by this fire.[34]

There are two different cultural interpretations for this event. From an academic historical perspective, the fire was probably the consequence of human activities. But the Gurindji historians see it as the result of the interaction between humans and the Dreaming. Historical agents are not always humans within the framework of the

Gurindji people's history. It is fact that Limbunya has been a country of many important Dreaming sites. It is also fact that settlers did not care about these sites when they used the land. Therefore, it is reasonable historical analysis that the fire at the Limbunya station was a punishment wrought by the Dreaming. The only (but serious) problem is that academic history has to be narrated in a secular manner, so the Gurindji historical analysis of the event cannot fully be accepted by Western-academic historical discourse. Therefore it is important to mark here that seemingly *universal* academic history has its limits in representing the past.

# CHAPTER 6

# CATTLE, DREAMING AND COUNTRY

*... fact may not be true, and truth may not be factual. The question of which parts of a story were factual and which were not was not a very important one for Cinnamon.*
*The important question was not what his grandfather did but what his grandfather might have done.*

HARUKI MURAKAMI 1997

## 'JAPARTA BULUKI-WAJI'

Ann McGrath argues, 'With the totemic system so important in Aboriginal life, it would be expected that cattle would eventually be incorporated in song cycles or dreamtime stories, like all other animals occurring in their country.'[1] Although I share similar expectations, cattle are not yet part of Dreaming in the Gurindji country. The

Gurindji historians instead have the clear idea that *kartiya* brought cattle to their country.

Jimmy Mangayarri said to me, 'No *buluki* [cattle] Dreaming. *Kartiya* bin bring 'em up this country.' Old Jimmy differentiates between two different types of animals: kangaroo, goanna and emu are 'on history', but cattle, horse and camel are 'not on history'; 'You never see history belonga bullock.'

According to Old Jimmy, the first cattle appeared in his country from Seven Mile Creek. This indicates that cattle appeared from east of Jimmy's country (Limbunya). This story roughly corresponds to the documentary evidence, which states that the first stock arrived in the area from Queensland in May 1883, and thousands of cattle were brought from Queensland in the following years.[2]

The first *ngumpin* who ate cattle was called 'japarta buluki-waji' – a rough translation would be 'cattle-man whose skin name is japarta'. He speared a cow and killed it. He wanted to see what its meat tasted like, 'maybe *punyu* [good], maybe *wankaj* [bad]'. He made a fire and cooked the cattle meat.

He tried it ............ 'Good *ngarin* [meat]!'

This japarta told *ngumpin* that this foreign animal had good meat. This was how *ngumpin* started to 'steal' cattle from *kartiya*. As already discussed, Old Jimmy explained that *kartiya* did not like *ngumpin* 'stealing' cattle because cattle came with *kartiya* and belonged to *kartiya*, and naturally it caused violent conflict between *ngumpin* and *kartiya*.

## THE QUESTION OF CATTLE KILLINGS

In order to understand the cultural and historical meaning of cattle for Aboriginal people, it is crucial to note that Old Jimmy explained that the reason behind cattle killing was to eat the cattle's tasty meat.

Old Jimmy's historical analysis is quite different from academic historians' discussion about the cattle killings. For example, McGrath explains that Aboriginal people speared cattle because it was 'one of the most effective means of resistance'.[3] She writes:

> While Europeans were frustrated by Aboriginal 'lawlessness',
> blacks were undoubtedly infuriated by the settlers' wastage of
> natural food resources, total disregard for sacred sites and the
> pollution and depletion of waterholes.[4]

However, this part of her work is based on documentary evidence that comes from a settler's perspective, not on Aboriginal oral accounts.[5] Dawn May's argument is more radical. She writes:

> While in some instances the killing of stock proved an
> additional source of food, there is clear evidence out of the
> district [Queensland] that in many cases Aboriginal attacks
> were aimed at driving Europeans out of the district.

But her 'clear evidence' is also drawn from historical documents.[6] On the history of the Gurindji country, the Daguragu land claim book also says, 'by 1886, cattle killing as a response to invasion had begun in earnest', but again this statement is based on documentary evidence.[7]

Old Jimmy said *ngumpin* killed cattle because it provided tasty meat, not because they wanted to demonstrate their agitation against *kartiya*. During my fieldwork, I never heard anyone saying that they killed cattle in order to fight against *kartiya*. Was killing cattle really an act of 'resistance'?

It could be true that for Aboriginal people, defending the waterholes was crucial for both economic and cultural reasons.[8] It is also obvious that the introduction of cattle rapidly changed soils and plants, which caused economic crises in Aboriginal societies.[9] However, what if Aboriginal people's purpose was not 'resistance' but simply the desire to ensure their food supply and take opportunities to eat 'good *ngarin*'?

When I saw the Gurindji people's attitude towards animals – regardless of whether they are 'on history' or 'not on history' – I could not picture Aboriginal people killing animals not for eating but for 'resistance'. The Gurindji people are very friendly towards cattle, horses and many other animals. While driving around the country, they often wave their hands and call out to cattle, donkeys or horses.

When cattle sit on the road, the way they disperse them – shouting at them to move away – is quite similar to the way they act towards relatively domesticated community dogs. When we visited one of the Dreaming waterholes, they explained to me without any hesitation that *kurraj* [rainbow snake] lived there and bullock came to drink water. These episodes remind me of what McGrath writes: 'They acknowledge the ecological damage done by cattle and buffalo, and try to prevent them fouling sacred sites, but are basically tolerant of them.'[10]

Did they really kill animals only to show their agitation towards settlers? Although specifying only 'station blacks' not 'bush blacks', McGrath writes:

> [T]hey do not view them [cattle] as a symbol of European
> usurpation of their lands, but are calmly accepting of their
> presence. The Aborigines' relatively non-aggressive attitude
> to indigenous animals (in the sense that they rarely kill for
> 'sport') now extends to the non-indigenous.[11]

Deborah Bird Rose also told me that an Aboriginal person said to her that cattle had done nothing wrong. It was whitefella who held responsibility for Australian colonisation.[12]

If oral historians want to stick to historical 'factuality' in the conventional academic sense, the best we could do is provide arguments which question (but do not disprove) the history constructed by the documentary evidence. It is possible that Aboriginal people's attitude to cattle has changed. Old Jimmy's perspective may be just a 'present view of the past'. They may have been as aggressive towards cattle as they were towards settlers in the earlier stages of colonisation. We do not know. However, at the same time, the Gurindji historians' perspective suggests that we may need to take a more critical approach to historical documents. It opens up the question of whether documentary evidences were recorded in an 'objective' manner.

The documents used for the evidence of cattle killing as 'resistance' were mostly written and reported by pastoralists and police. We should not forget that they were the people who often tried to 'clean up' or 'keep out' Aboriginal people, especially in the earlier stages of colonisation. It is reasonable to suspect that they exaggerated the number of cattle killings, or even made up the story of Aboriginal people killing cattle not for food but for 'resistance'. Why would they do this? They could have wanted to justify their 'reprisals', or their fear of Aboriginal attacks could have made their perceptions of the number of cattle killings inaccurate.

Document-centrists often argue that oral evidence could be made up later, and therefore you cannot prove the historical fact. However, documentary evidence could have been made up *at the time*, and we cannot prove it either. In this context, I suggest that historians can effectively utilise oral evidence to make history more open to different interpretations of the past.

## STOCKWORK

Before exploring the Gurindji elders' stories of stockwork at Wave Hill and other cattle stations, let me give you my impression of Daguragu's 'fashion scene'.

While I was in the Gurindji country, the young people's standard fashion was mainly basketball or football uniforms and sunglasses. On the other hand, the important Gurindji elders' 'fashion' was the cowboy hat. Many elders, if not all, wear very old cowboy hats which are deeply ingrained with their sweat and dirt, and also probably with their experiences of the 'hard time'. The Gurindji elders used to be stockmen. They are proud of their history. I have no doubt that cowboy hats are part of their (historical) identity. Today, young people do not even know how to ride horses. The young Gurindji don't wear cowboy hats.

Many elders who used to be stockmen are now pensioners. Some younger elders and young people in the community today work on Community Development Employment Projects (CDEP) which include road construction, making bread, building and repairing houses, making arts and crafts, cleaning the community, etc. I found that elders viewed CDEP in a very negative way compared to the stockwork of their 'early days'. For example, Tommy Wajabungu said:

> When I was young, I work everywhere. I like stockwork. I
> don't like CDEP. Stockwork all I can do. Mustering cattle
> everywhere. They [younger generation] use *motika* [car].
> They don't like riding horse. Young people don't like horse,
> mustering cattle.

Teddy Crew, who used to be a stockman, now works at the 'Vincent
Bakery' baking bread. I asked him which he preferred – being a stockworker or a baker. His answer was clear: 'I like stockwork.' Stanly
Sambo said CDEP was 'useless' but stockwork had been a 'good life'.
I was surprised, because he made this statement right after telling me
how bad Vesteys were. Harry George's narration had a similar structure: he started to tell me that today is much better than 'Vestey time',
but then he said stockwork was a good job, better than CDEP. Then
his story returned to how 'rough' *kartiya* were in 'Vestey time'.

Even the older generation of elders like Mick Rangiari, who
is probably more aggressive about *kartiya* than the others, said that
'Cattle work more better than CDEP work ... Longa [being in the]
bush, a lot fun.' Jimmy Mangayarri was more careful, and considered
the possibility of damage to *mangaya* [Dreaming sites], but he still said
stockwork was 'good job, branding cattle, mustering' and '(stockwork
was) alright. (But) you gotta careful. You never kill 'em Dreaming ...
Mustering, droving, that's alright.'

The Gurindji elders also repeatedly told me that stockwork was very
hard. In the very early morning, *kartiya* came to the *ngumpin* camp and
announced the work. In the dry season, they took cattle 'everywhere'.
They worked at making yards, did mustering, branding and droving.
Steven Long told me that sometimes *ngumpin* had to work in the bush
for eight months – the whole mustering season. Tommy Wajabungu
said, 'Ride 'm horse everywhere. Hard time ... but I like it.' Old Jimmy
said *kartiya* needed *ngumpin*'s help for stockwork because *kartiya* could
not work by themselves. *Ngumpin* were better stockworkers; it was
*ngumpin* who made *kartiya* rich.

For a stockworker, joining a long droving trip was something he was very proud of. The Gurindji elders told me with great pride about their experiences droving to Queensland. This was how Vesteys took their cattle to the market and sold them. Stanly Sambo said it was *ngumpin* who took *buluki* to Queensland and 'made money, made 'em [Vesteys] rich'. Although the Gurindji elders told me how hard the droving was, the manner in which they described such experiences was quite similar to how they proudly talked, with excitement, about our ceremonial journey to the Docker River in 1997. It was about their mobility, about an adventure, and droving was about the stories of experiences in the countries away from their own.

To sum up, although many Gurindji historians said most of the 'Vestey mob' had been bad people, the elders also agreed stockwork had been a hard but good job. There was no contradiction between bad Vesteys and good stockwork in their mind. The words 'hard time' were used by the Gurindji historians in both positive and negative ways. Listening to the Gurindji elders' stories of stockwork experiences, I felt exactly the same as the way Ann McGrath described in her *Born in the Cattle* (1987): 'when Aboriginal men describe their cattle work, they do so with pride; they speak with a sense of propriety, as though describing something of deep significance'.[13] Teddy Barry once told me, 'I bin grown up with cattle and horse. There was no *motika* [car], only horse.' Yes, McGrath was right: they were 'born in the cattle'.

### 'ALL HISTORY MAN GONE'

As I will discuss in the next chapter, the purpose of the Gurindji walk-off was to run the cattle station by and for themselves in their country. However, even though a few *ngumpin* are still working at Mistake Creek and some other stations, the Daguragu community does not run the cattle station any more. Why, if they like stockwork so much? Mick Rangiari told me how they set up the Daguragu cattle station:

> [W]e set up stock yard … people [supporters?] give us
> paddock … We bin make 'em stockman. Murramulla Gurindji
> Company … put 'em cattle together … Put bore, fence …
> after that put cattle in paddock. Mustering the country …

Then I asked him why they stopped cattle work. He told me, in a disappointed tone:

> Losing gear, brand, … missing out. We still have cattle this
> country, but everyone steal gear. We couldn't do nothing more
> … Horse still running around …

Aboriginal people in Daguragu – both young and old – sometimes told me that there has been a plan to restart the cattle business. However, while I was in Daguragu I did not hear about any organised or funded plan for this project. At the moment, the situation is closer to what Stanly Sambo described to me: I asked him, 'Why did you stop cattle work?' Stanly answered, 'All history men gone … Young people not good enough (for stockwork).'

The history people have all gone! Today, stockwork is history. It was part of the story of 'early days'. Those who used to be stockmen became 'history men'.

### KAYA

As McGrath says, 'The bush contained many hidden and different dangers for Aborigines which were unknown to Europeans.'[14] In the Gurindji country, one of those dangerous beings in the bush is *kaya* [ghosts].

I went for a three-day hunting trip with Peter Raymond, Harry Sambo and George Sambo. We could not catch anything on the first day, but the following day was a big catch. We caught so many *polan* [turtle], *yawu* [fish] and *chamut* [wild turkey] that there was a lot of *ngarin* [meat] left over that night. When we set up camp near the river, I realised that George and Harry had built fires in many different places in order to surround our camp with fire. They explained to me that *kaya* were close to us and trying to steal our *ngarin*. Peter had a bad headache and asked me for an aspirin. His headache was caused by the *kaya*, and I was surprised to know that European medicine like aspirin would help to ease this kind of headache. I asked them to tell me more stories about *kaya*, but it was already so dark that they were afraid of attracting the *kaya* to our camp by telling stories. I had to wait for the next day.

*Kaya* never die. Some say a *kaya* is just a skeleton, or you can see its eyes sparkling in the bush, and others say you cannot see a *kaya* at all, but can only smell it. They often live in caves and move around the country at night. When *kaya* find people camping in the bush, they kill the people and eat their flesh. *Kaya* also kill *buluki* [cattle] and eat the meat. Furthermore, *kaya* make people 'go bush [crazy]' and transform them into *kaya*. People in Daguragu were terribly frightened of *kaya*.[15] During the ceremonies that were held at night, I was told not to stray far away from other people because *kaya* were around. At other times, *kaya* appeared in Daguragu township, and people tied up the door so as not to allow *kaya* to come inside the house.

Naturally, *kaya* are historical actors as well. During the 'Vestey time', *kaya* sometimes took people away from stock camps. One of Old Jimmy's nephews was one of these victims. The most amazing story I heard was that of a *ngumpin* cook who worked at the stock camp and was taken away by *kaya*, but managed to survive. According to Peter and Harry, his name was Barshem and he still lives in Darwin. At the stock camp, he had to wake up earlier than the others because he had to prepare breakfast. But this time the cook woke up too early, and it was still too dark; *kaya* were still around the stock camp. Peter explained that the *kaya* wanted to take this cook with them because the *kaya* knew he was a good cook. When the others woke up, the cook had already disappeared. Other *ngumpin* looked for him, and a few days later they found him on the top of a big tree. He was pulled down from the tree, and managed to survive.[16]

## MUNGAMUNGA AND *KARRKAN*

*Mungamunga* and *karrkan* are also living in the country and trying to catch people, but they seem to be much less harmful than *kaya*. *Mungamunga* are 'bush country women' and *karrkan* are 'water country women'. *Mungamunga* are in fact *ngumpin* women living in the bush who never come close to the community or homestead. *Karrkan* are like mermaids; they live underwater and eat fish. They have a fish tail, but also walk around the bush during the night.

When I asked about stories of these mysterious women, people explained to me with impish eyes that they seduced men and slept with them. Peter Raymond said he had experienced sleeping with a *mungamunga* near Cattle Creek outstation during stockwork time. But since he said this half in jest, I was not sure if he was telling me a 'true story'. Old Jimmy said there is a song for *mungamunga*. If you sing this song all day, a *mungamunga* will come up to you at night. The Cattle Creek area seems like the country for *mungamunga*. Banjo Ryan told me about an old man who used to live in Daguragu but had now passed away.[17] Banjo told this story to me with a burst of laughter: when this old man was sleeping near Cattle Creek at night, he realised *mungamunga* were on each side of him. These two *mungamunga* started to touch his chest … and then slept with him. The next morning, he followed the *mungamunga*'s track and chased them over to the cave (why?!), where he realised he had lost his way. He was nearly caught by *kaya* there.[18]

## WAVE HILL FLOOD AND DREAMING

Even though I learned a story of how *ngumpin* started to work for *kartiya*, the Gurindji people did not tell me how the first Wave Hill station was established. Instead, their favourite story was how it was washed away by a flood.

In February 1924, the first Wave Hill station – at Lipananyku, near the Victoria River bank – was washed away by a big flood. Newspapers reported this disaster as follows:

A wire from Mr. (Alex) Moray who has arrived at Katherine, states that disastrous floods have occurred at Wave Hill. Everything on the station in the shape of improvements has been destroyed. The damage is enormous but there were no casualties ... [*Northern Territory Times and Gazette*, 29 February 1924]

... the Wave Hill homestead has been completely washed away by the flood and only the kitchen, a hut, and a waggon [*sic*] shed are left standing. Fourteen people comprising whites, Chinese and blacks who were at the homestead at that time were compelled to take shelter on the roof of the waggon shed during the night ... It is not known how the cattle fared, but stockmen consider that as only about four inches of rain had fallen in that locality prior to the flood, most of the cattle would be on the flats adjacent to the river and with such a flood as reported, hundreds, perhaps thousands, would perish ... [*The Northern Standard*, 4 March 1924]

... Other aboriginals in the vicinity lodged their women folk in the high growing timber and (stood?) by stoically until the torrent took them off their feet, and carried them in some instances 10 miles down the river. The dairy herd shared the same fate but in neither case was there any loss. Cattle in other directions were not so fortunate, and the probabilities are that a large number were drowned. Mr. Moray saw carcases on his road into Manbulloo, and the loss in this direction, combined with the damage to fences and buildings is estimated at £10,000 ... [*Northern Territory Times*, 13 March 1924]

The above newspaper reports certainly explain how disastrous the flood was. However, they do not explain why this flood occurred. Of course, it was because of heavy rain. But why did such heavy rain fall in that particular area in that particular year? The Gurindji people have an answer: one of the Gurindji men made it happen. The flood was the 'fault' of George Karlipirri's father, Tinker.

It was one of those years when the Gurindji people were working for *kartiya* at Lipananyku – the first Wave Hill station. In that particular year, there was little rain for a long time in the area. As shown above, the newspaper said, 'only about four inches of rain had fallen in that locality prior to the flood'. There was no grass for *buluki* [cattle] and horses. Tinker was 'a proper clever man [sorcerer, witchcraft]', and he decided to make a big rain.

In order to make a rain, you need a 'rainstone'. When I was in Daguragu, George Karlipirri's rainstones were taken by his nieces, so he did not have any. Instead, Mick Inverway showed me some rainstones. They were crystal stones, which you can find in certain places in their country.

The easiest way to make a rain is to fill up a billycan with water and put ('cook 'em') a rainstone underwater. Then, rain will start. However, what Tinker did at that time was much more elaborate. Tinker went to the Seven Mile waterhole where a *kurraj* [rainbow snake] had been living. He dived into the water and found the *kurraj*. Tinker explained how dry the country was and then handed over the rainstones and asked the *kurraj* to make a big rain.

The next day, the rain started and it kept raining for four days and four nights. Soon Tinker realised that the rain was too heavy. He stopped it by warming both his hands at the fire – this is how to stop the rain. But it was too late. The Old Wave Hill station was washed away.[19] According to the police report, the rain started on 9 February, the Wave Hill homestead was flooded by the 11th, and the rain stopped on the 13th – it was four days and four nights.[20]

Tinker's intention was to make a rain for *buluki*, but he ended up drowning them. Giving rainstones to *kurraj* causes too much rain. Tinker should not have done that. The elderly women discussed this and told me, 'Give 'm rainstone make 'm too much rain. No good!' When Peter Raymond took me to Lipananyku, he told the story of the Wave Hill flood and also said to me, 'Karlipirri father (was) no good.' However, even though the Gurindji elders agree that

Tinker did too much, they told me about Tinker's 'fault' with some amusement.[21]

This story gives us a better understanding of the historical reality of the Gurindji people. Gurindji historical practice describes their colonial history as the interaction between historical actors which include not only *ngumpin* and *kartiya*, but also Dreaming. It is obvious and rational in the Gurindji country that Dreaming beings have been as active as humans throughout the colonial history. *Kurraj* [rainbow snake] is one of those active historical agents. Even in January 1998, the Katherine township was flooded because someone killed *kurraj*. Since Dreaming has always interacted with people, the Gurindji people have always interacted with Dreaming over the country, even under colonial rule.

The Old Wave Hill station at Lipananyku was completely ruined by the flood, and later the new Wave Hill station was set up at Jimparrak, where many of the Gurindji elders spent their lives – until the 'walk-off' started in 1966. In 1967, the homestead was again moved, to its present place, which used be a No. 1 Bore and stock camp. McConvell and Hargen write:

> [I]t was a source of some amusement to the Gurindji that the Europeans take the name 'Wave Hill' with them every time they move; it contrasts strongly with the Gurindji view that a name belongs to a site forever 'in law' and obviously could not be applied to another place.[22]

## TINKER'S ESCAPE

Why did Tinker, the father of George Karlipirri, decide to make a heavy rain over the Wave Hill station? One story explains that the Gurindji people were worried about *buluki* dying due to lack of water. However, there are several alternative, but co-existing, versions of the story.

Another story explains that Tinker made a big rain because *kartiya* did not believe *ngumpin* could control rainfall. The *kartiya* manager at that time, Mr Rankin, made a bet with Tinker that he could not make rain. Another story says that 'kartiya asked ngumpin' to make rain because the country was too dry. In contrast, there is a version that Tinker made it flood in order to drown kartiya. These different versions seem to imply some aspects of race relations in the cattle station: settlers did not trust Aboriginal people, settlers needed Aboriginal people's help, and Aboriginal people generally did not like settlers.

Tinker dived into Seven Mile waterhole and gave some rainstones to the kurraj, and then it became a big flood. He stopped the rain, but it was too late. When the Old Wave Hill station was washed away by the flood, the kartiya got so angry that they decided to kill Tinker. Tinker ran away into the bush and two kartiya trackers followed him. When the kartiya found Tinker, they prepared a big fire to burn his body and said to him, 'We gonna shoot you!' However, Tinker, 'a clever man', sang a song to put them to sleep. When the two kartiya had fallen asleep, Tinker picked up mangarri [food] from their camp and vanished into the bush. Later (a few years later?), Tinker walked all the way back and appeared at the new Wave Hill station at Jimparrak.

Kartiya did not trust Aboriginal people, but the Gurindji proved they could control the weather by using rainstones. It is noteworthy that kartiya later admitted ngumpin could do it. Otherwise, why did kartiya get angry with Tinker and try to kill him? However, once again, ngumpin had more power than kartiya in terms of sorcery. Tinker managed to run away from the kartiya trackers.

This episode is an example of both Dreaming and ngumpin actively interacting with kartiya and being involved in colonial history. Of course, if you prefer, one may change this sentence to a more academic style: Gurindji historians tend to interpret their pasts much more actively than academic historians do. And the Gurindji people's historical interpretation probably implies their struggle for survival and calls for the recognition of their dignity under the oppressive colonial regime.

\*

Dreaming – and many other living beings in the bush – were all active before, during and after the 'Vestey time'. In other words, it is evident that the Gurindji country has been alive and actively interacting with *ngumpin* throughout the colonial history. I did not hear the Gurindji historians saying that the stockwork was part of *ngumpin* way. However, there is no doubt that the lifestyle and mobility of stockwork maintained the Gurindji people's interaction with Dreaming and other beings over the country.

## WALKABOUT ECONOMY

The Gurindji people's strong commitment to their country continued even after they started to work for cattle stations. In particular, 'holiday time' – or walkabout season – became a crucial period for the station *ngumpin* to intensively interact with their countries.

The pastoral industry in northern Australia was regulated by the dry–wet seasonal cycle, so most Aboriginal stockworkers were laid off temporarily during the rainy season. For example, the following figure shows a case study of Wave Hill station in 1952–53. It indicates that while the same number of female workers were employed throughout the year, the number of male workers varied considerably according to the season. We can infer that while Aboriginal female workers were employed for the domestic jobs at the homestead, and thus worked continuously for the whole year, men in stockwork were concentrated only in the dry season, and then they were on annual holiday. It is well known that during the lay-off period, most Aboriginal people (male and female) left the station and returned to the bush for hunting and gathering, visiting neighbours, and holding ceremonies. I defined this as the 'walkabout economy' in my previous study of the Aboriginal economy in the pastoral area.[23]

It is true that this walkabout economy was ultimately subordinated to the pastoral economy. Tim Rowse argues that the models of 'internal colonialism' and 'articulation of mode of production' are more appropriate than McGrath's exposition of the 'dual economy'[24] – yet this is only if one aims to show the logic of pastoral capitalism.

The Gurindji historians do not think that *ngumpin* were exploited by *kartiya* during the 'holiday time'. The Gurindji's historical view is

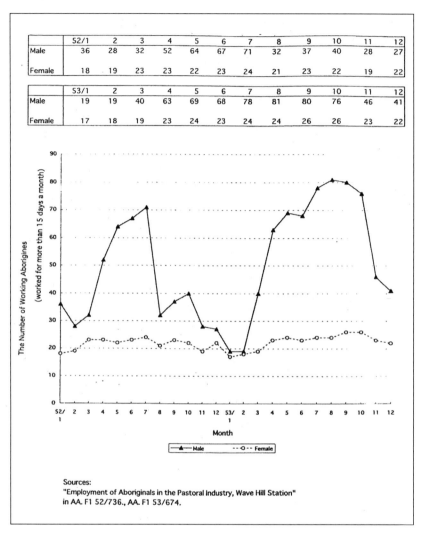

| | 52/1 | 2 | 3 | 4 | 5 | 6 | 7 | 8 | 9 | 10 | 11 | 12 |
|---|---|---|---|---|---|---|---|---|---|---|---|---|
| Male | 36 | 28 | 32 | 52 | 64 | 67 | 71 | 32 | 37 | 40 | 28 | 27 |
| Female | 18 | 19 | 23 | 23 | 22 | 23 | 24 | 21 | 23 | 22 | 19 | 22 |

| | 53/1 | 2 | 3 | 4 | 5 | 6 | 7 | 8 | 9 | 10 | 11 | 12 |
|---|---|---|---|---|---|---|---|---|---|---|---|---|
| Male | 19 | 19 | 40 | 63 | 69 | 68 | 78 | 81 | 80 | 76 | 46 | 41 |
| Female | 17 | 18 | 19 | 23 | 24 | 23 | 24 | 24 | 26 | 26 | 23 | 22 |

Sources:
"Employment of Aboriginals in the Pastoral Industry, Wave Hill Station"
in AA. F1 52/736., AA. F1 53/674.

Figure 6.1 Number of Aboriginal workers at Wave Hill station (1952–53)

probably quite similar to the notion of 'dual economy'. For example, Mick Rangiari said they used to 'live on *kartiya* food' at the station, then 'live on bush tucker' during the 'holiday time'. I was never told that the Gurindji people lived on bush tucker because *kartiya* did not feed them.

Today, even though most of the community food supply comes from a shop, bush tucker has higher priority than *kartiya* food. This is not just true of the elders; while living in the Gurindji country, I was mostly asked by younger people to go hunting, fishing and gathering. When we were collecting *muyung* [*Vitex glabrata*, or 'bush plum'],[25] Teresa Yiboin told me an excellent analogy: bush tucker is good food because it 'come up from sun', but *kartiya* food is bad because it 'come from fridge'. Mick Rangiari said during the 'holiday time' *ngumpin* ate good food because they 'find 'em bush tucker, live on bush tucker'. Many people liked to tell me with great pride about what kinds of bush tucker they hunted and gathered during the 'holiday time': kangaroo, goanna, porcupine, crocodile, emu, fish, snake, turtle, sugarbag, bush plum, bush banana, bush yam …

The walkabout economy was not just the survival economy during the wet season; it was also the 'cultural economy' that gave them the opportunity to interact with bush tucker, and thus with their country. Bush tucker is not just food. It is 'cultural' food which is 'on history' (Old Jimmy), or 'come up from the sun' (Teresa). Bush tucker has Dreaming stories and songs, and therefore has a direct connection to their country. This is what I mean by cultural economy – *ngumpin* and bush tucker have kept a dialectic relationship through the Dreaming geography over the countries. Hunting and gathering bush tucker is fundamentally different from buying *kartiya* food. Likewise, eating bush tucker is fundamentally different from eating *kartiya* food. *Ngumpin* buy and eat *kartiya* food because they are hungry, but they hunt, gather, fish and eat bush tucker not only out of hunger, but more importantly, because this is one of the ways of communicating with their countries.

## FOOD SUPPLY AND CEREMONIES

However, were they really well fed only by bush tucker during the 'holiday time'? This question should be raised not only because ecological conditions had been changed by the cattle grazing over the country, but also because, as the Berndts had already found in the 1940s, Aboriginal employees 'tended to lose some of their skills in hunting and food-collecting'.[26]

Although the Gurindji elders emphasised that there had been plenty of bush tucker in their country and they used to 'live on bush tucker' during their walkabout, they did not deny that they had also received 'holiday ration' from the station. According to the Berndts, in 1944 at Wave Hill station, 'walkabout rations', which were officially supposed to last them for a month:

> consisted of half a bag of flour (25 pounds), eight pounds of sugar, one pound of tea, one tin of baking powder, twelve sticks of tobacco, one handkerchief, and three boxes of matches ... Dissatisfaction was at its highest at that time, when they received what they regarded as the result of their year's labour ...[27]

Mick Rangiari said that the ration was so little that they soon finished it and had to rely on bush tucker. It was probably the case that, as McGrath points out, '"walkabout supplies" were used up near the station before the real travel began'.[28]

Before discussing another method of food supply during the walkabout season, let us shift our focus from food to ceremony. When I asked the elders about the 'holiday time', they told me mainly about their bush tucker hunting, but they also talked about the ceremonies they had in the bush.

During the 'Vestey time', *ngumpin* were not allowed to hold *business* [ceremony] while working for *kartiya* in the dry season. Naturally, they had to practise lots of *business* during the 'holiday time'. Victor Vincent said that it was a 'good holiday' walking around the country, using foot and spear wherever you went. Then, when *business* started, they made a 'big camp' in the bush, and held a big ceremony. As Stanly Sambo said, 'Whitefella don't care land, (but) blackfella take care land.' I probably do not need to explore how important it is to hold initiation and many other ceremonies to keep the connection with the country as well as to meet people from different places and exchange information. These issues have already been emphasised and well argued by anthropologists and historians.[29]

If the walkabout ration was consumed near the station, how did they manage to collect enough food in the bush after such ecological damage, as well as the loss of their hunting skills? It is not difficult to assume that food would have been harder to obtain, especially at times when they held a ceremony, because more of the population gathers at one place.

Naturally, they stole cattle. The Gurindji elders did not often tell me about stealing cattle during 'holiday time'. This was probably because they knew their act was an offence. Roy Yunga once told me that they sometimes killed cattle and ate them at the bush camp. When they finished eating, they threw the bones into the river: 'Next year, *kartiya* find camp, but no bone (no evidence).' I believe cattle meat greatly contributed to the holding of a big ceremony during the walkabout season. In the earlier stages, its contribution was perhaps limited to supplying enough food to the participants of the ceremony. However, cattle was not just food. I often participated in ceremonies where beef 'fat' was used for the purpose of medication or sorcery. Today, securing enough beef to supply the ceremony is one of the important concerns among the Gurindji elders. They spend a lot of money to buy a huge amount of beef for the ceremonies.

As I discussed, cattle are not (yet) a part of Dreaming. Nevertheless, cattle meat has become an essential part of the Gurindji ceremonial practice. Even though *ngumpin* left the station, and were physically and culturally separated from *kartiya* during the 'holiday time', *ngumpin* did not ever lose their connection with cattle.[30]

# CHAPTER 7

# THE GURINDJI WALK-OFF

*A brother of yours has took his stand*
*For no longer he's sick with shame*
*Come on let's shoot this old image down*
*Let's push away our pain*
SELWYN HUGHES 1988

## RE-THINKING THE GURINDJI WALK-OFF

In learning the history of the Gurindji people and their country, it is crucial to explore the walk-off from the Wave Hill station (Jimparrak) and the subsequent establishment of the Daguragu community at Wattie Creek. The Gurindji walk-off is an iconic event in Australian race relations, particularly in terms of the Aboriginal land rights movement. This episode succeeded in gaining the wide public attention of contemporary Australia, has been spoken of at length among the Gurindji people, and has also been discussed by academic historians.

It remains an event that is deeply engraved in the memories of both Aboriginal and non-Aboriginal people in Australia.[1]

My aim in this chapter is basically the same as in other chapters: to learn the walk-off movement from the Gurindji historians. From this perspective, it is crucial to think about the story that the American President, John F. Kennedy, visited the Gurindji country to support their movement. However, since the Gurindji walk-off episode has been discussed by many historians and I do not necessarily agree with these previous studies, I also want to engage with debates related to Western-academic-oriented historical 'factuality'.

There are many questions to investigate in order to understand the Gurindji people's perspective on the walk-off event. I focus on three main questions. The first question relates to how the Gurindji people formulated the idea of the walk-off. Who invented or brought about the idea of the walk-off? This discussion will also examine the reasons why the Wave Hill Aborigines, and not those from other stations, were able to begin the struggle towards regaining their country. Second, I will examine the Gurindji people's action, which has most often been referred to as a 'strike' and as part of a 'land rights movement' in the popular sense of these terms. The question here is: to what extent was the Gurindji walk-off a 'strike' and part of a 'land rights movement'? The third question is: Why did they choose Wattie Creek and move there to establish the new community? The simple answer has already been given by previous studies: Wattie Creek is a sacred place for the Gurindji people. But no one has explained why they did not move to another sacred place, and why they specifically chose Wattie Creek. In accordance with the above three questions, three sequences must be examined: (1) before the walk-off, (2) the walk-off, and (3) the establishment of the Daguragu community.

Following what the Gurindji historians told me about the event, I want to demonstrate that the Gurindji walk-off was neither a 'strike' nor part of a 'land rights movement'. In my understanding, from the very beginning of this event, it was a process of reconstructing the healthy relationship between the Gurindji people and their country by freeing themselves from the authority and control of the settlers. In the course of my analysis, I will show a Gurindji geography that is historically situated, and that comes into being as a dimension of colonial residence within an existing Dreaming landscape.

## THE UNLUCKY AUSTRALIANS

Before exploring the Gurindji people's historical narratives, I shall briefly examine studies related to this event.

Among written accounts of the Gurindji walk-off, the first and most significant report is probably Frank Hardy's *The Unlucky Australians* (1968).[2] As a journalist, Hardy was personally involved in this event and supported the Gurindji people. Encountering the Aboriginal struggle with white pastoralists, Hardy decided to help Aboriginal people in his own way: by writing articles, seeking a way to raise funds for their survival during the 'strike', writing a petition to the Governor-General of Australia for the return of their land, and so on. His standpoint is clear: he actively assisted Aboriginal 'strikers', but did not initiate their movement.

Even though there is no doubt that Hardy's commitment to the cause greatly encouraged the Gurindji elders' decision making, his restraint in terms of respecting Aboriginal initiative is admirable. Hardy conscientiously resisted paternalism in his relationship with the Gurindji people. My discussion does not intend to dismiss the extremely important role of Hardy as a supportive participant in the event. Nevertheless, I want to make it clear that Hardy's role was not to explore and interpret the background of the walk-off, but to immediately respond to the Gurindji people's requests in an appropriate way. He played his role effectively, and thus the Gurindji people respected him greatly. *The Unlucky Australians* is the product of his actual experience at that time.

However, when readers aspire to understand the Gurindji people's view of the walk-off, Hardy's book gives us a limited perspective. For instance, readers are not privy to the actual process involved in the development of the Gurindji's demands and decisions. Hardy simply presents the chronological order he experienced. In *The Unlucky*

*Australians*, the Gurindji people first demanded (1) equal wages, then (2) social justice in every aspect, until finally they wanted (3) the return of their land. If you read this book without supplementary information, you would probably accept this as the chronological order in which the Gurindji people developed their ideas. However, it is crucial to emphasise that this was the order *in which the Gurindji people told their story to Hardy*, and was therefore reflected in what he and others were able to observe at the time.

Most of the research literature follows Hardy's chronology. This order often describes the Gurindji walk-off as moving 'from a strike to a land claim'. For instance, Stuart Macintyre says, 'What had begun as a strike had become a land claim.'[3] Similarly, Lyn A. Riddett titled her article 'The Strike That Became a Land Rights Movement'.[4] Bain Attwood's study focuses on Hardy's role in this event and argues that both strike and land claim were not ideas that originated from the Gurindji people but from 'conversation' between the Gurindji strikers and Hardy.[5] Attwood's analysis leads us to re-evaluate the initiatives of outside supporters such as the workers' union and Hardy himself.[6]

However, my study has convinced me that the Gurindji walk-off was never principally a 'strike' or a 'land claim', but rather that their main purpose, consistently, was to re-establish and maintain a better relationship with their country.[7] The development of Wave Hill station certainly dominated the Gurindji people's lives and their land, but settlers' domination did not mean that the Gurindji people were totally disconnected from their country as 'nourishing terrains'. Nonetheless, their activities towards having a healthy relationship with their country were largely restricted by the settlers' control over Aboriginal labourers. I would argue that the Gurindji walk-off was planned to alter this situation. Despite these concerns about Hardy's understanding of the walk-off's purpose, *The Unlucky Australians* contains a lot of oral accounts. In later discussion, I use Hardy's book as one of the primary contemporary sources.

## OTHER ACADEMIC STUDIES

In other more academic studies there are, broadly speaking, two approaches towards the Gurindji walk-off: economic historical and socio-historical. Hannah Middleton was probably the first person to explore the economic historical view. As a Marxist anthropologist, she sees the class conflict between the Gurindji stockworkers and white pastoralists.[8] Gordon Briscoe also asserts the importance of class analysis based on Marx's theory of the mode of production.[9] Tina Jowett applies the theory of 'internal colonialism'[10] to explain the process of exploitation of the Aboriginal workers at Wave Hill station.[11] My previous work rejected theories such as 'internal colonialism' or 'articulation of mode of production'[12] because these theories cannot adequately describe the active participation of the colonised Aboriginal economy. Alternatively, I have emphasised the Gurindji people's continuous struggle to maintain economic autonomy not only during, but also before the walk-off.[13] These economic historical analyses are necessary for understanding the economic status of Aboriginal people living on stations and for explaining the economic aspects of their motivation for the walk-off. However, at the same time, this economic consideration is just one of the many issues involved in understanding this event.

Socio-historical approaches emphasise racial conflict and its social complexity. Jack K. Doolan's report clearly points out that the Aborigines' struggle was not for wages but for an equal relationship between the two races.[14] The land claim book written by Patrick McConvell and Rod Hargen shows a good integration of both economic and sociological perspectives.[15] The Aboriginal Land Commissioner's report on the Daguragu claim is also based on this book.[16] Using *The Unlucky Australians*, Ann McGrath emphasises 'white men's unfair sexual monopolisation of Aboriginal women' as one of the key reasons for the walk-off.[17] Riddett reflects on aspects of non-Aboriginal support, including her personal commitment.[18] These socio-historical approaches give us a wider view of the walk-off episode than the economic historical approach. However, we still do not know much about what the walk-off meant to the Gurindji people, a question to which I believe only an oral historical approach can provide an answer.

Jowett and Riddett used oral historical accounts from Daguragu, yet these were not presented as a major source in the construction of the history of the walk-off, but were treated more as supplementary sources.[19] McConvell and Hargen's work and a number of other reports were based heavily on the Gurindji people's oral accounts.[20] The Aboriginal Land Commissioner's report especially dealt with the Gurindji people's oral testimonies to justify the Aboriginal ownership of the claimed area and its historical background.[21] However, the questions I seek to address – Who invented the idea of the walk-off? Was the walk-off a strike in the European sense of the term? Why did they choose Wattie Creek as their new community? – were not discussed at length in these works. Deborah B. Rose's *Hidden Histories* (1991) includes a chapter on this 'strike' movement, in which she argues that the Aboriginal people's primary demand was the return of their land.[22] In 1982, Hobbles Danayarri, a Mudburra man of Yarralin, said to Rose, 'Tommy Vincent (Lingiari) told Lord Vestey: "You can keep your gold. We just want our land back".'[23] However, Rose primarily explored the perspective of Aboriginal people from Victoria River Downs rather than those from Wave Hill.

Thus the purpose of this chapter becomes clear: it addresses the need to discuss the walk-off episode more thoroughly, with specific questions based on the oral historical accounts of the Gurindji people. Only through this approach can we understand the meaning of the walk-off from the Gurindji perspective.

## 'WISH WE HAD SOMEONE BEHIND US'

A leader of the Wave Hill walk-off, Tommy Vincent Lingiari, a Gurindji elder, told Hardy what he had been thinking during the 'Vestey time'– that is, before the walk-off:

> The manager of Wave Hill was Tom Pisher. Besty [Vestey] man, Tom Pisher. Always when big plant start to go out from station when mustering start, they go out two, maybe three month. Aboriginal men out in bush all time. White ringers

come back to station ebry Friday night. That not right. I think to mesel' about that longa time. And think them Bestey mob don't treat Aborigine native people right way.[24]

A similar story is also told by Captain Major (Lupgna Giari or Lapngayarri), another Gurindji man who led the Aborigines of Newcastle Waters station and walked off to the vicinity of Elliott; this was about three months before the walk-off at Wave Hill station. Captain Major told Hardy the following:

All around the Territory I bin working more than thirty year. And I bin thinking: white fella don't treat native people proper, don't gib him proper wages or nothing. He never teach you to read, only to count, to keep tally when the cattle go in the yard … I was thinkin' to mesel': I was reckon I only get ten dollar and all these other men only get six dollar. And them women might book a few things down at store, lucky if thirty bob left after two months. That not right. And I bin thinkin' agen: Wish we had someone behind us somewhere.[25]

Dexter Daniels, a young Aboriginal Roper River man who worked for the North Australian Workers Union (NAWU), also remembers that Captain Major 'told me he had often thought this. He told me about having someone behind him, someone who would help the Aborigines.'[26] These comments show us that both the Gurindji men, Vincent Lingiari and Captain Major, had been thinking about the poor situation of their people. It was before Dexter Daniels and Hardy arrived to support Aboriginal stockworkers that Captain Major was seeking to have 'someone behind him' who would help Aboriginal people.

I would like to explore this point: what did it really mean when Vincent Lingiari said, 'I think to mesel' about that longa time' and Captain Major said, 'Wish we had someone behind us somewhere'? What was behind these statements? This should be the starting point for exploring our first question: where did the idea of the walk-off originate?

## SANDY MORAY

Most of the Aboriginal elders in Daguragu remember a Gurindji man, Sandy Moray Junganaiari, who seems to have been well known throughout the region.[27] Frank Hardy met and wrote about him, describing Sandy as 'an ancient thin man'.[28] Hardy also drew a portrait of Sandy Moray on the front page of *The Unlucky Australians*.

Among the Gurindji elders in Daguragu community, I held intensive discussions with Jimmy Mangayarri, Mick Rangiari, Peanut Pontiari and Stanly Sambo. They convinced me that Sandy Moray was the founder of the walk-off, before Vincent Lingiari took the real action.

They told me that Sandy Moray was called 'Tipujurn' among the Gurindji and his country was Seale Gorge and Wattie Creek. During the mustering time, he did stockwork on Wave Hill station, then he went back to his country, Seale Gorge, when the wet season ('holiday time') started.[29] Sandy Moray also worked for Alex Moray, a pastoral inspector for Vesteys, whom they called 'Vestey's big boss', or 'travelling boss'.[30] Tipujurn's European name, Sandy Moray comes from Alex Moray. Since Sandy Moray worked for Alex Moray, 'he bin all over' Australia. His frequent interstate trips gave Sandy Moray an unusual opportunity to observe the race relations at cattle stations in other places, such as Queensland and Western Australia. In other states, especially in Queensland, Sandy Moray was impressed to see that Aborigines and white Australians worked together and the conditions of the Aboriginal people were better than in the Northern Territory. Sandy Moray wanted to show the better race relations in Queensland to his 'mate', Vincent Lingiari. One day ('holiday time'?) they went to the Northern Territory/Queensland border to meet some Queensland Aborigines. However, local police denied them entry because they did not have permission to travel into Queensland.

Eventually, Sandy Moray started to think about changing the Aboriginal situation in his country: 'He [Sandy] bin start think'n, (and said) "I gonna get somebody. I got a bit of idea."' The Gurindji elders with whom I spoke could not fully explain to me how Sandy Moray developed the idea of changing the situation of his own country. They did suggest that Tipujurn was good at following the white man's ideas

Figure 7.1 A portrait of Sandy Moray by Frank Hardy

and practices because he had known Alex Moray for a long time. They also told me that Sandy Moray may have met unionists in Queensland and learned how to fight. Mick Rangiari suggested that Sandy Moray had a good 'brain' so that 'maybe he bin think'n himself'.

On the other hand, what they clearly remembered is that Sandy Moray called meetings under the '*partiki* tree' [*Terminalia arostrata*, or 'nut tree']31 at Wattie Creek. Jimmy Mangayarri was one of the participants. Other participants he remembered were Vincent Lingiari, and Peanut Pontiari's father, Bob Warriyawun.32 Mick Rangiari was a little boy at that time. Pincher Nyurrmiyari (Manguari) was not there because he was not yet a member of this project.

At these meetings, Sandy Moray told them:

What's for we work'n langa *kartiya* [white people]? We wanna
fight the *kartiya*. Get the country back! Don't worry about it.
You gotta [will get] land, no worry. You gotta land, you gotta
station, you gotta horse, you gotta *buluki* [bullock], you gotta
*motika* [car].

Initially, most of them did not believe him. However, Sandy Moray
patiently explained his idea to people. He said, 'We gonna do something', and explained his plan every night. He talked 'all night, and get
old men made 'em understand'. As I discussed in Chapter 6, the Gurindji
people maintained their relationship with their country through the
ceremonies held during the 'walkabout season', so we should understand Sandy Moray's 'get the country back' not as 'returning the lost
country' but rather as 're-establishment of the healthy and continuous
relationship with the country regardless of seasons'.

Jimmy Mangayarri and Mick Rangiari confirmed that these meetings had been held a long time before Hardy visited the Gurindji
country. Therefore, it is evident that the ideas of keeping settlers out
of their country and running the cattle station by themselves were
formulated by Sandy Moray and had been in the Gurindji people's
consciousness long before the actual walk-off occurred. Riley Young
of Lingara told Rose that Sandy Moray also went to the Ngarinman
country to explain his plan. This, according to Rose, appears to have
been around 1950:

> And old Sandy Moray used to come out from Wave Hill …
> Sandy Moray, Jangala [skin name] bloke. He used to come out
> there and tell us this story for us. Tell us. Ohhh, myall time.
> We were working for whiteman yet. He used to come out and
> tell us. He used to come out from Wave Hill for holiday, you
> know.
>
>    'Ah,' he told us, 'ah, you gotta change the law now. Eh?
> Might be four years' time, might be five years' time.' He (had
> had an) education for whiteman before. Working (for) the
> whiteman too long. He used to go down to Canberra, talk

with them Waterside Union. Talking with them. Telling them. Sneaking without no permit ... He used to come out telling us: 'We gotta get this land back. Don't tell anybody.'[33]

However, if Sandy Moray was the person who conceived the project, was there a reason that prevented him from leading the walk-off? Peanut Pontiari explained that he was already too old to become a leader of all the actions they would take. Instead, Sandy Moray said to Vincent Lingiari, 'You gotta do something.'

This story of Sandy Moray holds the answer to the question I raised above. When Vincent Lingiari said, 'I think to mesel' about that longa time' and Captain Major said, 'Wish we had someone behind us somewhere', they meant that they had been thinking about how to put Tipujurn's plan into practice and were looking for someone to facilitate their project. Their project was, from the very beginning, to keep settlers out of their country and to establish their own cattle station.

*

One may wonder why the story of Sandy Moray has been neglected by the many previous oral accounts of the Gurindji people. We heard much about Vincent Lingiari as a leader of the walk-off, but rarely about Sandy Moray as a founder of the walk-off. As oral testimonies are often criticised, it is natural to cast doubt on the Gurindji people's memories of Sandy Moray. Was this aspect made up by the Gurindji people decades later? Is it likely that previous studies are more accurate than my research, conducted 30 years after the events?

To answer this, I have already mentioned that there was little oral historical research which explored the specific question of 'Who invented the walk-off?' instead of 'Who led the walk-off?' As shown above, Rose was one of the few people who collected a story of Sandy Moray. In addition, Patrick McConvell, who did intensive fieldwork at Daguragu in the mid 1970s, was also told that Sandy Moray formulated the idea of the walk-off. According to McConvell, he was referred to as 'jangala' – his skin name – since his name was taboo at that time. McConvell found out later that 'jangala' referred to Sandy

Moray.[34] Because of the nature of oral accounts, every detail of the story of Sandy Moray may not be accurate, but it is compelling that the essence of the story has remained identical over the decades spanning the research done by McConvell, Rose and myself.

It is also interesting to note that the story of Sandy Moray has been gradually revealed to non-Gurindji; first, briefly to McConvell in the 1970s, then to Rose in the 1980s, and to me in more detail in the late 1990s. I found that Gurindji people today have become more comfortable telling the stories about the deeper background to the walk-off episode. I will return to this point after discussing the whole event.

## THE GURINDJI NETWORK SYSTEM

In order to explore the sequence prior to the walk-off in more depth, it is also important to examine Aboriginal relations and networks in different stations. I would especially like to explore the relations between the Gurindji elders of different stations.

It is interesting to note that Captain Major also worked for Alex Moray. In *The Unlucky Australians*, Captain Major told Hardy: 'I bin droving sometimes and I worked in Queensland. I worked for Alex Moray, Vestey man but very good.'[35] In addition, in 1977 he told Ann McGrath that he used to work for Alex Moray.[36] Jimmy Mangayarri also confirmed that Alex Moray used to take two 'boys', Captain Major and Sandy Moray. There is a strong possibility that the two Gurindji men from different stations, Captain Major from Newcastle Waters and Sandy Moray from Wave Hill, discussed what they had seen in Queensland and Western Australia and how to change the situation in their own country. They may also have visited or heard about the Pilbara (Pindan) walk-off in 1946 in northern Western Australia.[37]

Eventually, Captain Major took the first action, at Newcastle Waters, and Sandy Moray told Vincent Lingiari to lead the walk-off at Wave Hill station. When reading *The Unlucky Australians* without such background knowledge, readers probably assume that Dexter Daniels was the one who chose Newcastle Waters as the first place to strike, and that Wave Hill station was chosen as the site of the second strike through discussion between Hardy and Dexter Daniels.[38] This point is especially emphasised by Attwood, perhaps to convince readers that the idea of walk-off originated from the 'conversations' – or more – of outside supporters.[39] However, we should not ignore the fact that Dexter Daniels had been to many stations to encourage Aboriginal workers to take action. In addition, conditions at Newcastle Waters were far better than at other stations in the area.[40] Captain Major even said the manager of Newcastle Waters, Roy Edwards, was the 'best boss I ever work for. We had good house at Newcastle Water, cement floor and 'lectric light, good buildings. Better than other stations.'[41] Nevertheless, the Aborigines' response to Dexter Daniels' offer was much swifter and more organised at Newcastle Waters than at many other stations.[42] It is logical that if you are looking for help and waiting for the right moment, your response to the right offer will be quick.

It is also noteworthy that when Dexter Daniels met an old man called 'Double-O' from Newcastle Waters, he suggested that Daniels meet Captain Major.[43] Why did Double-O tell him to see Captain Major? It is reasonable to assume that, through the network among Aboriginal people, they knew of the Gurindji project, and in particular that Captain Major (and Sandy Moray) were looking for 'someone behind them'. Before Captain Major received a letter from Dexter Daniels, he already 'bin hear about that young Dexter, an Aboriginal who work for that Union mob in Darwin'.[44] Here you can see how the Aboriginal people were trying to make a 'connection' between people who were looking for assistance, and a person who was willing to help them. Hardy may have been unaware of, or have underestimated, the amount of planning among the Gurindji people prior to his involvement. In fact, Captain Major expresses this point of view in *The Unlucky Australians*:

> Some white fella bin say Dexter tell me to strike because him higher man in tribe. That not right. Dexter Roper River man, me Gurindji; nothing to do with Roper River mob. We strike because we sick of small money. We had someone behind us.[45]

One may interpret this to mean Captain Major was asserting his authority over the Gurindji 'strikers'. But the oral historical approach gives us the deeper meaning of his statement: Dexter Daniels and Frank Hardy were the *external conditions* which ignited the Gurindji's long-awaited project.

The above discussion reflects the Gurindji temporal and networking system discussed in Chapter 2: the Gurindji people had been waiting for the 'right time' to come. When the Gurindji information system confirmed the 'right time' for their project, their action was immediate and well organised.

## JFK VISITED WAVE HILL: INTERNATIONAL NETWORK

In order to understand the Gurindji network system better, it is also crucial to explore the Gurindji people's 'international network'. However, in order to explore this Gurindji internationalism, once again I have to confront the 'gap' between the Gurindji and academic histories.

*Ngumpin* were desperate to find 'someone behind' them in order to fight the Vestey mob or 'English *kartiya*' and to realise their project of keeping *kartiya* out of their county. They needed allies who had more power than 'England'. One of these allies, such as Hardy or the NAWU mob, came from 'union country'.[46] Old Jimmy also told me 'Mr Berndt', who was one of the 'union mob', visited Limbunya station to study how *kartiya* treated *ngumpin*.[47] Union members became one of the international allies supporting *ngumpin*'s fight for their land.

Furthermore, we also need to understand the role of 'America'. Even though I learned of this Gurindji–American relationship from Old Jimmy and Dandy Danbayarri, I realised that this was not a story that every Gurindji person knew. Rose learned a similar story from the Yarralin people, but she was asked to conceal some parts of the story. She writes, 'Because some stories are not fully for the public, and some story tellers worry about publicity, I cannot discuss these matters further.'[48] The stories I learned may not be exactly the same as Rose's. However, in respect for their concern about publicity, I confirmed many times with Old Jimmy and Dandy that I could write the following story.

Old Jimmy told me that America or 'Yankee country' is 'just like rangers country'. Yankees live in '*ngurra punyu* [good camp/country]' and they are 'same as *yunmi* [you and me]'. This implies that Americans are different from English *kartiya*. As Rose suggests, 'Americans' represent one of the most powerful moral Europeans.[49]

During the 'Vestey time', President Kennedy – or 'Big American Boss'[50] – visited Wave Hill station. Dandy told me that he saw a huge airplane arrive on Wave Hill airstrip. According to Dandy, there was a star mark on the tail of this plane. The plane was so big, he explained, that there were two *motika* [cars] loaded inside.

President Kennedy came to Jimparrak (Wave Hill station) in order to talk to and help *ngumpin*. According to Old Jimmy, President Kennedy met Sandy Moray at the No. 1 Bore. There, Sandy Moray told President Kennedy how badly English *kartiya* treated *ngumpin*. 'He [Kennedy] bin sorry for *ngumpin* … (He was) good *kartiya*.' After their long meeting, President Kennedy agreed to support Sandy's idea of returning their country. He said to Sandy, 'You gotta your country back soon … You gotta your money, you gotta your *motika*.' Dandy told me that President Kennedy met not only Sandy Moray but also Vincent Lingiari, and promised to support their walk-off project. Hobbles Danayarri gave a detailed description of the final meeting between 'Big American Boss' and Vincent Lingiari to Rose:

> *Big American Boss (B)*: You know all these Australian people really bad men. We don't know Northern Territory. We only hear Australian people take it away longa you. You want it back?
> *Vincent (V)*: Course.
> *B*: You want help?
> *V*: If you can give me help.
> – *they shake hands* –
> *B*: I'll help you. You keep going. Union strike (will) tell 'em Vestey mob finish. Don't you worry. Any day I might

(be) hearing what you do now. You been fight for your land (before, and) you lost your land. Right we'll fix it up. Thank you, old Tommy Vincent. I'll really work for you. I'm behind you. Goodbye Tommy Vincent.[51]

How did President Kennedy help *ngumpin*? Old Jimmy said President Kennedy started 'the biggest war' against England in order to 'kill 'em all (English) *kartiya*'. From an academic historical perspective, one may speculate that this story corresponds with the Vietnam War (1961–75), in which the American president John F. Kennedy was heavily involved. In Gurindji people's history, the battlefield was not Vietnam but 'England', and the purpose of the war was to kill immoral English *kartiya*.

Let us put aside our naïve conviction of 'We know JFK never came to the Gurindji country.' Rather, we may need to ask ourselves *what it really means* that 'we know' JFK never came there. If a history of JFK has been 'localised' by the Gurindji historians, instead of calling it 'wrong history' from a universal-Western-positivist perspective, can we not relate to the Gurindji historical analysis by sharing the 'truthfulness' of this episode?

What is the significance in the Gurindji history of these international networks? I think the Gurindji people's history helps us understand how much *ngumpin* looked for strong supporters from the outside to help realise their project. I believe that Gurindji and academic historians can share the 'historical truthfulness' of a history of JFK visiting Wave Hill station in terms of how scary, adventurous and challenging it was for *ngumpin* to fight the oppressive colonial regime. Without confirming these international supporters, the Gurindji elders probably could not make a decision to take action.

## HISTORIC MEETING AT DARWIN HOSPITAL

It was in early August 1966 that Dexter Daniels met Vincent Lingiari for the first time – in the Darwin hospital. Vincent Lingiari explained that he had been kicked by a donkey, which broke his foot. Hardy describes this meeting as if Dexter Daniels knew Vincent Lingiari was at Darwin Hospital and so knew that he could visit this Gurindji leader of Wave Hill station in order to discuss the conditions at the station.[52]

It is probably true that, as Jowett writes, 'this discussion was the catalyst for fundamental change to Aboriginal political rights in Australia'.[53] However, she as well as Hardy and other writers do not explain how this historic meeting was made possible. Was it too coincidental that while the strike had been going on at Newcastle Waters station, a leader of the Wave Hill Aboriginal people broke his foot and went up to Darwin, and that Dexter Daniels happened to know he was in the hospital? There could well be something more behind this event.

Mick Rangiari told me another story about this meeting. Sandy Moray told Vincent Lingiari to pretend to be 'sick' (injured?) in order to go to Darwin to see Dexter Daniels. We might believe that this story was made up later by the Gurindji people in order to control their own past more actively. However, his story may be true. As I discussed, if the Gurindji people were ready for the action and looking for 'someone behind them', and then found out what Captain Major did at Newcastle Waters station, it is reasonable that they wanted to hold discussions with Dexter Daniels about action at Wave Hill station. Captain Major may have sent a message to Sandy Moray or Vincent Lingiari to come to Darwin to see Dexter Daniels. In the same manner, it would not be surprising if Vincent Lingiari intentionally let a donkey kick his foot to create a reason to contact union members in Darwin.

## WAS IT A STRIKE?

It was on 23 August 1966 that Vincent Lingiari organised the Aboriginal people at Wave Hill station. They walked off the property and went 16km away, to the banks of the Victoria River near the Wave Hill Welfare Settlement. Why did they walk off? If the Gurindji's action was literally a 'strike', the aim of their action must have been equal wages or improvements in their living conditions. In that case, it would not be necessary to leave the station. They should have stayed there and simply stopped working in order to force the manager to negotiate.

An approach from Gurindji perspective gives us two key reasons why they wanted not only to stop working but also to leave the station. First, physically moving and shifting their living space is a Gurindji cultural tactic for solving problems. As discussed in Chapter 2, mobility is one of the fundamental social modes of being in the Gurindji and many other Aboriginal societies. To change places for economic reasons is a common practice in hunter-gatherer societies. Mobility is also fundamental to maintaining their ceremonial exchange system. One cannot underestimate the importance of the physical and metaphysical functions of movement in Aboriginal social practice.[54] Furthermore, the importance of Aboriginal mobility, even within the context of relatively settled contemporary lifestyles of Aboriginal communities, should not be underestimated.[55]

For the Gurindji people, the 'strike' did not mean negotiating with the Wave Hill manager; instead it meant leaving the station and shifting their living location. It is noteworthy that, from the beginning of their action, the Gurindji people did not want to stay at Wave Hill station. Changing their living space or 'camp' was seen as the first step to independence from European authorities: be nomadic and white settlers cannot catch up with you!

This idea gives us the second reason: since their purpose was to regain the authority in their country, the first thing they had to do was leave the European authority. For example, Pincher Nyurrmiyari says, 'We go back to Wave Hill if that Tom Pisher [the manager] leave, alla that Besty [Vestey] mob leave.'[56] What they wanted was not an improvement in the conditions at Wave Hill station, but to remove Vesteys from their country and run the cattle station. Vincent Lingiari explains more clearly why they did not stay at the station. He told Hardy that one Aboriginal person suggested they go back to Wave Hill:

> He [an Aboriginal man] said: 'When white fella go on strike,
> they don't walk off straight away, they see their boss and
> talk things over. I worked for white man myself and start for

sixpence maybe, or five bob, now I got proper money.'

'You work for that Welfare?' I (Vincent Lingiari) said. And
he said: 'Yes, them Welfare blokes are all right. And Tom
Fisher a good man. Why can't you fellas go back to work? And
I said: 'I won't go back.' That's all I said. I never said no more.[57]

Vincent Lingiari implies that the Gurindji 'strike' was not like a white
workers' strike. He did not want to negotiate with the manager; he
wanted to leave the station. Peanut Pontiari remembers that Vincent
Lingiari once asked people if they wanted to go back to the station,
but they said, 'No, we don't wanna go back. No more station. One way
walk-off, that's it!'

The memorable day of 23 August 1966 was not the day that the
Gurindji people started negotiations with the white authorities, but
the day they physically left foreign authority and returned to their
own. In other words, the walk-off was not really an agitation against
Wave Hill station, but *a spatial movement* which allowed them to regain
the power to establish their own community. They did not want to
return to Wave Hill unless Vesteys left the property. Higher wages
and improved conditions may have been secondary considerations, but
neither was the original or main purpose of their action.

Therefore, one needs to be careful when referring to the Gurindji
walk-off as a 'strike' or a 'land claim'. I do not object to the usage of
the expression 'Wave Hill strike' or 'land rights movement', not only
because it has already become part of the Australian lexicon but also
because the Gurindji people also express their walk-off as the 'strike'
or 'land rights'. However, the Gurindji people do not describe the
sequence as moving 'from a strike to a land claim'. The words 'strike'
and 'land claim' should be understood in Gurindji Creole as meaning
their physical walk-off from European authority in order to re-establish a healthy relationship with their country. Later, Hardy himself
admits that the key issue was their land, not wages. He:

discovered that wages were not the only, perhaps not even the
main, issue for the Gurindji men. They were concerned about

their women, about the children getting an education, about housing, about dignity and self-respect, about tribal identity – and there hovered vaguely behind every thought a desire to live alone in their own land.[58]

As already discussed, it would be remiss to read this change in Hardy's impression as a change in the Gurindji people's demands. Their aim was consistent, but their strategy was to avoid discussing their central project with white people in the beginning. They did not explicitly challenge the agenda or politics of unionists. Rather, they simply followed their own initiative in not returning from the walk-off once outside support for their action had been secured.

However, if their aim from the outset was to run their own community and cattle station, why did they not express this to outside supporters at the first stage? To answer this question, Rose provides us with the insight that for the Gurindji people, 'wages were a language which Europeans could understand, and constituted an issue which trade unions were known to support'.[59] They were looking for allies who could help them realise their plan, and finally found unionists such as Dexter Daniels, and a writer like Hardy, who were willing to help them (and President Kennedy from 'America'). The Gurindji people knew that unionists were keen about the issue of equal wages. They knew that 'equal wages' was the key term for gaining support from outsiders. After the walk-off leaders confirmed these people's support, the Gurindji people gradually started to educate them to understand the real purpose of their action.

This educational process can be observed in the supporters' confusion, as narrated in *The Unlucky Australians*. From Hardy's point of view, he was the one who knew how to fight and that was why Dexter Daniels, as well as the Gurindji people, asked him to help. However, he eventually discovered that the Gurindji's plan extended beyond his own conception. When the Gurindji leaders told Hardy about their desire to run their own cattle station, Anne Jeffrey, the wife of a welfare officer at Wave Hill, asked Hardy if this was originally Hardy's idea:

Anne asked: 'Did you have this in your mind when you came here, Frank? … Are you sure you didn't prompt them? If you did, they'll agree just to please you because you want to help them. Right?'

(Frank said) 'No, Anne. Vincent mentioned it first on the way to Mount Sanford and I didn't take much notice. Then Pincher approached me. I'm positive I didn't plant it in their minds. It wasn't even in my mind. I was thinking of wages and conditions and strikes.'[60]

Later, when Hardy found their 'strike' seemed neverending, he was confused about what the Gurindji people were really thinking regarding their future, and wondered if he should tell them to stop the struggle:

Is anything going on in the Aborigines' mind? Have they really any plans for the future? Should I try to end their travail by urging them to go back to work at Wave Hill?[61]

Vincent Lingiari soon told Hardy about their plan to move their camp to Wattie Creek and establish their own community.[62] Through all these processes, we can see the Gurindji people's initiative. At the same time, Hardy's constant support for their self-determination must also be acknowledged. There is no doubt that his non-paternalistic attitude towards the Gurindji people facilitated the establishment of a firm rapport between Hardy and the Gurindji. Accordingly, Gurindji leaders gradually told the supporters about their plan and the final destination of their walk-off movement.

## FROM STATION TO WELFARE SETTLEMENT

I would like to discuss the sequence of the establishment of the Daguragu community at Wattie Creek. We will see how the Gurindji people finally accomplished their long-term project. However, I must start by looking at the first sequence of their movement near the Wave Hill settlement.

This is because the fact that they did not go directly to Wattie Creek may be regarded as 'evidence' that the establishment of their own community was not the plan at the beginning of the walk-off.[63]

The most immediate need following the walk-off was to maintain access to an adequate food supply. Vincent Lingiari told people to look for bush tucker.[64] They certainly relied on bush food, but at the same time, a sedentary camp could not support over 200 people on bush tucker alone. Mick Rangiari often told me how relieved they were when a truck with plenty of food arrived in the walk-off camp. *The Unlucky Australians* also notes the urgency of keeping enough food to feed the walk-off mob.[65] When they left Wave Hill station, the nearest place they could get enough food was, obviously, Wave Hill Welfare Settlement. They also had to camp there, because they definitely needed access to the white settlers' information network. It was essential to keep in touch with outside supporters such as Daniels and Hardy. When the Gurindji people left the station, Wave Hill Welfare Settlement was the only place for them to access the telegram and other mailing systems by which they could communicate with the outside world.

Furthermore, their plan remained flexible at its initial stages. If Vesteys left their country, they could regain their authority over the country simply by going back to Wave Hill station and running the property by themselves. The Gurindji people needed to see how Vesteys, as well as outside supporters, reacted to their initial action. Therefore the riverbank near the Welfare Settlement was ideally suited as a temporary camping place.

## REACTIONS OF NON-GURINDJI ABORIGINAL PEOPLE

I would also like to briefly discuss the relations between Aboriginal people at Wave Hill and those at Victoria River Downs (VRD) during the Gurindji walk-off movement. Sandy Moray went up to VRD to tell the Aboriginal people there about his plan. *Ngumpin* at VRD must have discussed Sandy Moray's plan. However, their attitude towards the Wave Hill walk-off had been equivocal.

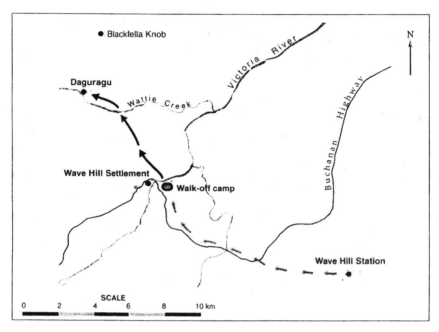

Map 7.1 Movement of the Gurindji walk-off

In *The Unlucky Australians*, a main figure among the VRD mob is King Brumby, probably a Bilinara or Ngarinman man. In Hardy's book, it is not clear if King Brumby really wanted to lead *ngumpin* and leave VRD and Humbert River station. Dexter Daniels believes that Aboriginal people there wanted to walk off, but the station manager interrupted them.[66] Some VRD Aboriginal workers left the station, but then some of them returned to work. It was not until 1972, six years after the Gurindji had started their walk-off, that the VRD people finally joined the movement.[67]

In *Hidden Histories*, Rose says she has 'never fully understood precisely why it took (VRD) people so long to make the decision, for it seems clear that their commitment to change and their desire for their own land were as strong as those of Wave Hill people'.[68] She suggests that VRD people may have 'wanted to see what would happen at Wattie Creek because for them, ... going to Daguragu meant leaving their own country, and many were loath to do so'.[69] Rose's speculation explains why VRD and Humbert River people did not join the Gurindji walk-off for six years. However, it is still not clear why they did not walk off by and for themselves and move to their own sacred place.

In my opinion, VRD people did not move straight after the Gurindji walk-off because, among the Aboriginal people of this area, there was a feeling that this was a business of 'the Gurindji people and their country'. For example, when eight to ten young Aboriginal men left the walk-off camp and went back to Wave Hill station, Vincent Lingiari emphasised that they were 'nearly all Walbiri (Warlpiri), only two Gurindji', and said, 'Maybe them Walbiri (Warlpiri) not like listen word of Gurindji Kadijeri man, I reckon.'[70] He also stressed that the Wattie Creek project was for the Gurindji people:

> Gurindji people scatter now like bullocks, some eat here, some eat there. That not right. After the wet season, when the riber go down, I gotta go to Camfield and Montejinni make sure them young fellas come back here later on … Gurindji I mean – Walbiri (Warlpiri) can go they own way, I won't touch them. But I'll tell young Peter and other Gurindji: We gotta do things right way now. All together in Gurindji country.[71]

A similar attitude was displayed by Captain Major. He had been working at Newcastle Waters station, which is in the Mudburra country. When he led the 'strike', his aim was to go back to the Gurindji country. He hoped to 'live in my own country with Gurindji tribe'.[72] This does not mean that Bilinara, Ngarinman or Warlpiri people did not agree with the walk-off. Instead it should be understood that this was not their countries' business. Warlpiri people in the Gurindji country had to follow the Gurindji elders' decisions, because they lived in a foreign country. For example, Gerry, a Warlpiri man, became one of the leaders. However, Hardy carefully notes that Gerry 'seemed to be accepted as a strike leader by the Gurindji'.[73] Initiatives were always made by the Gurindji.

The inter-group political situation of the VRD and Humbert River people was different from that of the Warlpiri in the Gurindji country. VRD people knew the Gurindji people would do something; Sandy

Moray was there to explain his plan to them. They knew the plan. However, it was their own choice whether to follow the Gurindji movement or not. As Rose says, the VRD people probably wanted to see what would happen at Wattie Creek, but I think this is not simply because they did not want to leave their country. Rather, VRD people initially regarded the walk-off as the Gurindji people's project. For them, there was no need to be in a hurry to follow the Gurindji way; they would observe the sequence, and then make their own decision later.

For the Aboriginal people in the Victoria River district, the walk-off was the Gurindji project, which was planned by the Gurindji old man (Sandy Moray), and conducted by the Gurindji leaders (Captain Major and Vincent Lingiari). It was a while before the walk-off became the symbol of Aboriginal struggles in general and Wattie Creek became the centre of not only the Gurindji but also other Aboriginal people in the Victoria River district.

## ESTABLISHMENT OF THE DAGURAGU COMMUNITY

In March 1967, at the end of the wet season, seven months after their walk-off from Wave Hill station, the Gurindji people shifted their camp to Wattie Creek near the Seale Gorge Dreaming site. The main question here is: why did they choose Wattie Creek?

Many scholars simply explain that the Gurindji people chose Wattie Creek because it was a symbolically central place for them. For example, Jowett states: 'This area was chosen because it was the main place of the Gurindji Dreaming and the geographical centre of the traditional Gurindji country.'[74] It is not surprising that people simply accept such an explanation, because the Gurindji leaders themselves explained their decision to the public in the same way. In April 1967, with the assistance of Hardy and Bill Jeffrey, the Gurindji leaders wrote a petition to the Governor-General asking for the return of 500 square miles (129,500 ha) of their country. In this letter, they explain that Wattie Creek is 'the main place of our dreaming'.[75]

However, their explanation of Wattie Creek as a main place for their Dreaming was probably a tactic to make white people understand how important it was to establish their community there. Such a tactic is similar to the way they used 'equal wages' to gain public attention in the first stage. They needed a public reason that could help outside supporters understand their decision.

If you study the sacred sites in the Gurindji country, it is not difficult to discover that Seale Gorge/Wattie Creek is only one of many Dreaming sites for them. For example, McConvell and Hargen suggest that there are over 200 sites in the Daguragu land claim area.[76] T.G.H. Strehlow explains that since the major totemic sites were 'linked according to the nature of their totems with the totemic sites of other subgroups and even of other tribes, not one of them was fitted in any sense to act as a sort of central "capital" site for a whole tribal subgroup or a whole tribe'.[77] In Dreaming geography, there is no such 'centre' or 'main' place. Dreaming sites are connected to each other through the Dreaming tracks and you cannot claim one of them as a centre of these Dreamings.[78] Certainly, Seale Gorge was one of the important Dreaming sites for the Gurindji people, so there must have been no problem shifting the camp there. However, in order to make settlers understand and win the favour of the Australian public, they – or possibly Hardy and Jeffrey – used the hierarchical terminology of settlers' language and culture, such as 'centre' or 'main', to describe Wattie Creek.

In 1968, the government announced the construction of a new village near the Wave Hill Welfare Settlement for Aboriginal people living in the area.[79] The area had been excluded from Vesteys' property. However, most of them did not leave Daguragu, and this governmental plan was ignored.[80] At this time Pincher said the following:

> Forty-five years I work for Vesteys – bread, salt beef, little
> bit of tea and sugar, that's all. Now I got nothing, don't even
> own this little bit of my land. Welfare do nothing for us. We
> don't want Welfare town, we don't want that dirty, stony
> place over on Common, that's only rubbish country. We want

Wattie Creek for ourselves and our children. This country belong to us, Wattie Creek our dreaming place, sacred ground belonging to Gurindjis.[81]

Pincher's statement implies that the Welfare township is a 'dirty stony place' and not a sacred Dreaming place. However, the Gurindji people today live in both Daguragu and the ex-Welfare township, which is now called Kalkaringi. I was also told by the Gurindji elders that Kalkaringi township is on a *karu* Dreaming track.

Therefore, as previous research shows, one of the reasons they refused the government's plan and adhered to Daguragu was probably because they did not like to be dependent on welfare, and they wanted to support their own economy at Daguragu, where water was plentiful.[82] Mick Rangiari also told Jowett that the Gurindji elders 'would get very angry with the way that they had been treated by Vesteys in the past and how the government ignored their wishes and continued to ignore their wishes throughout the strike'.[83] They refused the plan of the Welfare township not because Daguragu was the only sacred place, but because they refused government paternalism.

## FROM WATTIE CREEK TO WATTIE CREEK

We still do not have an answer as to why they chose Wattie Creek in particular and not an alternative Dreaming site. Jowett interviewed Mick Rangiari in 1990 and summarised his comments:

> [I]t was Vincent Lingiari's decision to walk off Wave Hill station, but that was only after he had consulted with senior members of the community. When they were at Wave Hill settlement the elders decided to move to Wattie Creek.[84]

There is no doubt that when it became clearer that Vesteys would never leave Wave Hill station, the Gurindji started looking for a place near the Dreaming site for the location of their new community. From Wave Hill Welfare Settlement, one of the closest sites is Wattie Creek.

This purely geographical factor may be one of the reasons for their decision.

However, Wattie Creek holds more meaning for the Gurindji elders and their walk-off project. It is important to note that even though the leader of the walk-off was Vincent Lingiari, he constantly 'consulted with senior members' about the decision and the destination. One of the elders would have been Sandy Moray, an original planner of this movement and the one who told Vincent to take action – and Wattie Creek was the country of Sandy Moray. Furthermore, the 'partiki tree meeting' during which Sandy Moray told his plan to the Gurindji elders for the first time was held at Wattie Creek. Jimmy Mangayarri took me to the big *partiki* tree where the meeting was held. The tree was located in the middle of the Daguragu township, only about 30 metres away from the memorial stone of Gough Whitlam handing over the Gurindji land to Vincent Lingiari. The Daguragu community was established beside the memory of their historic meeting. Sandy Moray told people, 'Before I die, you gotta do it.' Mick Rangiari proudly said to me, 'So we did it!'

The walk-off project had been formulated at Wattie Creek, and it returned to the same place at the end.

## FROM ILLEGAL OCCUPANCY TO LEGAL FREEHOLD

After the Gurindji people walked off Wave Hill station, it took nine years for them to legally get their land back. This also means that they illegally occupied Wattie Creek for over eight years.

It is not necessary for the purpose of this chapter to enter into a detailed discussion of these eight years. This is primarily because the Gurindji historians are not very interested in talking about this period. The Gurindji historians did not tell me much about these years. I think, for the Gurindji people, this eight years was more or less a period of clearing up the remaining business.

Of course the Gurindji people knew that they needed to regain their land legally, so they called for non-Gurindji supporters and went on their Australia-wide campaign in order to get 'land rights'. Finally, in January 1972, Vesteys, the owner of Wave Hill station, promised to give an area of land from Wave Hill to the Gurindji people. It took another three years of negotiation for a lease to be permitted, in July 1975.[85]

However, these legal issues and procedures were probably of relatively marginal importance to the Gurindji people. Practically speaking, the Gurindji people managed to hold their authority when they walked off the station. At Wattie Creek, the Gurindji leaders did not have to initiate the nation-wide campaign, the legal procedure and the negotiation with Australian authorities. Rather, such a process had already been conducted in a more collaborative manner with non-Gurindji supporters such as Actors Equity, NAWU and the Waterfront Workers Union, as well as student organisations such as Abschol[86] and the Melbourne Gurindji Group.[87]

Through this campaign, the Daguragu community became a cultural and political centre for the 'walk-off mob' in the Victoria River district and a symbol of the Australia-wide Aboriginal land rights movement. In 1972, Aboriginal people in VRD and Humbert River station walked off and stayed at Wattie Creek. Rose explains: 'people who walked off went there because that was the place where they could get food and other assistance, medical attention, publicity for their case, education for their children, and solidarity from their peers'.[88] The Daguragu Aboriginal community, however, was still directed mainly by the Gurindji people, and the leaders were the Gurindji elders such as Vincent Lingiari.[89] At the same time, Aboriginal people in New South Wales regarded the Gurindji people as the new allies of their own land rights movement.[90] The Gurindji walk-off now gained wider attention than originally planned by the Gurindji elders. On 16 August 1975, Prime Minister Whitlam attended the land-giving ceremony at Daguragu. This handing-over ceremony was memorable for the Gurindji people, and they still remember and describe Gough Whitlam as a 'good *kartiya* boss'.

Negotiations with Australian authorities for their country seemed like a neverending process. In 1981, the Gurindji people claimed Aboriginal freehold title under the *Aboriginal Land Rights Act 1976* (NT).

This time, academics such as Patrick McConvell and Rod Hargen helped their 'land claim'. It was in 1986 that the Gurindji people finally succeeded in holding the freehold title to Daguragu country.

## RUNNING THE CATTLE STATION: POSTCOLONIAL DYNAMICS

When learning the Gurindji history of the walk-off, one may tend to pay most attention to the aspect of 'getting the country back'. However, we also need to remember that the aim of their walk-off was not only to keep English *kartiya* out of their country but also to run their own cattle station. It is safe to say that the aim of the Gurindji walk-off was not to return to the precolonial hunting-gathering lifestyle, but to move living conditions forward: namely, to the post-colonial domain. Today, the Gurindji people often refer to the post-walk-off era as the 'New Generation'.

The Gurindji elders' aim of running the cattle business was very clear from the beginning. Sandy Moray explained his project at the *partiki* tree meetings as 'We gotta station, we gotta horse.' In addition, it is also clear that Vincent Lingiari was positive about their children receiving a Western education. He says to Hardy:

> That Besty mob neber bin teach Gurindji people to read, but
> now our childrens bin go to school house. Later on they bin
> learn ebrything and know what to do. Then, we bin want this
> ground, all belonga we Gurindji. Childrens grow up proper
> book work. We wait for that, then no white man here.[91]

Pincher's view is even stronger. He says that the Gurindji people 'work the cattle. Learn to build yard, lay concrete, build fence, sink bore. Lib same as white fella, have property.'[92] They were keen to run the cattle business, but they wanted to do it by themselves. Long Johnny Kitgnaari, another Gurindji elder, says:

> We know cattle business. We can do without white fella ...
> Bincent bin manager. White fella keep book. We like to

see something from books, him tell us. We do all the cattle.[93]

It is clear that for the Gurindji people, decolonisation did not mean going back to a hunting-gathering economy; it meant running the cattle business under their own authority.

## POLITICAL CONTEXT OF ORAL HISTORY

Before concluding this section, I want to return to the questions: why has the story of Sandy Moray rarely been told to the non-Gurindji? Why didn't the Gurindji people discuss Wattie Creek as the country of Sandy Moray in earlier research?

It is crucial to understand that the Gurindji people had been fighting for their land until 1986, when finally their inalienable freehold title was granted. Therefore what they thought was worth telling to the non-Gurindji during that time was probably not 'Who invented the walk-off?' or 'Who belongs to Wattie Creek?' Instead, their greater concern was letting outside supporters know about Vincent Lingiari as a leader of their movement and Wattie Creek as the country for all the Gurindji. It is indisputable that Vincent Lingiari was the leader of the Gurindji walk-off movement. It is also true that Daguragu became the symbolic place for all the Gurindji who fought for their land. These were the issues they wanted to communicate to non-Gurindji supporters at that time. Since then, the Gurindji people's political circumstances have changed and their rights over their country have become more certain. Today, the Gurindji people probably feel more comfortable telling the stories about different aspects of the walk-off episode. The story of Sandy Moray has been gradually revealed to non-Gurindji according to their situation at different times.

Therefore, one should be more critical of the naïve notion that the earlier oral testimonies are more accurate than later ones. We should consider the historical and political situation in which any – oral and written – accounts are located. The assessment of the oral historical evidence should not only be based on their temporal distance from the events, but also on their political context.

Accordingly, I cannot naively claim the 'objectivity' of my research and oral evidence. It is possible that there are untold political reasons why the Gurindji people have now begun to tell stories of Sandy Moray. Furthermore, my study lacks the Gurindji women's stories and viewpoints. I am hopeful that I, or other (maybe female) researchers, will explore the history of the Gurindji walk-off from female perspectives some time in the future.

## WHAT WAS THE GURINDJI WALK-OFF?

To sum up, I shall now answer the question: What was the Gurindji walk-off? From the very beginning, the Gurindji walk-off was not initiated by white people in order to protest against European authorities and gain better working conditions. Of course there is no doubt that the Gurindji people needed and looked for supporters from the outside. Without the presence of Dexter Daniels and Frank Hardy, the Gurindji project might not have happened. Without Australia-wide support, their project could not have been completed. Today, the Gurindji people remember Hardy and many other outside supporters as 'good *kartiya* helped *ngumpin*'. The Gurindji people are deeply grateful to them for their devotion in fighting for the Gurindji country. However, let me repeat here that these were the external conditions that the Gurindji people had long been waiting for.

What was the Gurindji walk-off?

The walk-off was the Gurindji way of re-establishing their relationship with their country by keeping the 'Vestey mob' out of their land. It was planned and conducted by the Gurindji people and those related to the Gurindji country. Their aim was to physically leave settlers' authority, to regain autonomy and sovereignty over their country, to establish their own community, and to run a cattle station by and for themselves.

# CHAPTER 8

# 'NEW GENERATION'

## 'HUNGRY TIME'

Before the Gurindji walk-off, it was a 'hungry time'. The phrase 'hungry time' was given by a Gurindji woman, Violet Donald, while we were collecting bush fruits near Kalkaringi, and later fishing at Ten Mile waterhole. According to Violet, 'hungry time' started when *kartiya* came to the Gurindji country and ended when the Gurindji walked off from Jimparrak (Wave Hill station).

Before *kartiya* came to the Gurindji country, *ngumpin* lived on bush tucker, and they were not hungry. It was a 'bush time', or as she also called it, 'bush *tanku* [well fed]'. However, when *ngumpin* started to work for *kartiya*, 'hungry time' began. In 'hungry time', only *kartiya* were *tanku* and *ngumpin* were hungry. *Ngumpin* worked for *kartiya*, but they worked for nothing: '(We used to) live like *warlaku* [dog] … *Kartiya* bin treat us wrong way.' When Violet was telling the story of 'hungry time', she was criticising the food situation in the cattle station. 'Hungry time' seems to me more localised in the cattle stations than the bush. Although it is evident that the introduction of cattle had a destructive impact on the ecological system,[1] it seems that the rations received from the station were much smaller than the food provided by bush tucker (and cattle they secretly killed) during the walkabout season or 'holiday time'.

People in Daguragu often told me how little food they received from the station. It was almost a fixed action and phrase among the Gurindji – forming a scoop with their hands and saying, 'little bit of sugar, flour, meat, tea, tobacco … that's all!' Mick Rangiari explained that after they received rations on Friday, they finished it in two days and had to live on river water. There was also not enough bush tucker to be found around the station.

These stories certainly correspond to the Berndts' report. The Berndts describe the food supply at Wave Hill station in the following way:

> The weekly amount for each adult was two or three pounds
> of white flour, sometimes with rising (to those requesting it);
> one half to one pound of sugar (often less), to which was added
> a small handful of tea (under one ounce); and one stick of
> tobacco (to those requesting it).[2]

When it came to meat distribution, Aboriginal employees received a certain amount of meat, but their dependants received only bones and offal. And this 'already meagre quantity of rations' was 'spread out over an even greater number than originally intended'.[3] The Berndts' conclusion was that the amount of food from the station 'was not sufficient to maintain a person in good health'. Furthermore, during the working season, 'there was no appreciable opportunity for anyone living on the station to look for "bush tucker" … (they) had no time for such activities'.[4]

The Gurindji people worked hard for *kartiya*, but the Vestey mob never recognised the Aboriginal contribution to their business. Here is another fairly fixed phrase they often said to me: 'We bin work for Vestey, made 'em rich. We work for nothing, no money!'[5] Stockwork was very hard work, but it seems to me that the worst part of it was not the stockwork itself but the way *kartiya* treated *ngumpin*. Even though they emphasised to me how 'hard' the stockwork was, it was clear that they were rather proud of it; it was not really a complaint. Instead, what they protested against was that *kartiya* did not give them enough food, enough money, and enough respect. Roy Yunga, from a younger generation who are now middle-aged, gave me another example of this treatment: *kartiya* never let *ngumpin* sit in the front seat of a truck. Even it was raining, *ngumpin* always had to sit in the back of a truck and get wet.

During my stay in the Gurindji country, I was told that only Alex Moray was a 'good Vestey man'.[6] In general, literally everybody said to me that the Vestey mob was bad: Vesteys did not like *ngumpin*, did not trust *ngumpin*, and *ngumpin* never liked Vesteys. The notion of 'Vesteys, the bad mob' could have been exaggerated through the Gurindji walk-off campaign. However, it was also clear to me that the Gurindji people did not remember, or did not think it was worth telling me about, any other exceptional friendly relationship with the Vestey mob, even if there had been one.

## (NOT) VISITING JIMPARRAK

A young couple, Noeleen Morris and Rodney Bernard, said to me that old people did not want to visit Jimparrak because of their traumatic memories. When one considers the Gurindji cultural and historical geography, it is important to know that, for elders, Jimparrak has become a location of not-willing-to-visit. Eventually, Victor Vincent, a son of Vincent Lingiari, took me to Jimparrak. He showed me, for example, how *ngumpin* workers received food from the kitchen and carried it to the tree near the creek – *ngumpin* were not allowed to eat inside the kitchen. Since the wind from the south was so cold, they made a stone wall around the southern part of the tree. Victor was moved when he realised that the tree and the ruins of the stone wall were still there.

He also pointed out to me roughly where the Aboriginal camps had been. The Aboriginal camp sites and the Wave Hill homestead were divided by the creek. Victor emphasised that there were no houses for *ngumpin*, only humpies. He also told me how hard it was to carry water the long distance from the bore to their camp. The problem of carrying water was also described by many other people in Daguragu. In 1947, a report explained it as follows: 'Water is obtained from a bore half a mile away and has to be carried up a grade to the camp.' According to this report, a director of the Native Affairs Branch discussed improvements to the Aboriginal camp with the manager, and these included, 'detailing someone to pay attention to the camp sanitation and hygiene, the provision of washing facilities, the making of water more readily available ...' The manager agreed with all of these suggestions, but the reporter doubted if he would implement any of them.[7]

The *kartiya* who treated *ngumpin* badly at the stations were the 'Vestey mob'. The Vestey mob were from 'England': Captain Cook and Jacky Pantamarra's country. Following Captain Cook, Vestey came to *ngumpin* country to establish cattle stations. Following Jacky Pantamarra's book, Vestey stole *ngumpin* country. The Vestey mob used *ngumpin* for their own purposes, but they never trusted them and treated them badly. Lots of *ngumpin* were killed by *kartiya*, and the survivors had to work for *kartiya*.

However, the Gurindji also knew that not all *kartiya* were from 'England'. Old Jimmy remembered, for example, that 'Mr Berndt' came to their country to see how *ngumpin* were treated by English *kartiya*. Old Jimmy explained to him about the Aboriginal situation at Limbunya station. *Ngumpin* had been waiting for help to change the situation for a long time. Later, President Kennedy from 'Big

America' came to Wave Hill to show his support for *ngumpin*. Then Sandy Moray organised to realise his plan of regaining their country from the Vesteys. When the Gurindji walk-off started, unionists from 'union country' also supported *ngumpin* fighting against the Vestey mob. Prime Minister Gough Whitlam came to Daguragu to hand over the Gurindji country. The Gurindji walk-off happened, and then the 'New Generation' started.

## 'HAPPY TIME', 'CITIZEN TIME'

After telling me the episode of the Gurindji walk-off, Mick Rangiari said, 'Today, we are happy, we got money, we are citizen.' Kennedy Ricky, a middle-aged man called today 'citizen time'; in 'olden time', Vestey men never trusted *ngumpin* and *ngumpin* were hungry all the time. However, Kennedy continued, 'We (did) walk-off. We got citizen time.' In 'citizen time', *ngumpin* can drive *modiga* [car], have money to buy a rifle. But most importantly, 'We got place, community to live.'

I was attending a men's ceremony at the secret place near Daguragu in September, still during the dry season. Billy Bunter and Mick Rangiari explained to me that *ngumpin* could not hold a ceremony during the working period (dry season), but could only afford to do it in the short period of the 'holiday time' or walkabout season. 'Now, we are free to do *business* [ceremony] anytime.' Stanly Sambo's comment was simple and clear: 'Today, (we live) more better. That's why we bin walk-off.'

The Gurindji people I talked with generally agreed with the idea that '*Kartiya* and *ngumpin* (should) live together, work together.'[8] In fact, it is quite a contrast to the Gurindji elders' original plan during the walk-off. According to Jack Doolan, when Vincent Lingiari was asked how many white advisers he needed for running the community and cattle station, he answered, 'None.'[9] While I was in Daguragu, I never heard statements about keeping out every *kartiya* from their country. They may have changed their view of *kartiya* after receiving so much support from them. Or what Old Vincent may have meant was that he did not want any *kartiya* related to the Vestey mob, who never wanted to work together with *ngumpin*.

I also want to note here that the Gurindji people today see that *ngumpin* are still 'behind *kartiya* government'. Although much better than before the walk-off, *ngumpin* and *kartiya* are not yet equal. Billy Bunter complained that the government told them about self-determination, 'but always we are behind the government'. He sees that this *ngumpin* situation is not only found in Australia. Although acknowledging that people like the Chinese, Indians and Africans still retain their strong cultures, Billy said, '*Kartiya* way everywhere (in the world).' Mick Rangiari also said to me, 'We are still behind the government. Government don't want us go front.' These statements by the Gurindji elders remind me of Dipesh Chakrabarty's argument about a '(hyperreal) Europe' or Michael Hardt and Antonio Negri's notion of 'Empire'.[10] Today, we all have no way of separating ourselves from '*kartiya* way' on this globe.

## STRONG LAW

While the Gurindji elders told me how hard the 'Vestey time' was, they also emphasised that the *ngumpin* law was much stronger at that time than today. This probably sounds contradictory: they started the walk-off project in order to regain autonomy and sovereignty. What happened to sovereignty?

For the elders, stories from 'early days' are the evidence that the *ngumpin* law was stronger then than it is today. They tell these 'early days' stories to young people and try to pull them back to the *ngumpin* way. Elders say with great pride that they used to move around the country by foot, and never used a car. Or they say they used a spear for hunting instead of a rifle. Today babies are born at the hospital, but they used to be born in the bush. In 'olden time', *ngumpin* did not go to a *kartiya* school, but learned more about the *ngumpin* law. Young people today go to the *kartiya* school and read books, but they are not following the *ngumpin* way any more. During the 'Vestey time', young men were not allowed to even look at young women at the camp.

Although Roy Yunga told me the way that cheating old men met girls in the bush outside the station camp, he also admitted that the law of promised wife was more strict in 'olden time'.

Old Jimmy said to me, 'When I was young, one bloke bin broke the (ngumpin) law. He (got) killed, tanpang [dead], got spear(ed). Family can't help 'em. He broke the law … Proper hard way … When I was young, malaluka [elders] like that …' At a meeting among elders, I heard someone say, 'We live on too much kartiya way today.' Billy Bunter also said: 'Before '66 [walk-off], law very strong …'

## GROG COMIN' UP

The Gurindji elders told me that ngumpin started drinking grog [alcohol] 'after walk-off'; 'Today, bad kidney. Too much grog.'

Old Jimmy views alcohol as a living being. He explained that grog (along with card playing) belongs to kaya. He could actually see kaya inside the bottle of beer: 'You can see the shadow, kaya shadow.' Grog is 'no history on this country … He [grog] get out life from everybody … He kill 'em everybody.' When you drink grog or play cards, kaya speak to you: 'Go on, go on, come on mate!' You play cards or drink grog all day and night. Kaya makes you 'go bush [crazy]'. He also said to me, 'Drink grog make 'em fight everywhere, no good all together … Before Keen Lewis [Jacky Pantamarra], we live good life. No grog, no fighting at that time … People live on proper food.'

Old Jimmy also explained the process of grog invasion in the ngumpin countries; Jacky Pantamarra brought grog from 'England' to ngumpin country.[11] Grog first came down to towns such as Halls Creek, Wyndham and Darwin. Then, 'slowly bring up every station'. When Old Jimmy was a young man, he was camping in the bush and saw a woman drinking grog every day. In front of him, this woman sprouted horns and hair grew on her body – she became kaya. Old Jimmy told me, 'I bin fuck'n frighten!'

Since the Daguragu Community Government Council started to operate a social club at Kalkaringi in 1998, community problems have rapidly increased: violence and abuse among families, breaking into shops or a clinic and stealing things, smashing windows of a school and a town council, breaking into a recreation hall or CDEP office and destroying community property. The community members agreed that most of these cases involved young people, and that the acts were directly or indirectly related to alcohol consumption.

There was a series of meetings to discuss these problems among the elders. When the community council offered a plan to remove community facilities from Daguragu to Kalkaringi for security reasons, the elders were firmly against it. Old men, women and young people, as well as a town clerk and other council members, all gathered at Daguragu to discuss this issue.

There, Billy Bunter, a member of *ngumpin* elders,[12] represented the pride of *malaluka* [elders], or the 'walk-off mob'. He was unusually aggressive and shouted, 'I don't wanna die out the history, walk-off story!' He continued, saying that if the Gurindji gave up having offices in Daguragu:

> That's *minirri* [shame]. People think Gurindji nomo [not] strong enough … I really worry about culture slow down. Gurindji get very bad news. People think we can't control property … I bin think of history we bin fight for. We had hard time for [against] government, (but) now we had hard time for own people.

Then Billy shared his experience of protecting the Daguragu community when Vestey men came to Daguragu with rifles. He concluded, 'We bin fight for this land!'

The elders showed support for Billy's talk, and the idea of shifting offices from Daguragu to Kalkaringi was shelved.

## YOUNG PEOPLE AND THEIR PROSPECTS

The Gurindji elders are worried about the younger generation. Using sand drawing, Billy Bunter explained their situation to me. He drew lines in opposite directions representing *ngumpin* way and *kartiya* way.

Then he put a circle in the middle indicating young people who could not go either way: 'Not go *kartiya* way to end, not go *ngumpin* way to end. They don't know which way to go.' He often said to me that young people today were 'stuck in the middle' between *kartiya* way and *ngumpin* way. Young people break both *ngumpin* law and *kartiya* law. He explained to me that 'olden time' was a hard time but *ngumpin* kept strong law. Today, young people were 'stuck in the middle'; 'that's why we teach 'em *business* [ceremonies], show them early days', and why the elders are trying 'to put the old law back'.

When ceremonies started, I never saw any participants – young or old – drunk. Ceremonies give elders the opportunity to teach young people the *ngumpin* way as well as tell them histories from the 'olden time'. It is also true that the elders are not very keen about Western education and sometimes even complain that the *kartiya* school takes young people away from the *ngumpin* way. However, at the same time, the elders generally agree that young people should learn and use both the *ngumpin* way and the *kartiya* way. At the community today, literally everybody wants more money to buy *kartiya* food, a rifle, an axe, and a car. No one wants to live in humpies any more. The elders and young people both seemed very happy and proud when the Daguragu football team won a game. They want both the *kartiya* and *ngumpin* ways under their control.

Billy Bunter is highly respected by people in Daguragu and Kalkaringi because he knows both the *ngumpin* way and the *kartiya* way. Since he had a Western education, he can read and write English, and thus

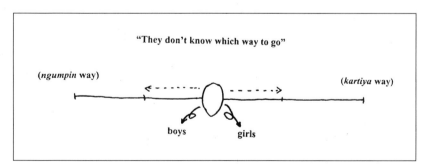

Figure 8.1 Billy's sand drawing

he has been an important representative in the Daguragu community from the time of the Gurindji walk-off.[13] Billy said to me that he has been a 'spokesman'. However, it should be noted that he is respected by community people not simply because he knows how to write and read, but because he also practises the *ngumpin* way very actively. He is an important figure in organising and running ceremonies as well. After telling me that learning the *ngumpin* way is lifetime work, he humbly said:

> For old people, I'm still child. Old people, they know every story and dance … I'm blind. I know *kartiya* way, but it's nothing for me. Aboriginal way first, *kartiya* way behind. Proper work [council job] nothing for me. *Kartiya* way (is) too light …

I understood that their fundamental question was how to integrate the *ngumpin* way and *kartiya* way in order to operate their community effectively as well as keep their country alive and *strong*. I personally did not fully agree with Billy's view of young people being 'stuck in the middle'. My young Gurindji friends often told me that 'We are New Generation!' They were trying to establish their identity as '*ngumpin* of the New Generation', and were struggling to find a way to create the 'third way' out of *ngumpin* and *kartiya* ways.

## CULTURAL POSITIONING OF CATTLE

I would like to briefly summarise the last four chapters by discussing the cultural positioning of cattle in the colonial history of the Gurindji country. This should bring us to the question: how can the position of 'cross-cultural' be realised?

Although the Gurindji historians have the clear idea that *kartiya* brought cattle to their country, cattle have been tolerated, even warmly welcomed by *ngumpin* throughout the colonial history. Despite their fear of *kartiya*, *ngumpin* established a peaceful relationship with cattle – and many other animals from 'England'. Obviously, *ngumpin* did not see cattle as being as oppressive as *kartiya*. Rather, cattle succeeded in being cross-cultural, bridging the gulf between *kartiya* culture and *ngumpin* culture.

Cattle belong to the settlers' pastoral colonialism: *kartiya* brought cattle from 'Big England'. Cattle have no Dreaming. *Ngumpin* were killed by *kartiya* because they stole cattle, and *ngumpin* did stockwork for Vesteys to make them rich. These aspects clearly show that cattle were part of *kartiya* way, or settlers' culture. However, the very same cattle also managed to cross the cultural boundary and move into the *ngumpin* world. It was ironic that *kartiya*, human beings who could communicate in language, were more intrusive and less communicative towards Aboriginal people than cattle. It was not cattle, but *kartiya*, who killed *ngumpin*. *Kartiya* did not give *ngumpin* enough food at the station, but cattle supplied extra tucker during 'holiday time'. *Kartiya* destroyed the Aboriginal economy without providing an adequate alternative source of supply. However, even though cattle destroyed the Aboriginal ecology, they also supplemented the Aboriginal economy with their own meat. Working for *kartiya* was a hard job, but working for cattle was a good job. Cattle even became a part of Aboriginal ceremonial practice. Through the interaction with *ngumpin* over the country, cattle established their position in *ngumpin* culture as well. To sum up, the *ngumpin*'s relationship with cattle was much more reciprocal than their relationship with *kartiya*.

How can we – non-Indigenous settlers – become as cross-cultural as cattle? It sounds odd, but Australian settlers may need to learn how to be cross-cultural from cattle. For example, academic practice is, without a doubt, *kartiya* way. Just as cattle are not part of Dreaming, this book is not part of Dreaming either. Therefore, this book inevitably belongs to *kartiya* culture. The Gurindji elders know it. They know and accept that I will use 'paper' to present their history in *kartiya* societies. The Gurindji people have been patiently cross-cultural as well.

However, naturally, what they expected me to do was to position my historical practice as close to *ngumpin* way as possible. The Gurindji people have been calling for such a dialectic partnership in many different aspects of Australian race relations. I believe Mick Rangiari's message is meaningful to anyone who participates in multicultural societies:

> Yes, you learn *kartiya* way and *ngumpin* way. Don't matter where you from in the world, we should live together, work together. Very hard, but gradually, we understand each other.

# CHAPTER 9

# FOR THEORY LOVERS ONLY (IF YOU ARE NOT, PLEASE SKIP TO THE NEXT CHAPTER)

*The theorizing operation finds itself at the*
*limits of the terrain where it normally functions,*
*like an automobile at the edge of a cliff.*
*Beyond and below lies the ocean.*
MICHEL DE CERTEAU 1984

Dipesh Chakrabarty notes that academic historians generally work within a framework which demands a positive answer to the following two questions: '[C]an the story be told/crafted? And does it allow for a rationally defensible point of view or position from which to tell the story?'[1] As long as one can meet these two conditions in one's narrative, historians welcome such a history as 'good history'[2]. After all, most academic historians are more concerned about 'the distinction between good and bad histories than with the question of who might own a particular piece of the past'.[3]

Decades have passed since postmodern history first challenged the naive idea of positivist historical discipline. Postmodern historians discussed the conditions of history from a new perspective. It has been well argued by Michel Foucault,[4] and many others, that a modern notion of history based on linearity, teleology and historicity was the invention of 19th century Europe. Through the postmodernists' works, one may say that history itself has been historicised. How far has postmodernism been successful in overcoming the idea of writing (only) a 'good history'? In my view, writing a 'good history' may still be the 'universal' foundation and condition of historical studies at academic institutions. It seems to be generally agreed that postmodernists have failed to effectively alter this.

In this chapter, my aim is to theorise what I have demonstrated throughout this book. Following the trajectory of what Chakrabarty calls the project of 'provincialising Europe', I want to explore the notion of 'dangerous history', or histories which are beyond the limits of history. From there, I seek alternative ways of exploring 'dangerous histories' as an academic historian.

## BRIEF HISTORY OF ABORIGINAL HISTORIOGRAPHY

Development of an Aboriginal historiography can be summarised as a process of 'moving as close as possible to Aboriginal pasts'. Although Aboriginal societies had been placed as a part of Australian history in 18th and 19th centuries' historiography,[5] Aboriginal studies had been practised mostly by anthropologists until the 1970s. Today, there seems to be agreement that it was W.H.E. Stanner's public lecture in 1968 that first challenged 'The Great Australian Silence' and called for the historical study of Aboriginal (colonial) pasts.[6]

The first generation of Aboriginal historical studies appeared. Their aim can be summarised as moving towards Aboriginal pasts by challenging the public ignorance of Aboriginal history. C.D. Rowley's trilogy,[7] Peter Biskup's *Not Slaves Not Citizens* (1973),[8] and Raymond Evans' *Exclusion, Exploitation and Extermination* (1975)[9] are probably the best examples of important works from this first generation. The contributions of these studies of Aboriginal history should be summarised on two different levels: public and academic. First, they succeeded in making the public recognise the omission of Aboriginal pasts from Australian history. Australian colonial history was not as peaceful as they had thought. There was a history of exclusion, exploitation and extermination of Indigenous Australians. These studies certainly reflected and reacted to public attention to the Aboriginal human rights and land rights movement at that time.[10] Second, these works opened up a new field in academic discussions of Aboriginal studies. Applying a dynamic approach meant that historians had a different perspective from the anthropological static approach, which tended to construct precolonial or 'traditional' aspects of Aboriginal societies.[11] The emergence of a historical approach in the field of Aboriginal studies challenged the monopoly over Aboriginal studies previously held by anthropologists.[12]

Anticipation of the second generation of Aboriginal historical studies can be found in Henry Reynolds' groundbreaking work, *The Other Side of the Frontier* (1981).[13] Claiming the importance of seeing events from the Aboriginal perspective, Reynolds described Aboriginal people not just as victims or passive objects, but also as activists or active agents of Australian colonial history. Although *The Other Side of the Frontier* and other related works emphasised violent conflict between the Indigenous people and the settlers,[14] historians also began to explore the ways in which Aboriginal people flexibly adopted the colonial regime, or their positive contribution to the shaping of colonial histories.[15] The project of 'moving as close as possible to Aboriginal pasts' opened up a new field in which Aboriginal people were considered historical actors.

The wave of the second generation became visible by the end of the 1980s. In terms of academic disciplines, it introduced two main new approaches: the oral historical approach and representation theory. The former aimed to be 'closer to Aboriginal pasts' and the latter began to cast doubt on the 'academic representation of Aboriginal pasts'.

Although the oral historical approach has never become mainstream in general academic historiography, one may say that it has been a growing method of practising history in the second half of the 20th century.[16] In terms of Aboriginal historiography, Bruce Shaw's *My Country of the Pelican Dreaming* (1981)[17] may have been one of the first triggers. The booming started from the late 1980s. In addition to Shaw's series of oral historical works,[18] Peter Read's *A Hundred Years' War* (1988)[19] and other works[20] greatly contributed to convincing an academic and public audience of the value of the oral historical approach to Aboriginal pasts. Among them, Ann McGrath's *Born in the Cattle* (1987)[21] probably received the strongest attention in the earlier stages of the development of oral historical disciplines. A decade later came the Human Rights and Equal Opportunity Commission's report *Bringing Them Home* (1997), which attracted enormous public attention to the Stolen Generation, and is one of the most influential oral historical studies in Aboriginal historiography.[22]

The project of 'moving as close as possible to Aboriginal pasts' was encouraged by the method of directly interviewing Aboriginal people, as opposed to searching for historical documents written by non-Aboriginal people. However, the oral historical approach inevitably had to face the question of the credibility of oral testimonies. Critiques of oral testimonies can be summarised by saying that Aboriginal oral evidence is not necessarily 'the reality of the past', but rather 'their present views of the past'.[23]

The other wave of the second generation was mainly generated by Bain Attwood's works: *The Making of the Aborigines* (1989) and *Power, Knowledge and Aborigines* (1992).[24] Following a trajectory from Michel Foucault to Edward Said, these studies about the 'European representation of non-Europe' also corresponded to the development of postcolonial studies in the general academic field of humanities. Attwood explored how European power and knowledge have constructed the Aboriginal subject, which was based on the essentialistic 'them–us' dichotomy. This historical study of the European representation of

Indigenous Australians certainly problematised anthropological practice once again. Anthropologists' authority over the representation of Aboriginal societies, and their appetite for constructing a nostalgic 'tradition' of precolonial Aboriginal 'Otherness', were historicised and criticised as modes of colonial practice.[25] However, even though these works criticised the essentialistic dichotomisation of 'Europe' and 'Aborigines', and called for 'effective cultural interchange, neither patronising or exploitative',[26] representation theory tended to emphasise the boundary between 'our representation of them' and 'them'. Thus it did not provide any solutions for 'moving as close as possible to Aboriginal pasts'.

Public desire for 'moving closer to Aboriginal pasts' and the question of 'our representation of them' provided an arena for Aboriginal representations of their own pasts. Even though Aboriginal writers often take an (auto)biographical approach and – probably for this very reason – do not make a distinctive impact on academic historical studies, their works certainly had an effect in the public arena.[27] I would like to note here that Sally Morgan's *My Place* (1988) was translated into Japanese in 1992, becoming one of the few Japanese publications about Indigenous Australians.[28]

In contrast, the academic desire to 'move as close as possible to Aboriginal pasts' and the question of 'our representation of them' have not yet found their destination. There are, however, some Indigenous academics who began to contribute to academic historical discourses. Gordon Briscoe has been one of the pioneering Indigenous academic historians since the 1980s.[29] John Maynard,[30] Jackie Huggins[31] and Tony Birch[32] are among those who have been greatly involved in Aboriginal historical studies since the 1990s. In addition to these Indigenous academic historians' works, there are studies which may give some hints as to a potential 'third generation' of Aboriginal historiography. Heather Goodall, for instance, calls attention to the gap between the positivist historical approach and the understanding of Aboriginal community memories; she suggests 'a more sensitive approach to research, which recognises the power and role of a community's own history making'.[33] Furthermore, there are some examples of the possibilities of 'effective cultural interchange' between Aboriginal people and academic writers. In the field of cultural studies, Stephen Muecke's *Reading the Country* (1984) emphasises putting the theory of communication into practice. Muecke's attempt to highlight the contrast between academic theories (of nomadology) and Aboriginal narratives is a unique experiment in communicating over the cultural difference.[34] To my knowledge, Deborah B. Rose's *Hidden Histories* (1991) was the first, and remains one of the few books to present Aboriginal oral historical accounts as analyses by Aboriginal historians. In this book, Aboriginal people are not interviewees or informants, not even just storytellers; they are the historians who analyse the Australian pasts.[35] Unlike many other academic historians' works, Richard Baker's *Land is Life* (1999), from the field of geography, applies the Yanyuwa people's own periodisation – such as 'wild times', 'cattle times' or 'land right times' – in order to explore the Indigenous notion of history and their cultural geography.[36]

The third generation of Aboriginal historiography is still emerging. In the same way that the second generation involved several different approaches to Aboriginal history, the third generation will be diverse as well. Nevertheless, many of the above-mentioned works, and new topics, tend to look into the complex cultural and social interactions between Aboriginal and non-Aboriginal societies. Thus I would like to point out that 'cross-cultural history' or 'hybrid history' may be a unifying theme among them. In these new styles of writing, historians often emphasise multiple voices from plural historical agents. Therefore, through the process of writing a cross-cultural history, Aboriginal history becomes less essentialistic and begins to interact with national history, non-Aboriginal ethnic history, even global history.

I, too, claim my work to be a part of cross-cultural history. However, my project is not simply a 'history of cross-cultural agents'. In my opinion, what needs to be cross-cultural is not only historical subjects, but also *history itself* as a discipline. The question I would like to raise now is this: can the very concept of 'history' be cross-cultural?

## POSTMODERNISM, MYTHS AND MEMORY

Since the 'linguistic turn' – when historians became more interested in and self-conscious about the construction of narrative and the way they draw upon the same techniques as writers of fiction – historical theorists have been facing a crisis of history. As Richard Evans argues, it is deemed a crisis because the question has become not so much 'What is history?' but rather 'Is it possible to do history at all?' Under the pressure of the linguistic turn, historians began to have doubts about historical truth and objectivity. Naturally, historical practice now faces an epistemological crisis that questions a scientific model of history based on the rigorous investigation of primary sources.[37]

Following the poststructuralists' arguments in linguistics, semiotics and deconstruction – typically tracing the theorists from Ferdinand de Saussure to Jacques Derrida – postmodern historians have argued that it is impossible for historians to construct the real past because 'history is never present to us in anything but a discursive form'.[38] Therefore, postmodern historians tend to conclude that there is no clear distinction between fiction and non-fiction, or imagination and reality when we practise history. Gabrielle Spiegel neatly summarises this perspective: 'If we cannot reach "life" through literature, we cannot reach "the past" through document.'[39]

I do not intend to dip into the numerous debates over postmodern history. What I would like to note here is that such postmodern relativism seems to be rapidly declining under the current circumstances of the rise of (right-wing) 'revisionist-denialist' historians. I may not need to elaborate this point in detail either. For example, deconstructionists had to move back from – or at least carefully annotate – their position when they sought to argue for the (im)possibility of representation of the Holocaust without considering so-called denialist history.[40] Another good example is provided by Joyce Appleby, Lynn Hunt and Margaret Jacobs, who call for the search for 'a workable truth communicable within an improving society' from pragmatic standpoints.[41] Many historical theorists today probably stand by what Ann Curthoys and John Docker argue: there is a distinction between fiction and non-fiction, but the distinction is not as clear as we used to think.[42]

Accepting this not-so-exciting but hard-to-disagree-with idea that historical reality is *to some extent* difficult to distinguish from historical imagination, I would like to shift our focus from the 'discourse of history' to the 'culture of history'. In fact, it is nothing new to say that history is just one of the many modes of understanding the past. One finds classic examples in Mircea Eliade's *The Myth of the Eternal Return*[43] and Claude Lévi-Strauss' *The Savage Mind*.[44] In their works, myth, or the 'savage mind', was suggested as an alternative way of constructing the past. History finds its cultural and methodological position distant from – if not opposite to – mythology. According to such arguments, history is not superior to myths any more; history and myth simply have different cultural and historical origins. Another heated discussion over 'memory and history' has been raging since the 1980s.[45] Here, the term 'memory' or 'remembering' instead of history has been suggested as an alternative way of approaching the past. Some suggest that history and memory exist in opposition,[46] others suggest that history is one mode of memory,[47] and probably many others suggest an interdependence or connection between history and memory.[48]

Through the discussion of history, myths and memory, contemporary historical thinking has engaged with the idea that (conventional academic) history has been culturally and historically specified as 'the Westernness of Western historical writing'.[49] In summary, history, as an academic discipline, has been provincialised as 'Western', historicised as originating in the 19th century, and has therefore lost its universality and been specified as just one of many modes of exploring the past.

Nevertheless, the practice of favouring certain historical disciplines as 'good history' has remained intact. The challenge of postmodern history staggered in the face of solemn 'facts' and 'truth' – we cannot accept the claim that 'the Holocaust never happened' because we eventually prioritise 'facts' more than 'discourse' or 'emplotment'.[50] Furthermore, however one emphasises the importance of 'memory' or 'myths', history's universality *as history* largely remains completely safe and unchallenged precisely because memory and myths are considered *not* 'history'. History may have lost its universality in the sense that there exist many different modes of representing the past. However, even if one emphasises the importance of studying memory or myths, such studies easily co-exist with 'history' as long as they are distinguished from the historical disciplines. In other words, history still demonstrates its Western-modern-universality without much trouble under the current power/knowledge structure of academic disciplines.

In this chapter, by introducing concepts of 'localised history' and 'post-secular history' I first aim to visualise the gap between 'good history' and 'dangerous history'. From there, I want to develop ways of accepting the gap but not abandoning the possibility of communication over the gap between *deeply plural historical spaces.* In other words, by demonstrating that histories exist in every society as much as myths and memories do, this chapter aims to seek the possibility of dialogue between Western-originating academic historical disciplines ('universal good history') and historical practices which academic historians hesitate to accept ('un-universalisable dangerous history').

## LOCALISED HISTORY

Let us talk about a history of Captain Cook as an example. The Gurindji people often taught me about how Captain Cook came to the Gurindji country to shoot Aboriginal people in the early stages of colonisation. What we need to remember here is that from an academic historical point of view, Captain James Cook 'discovered' the eastern coast of Australia in 1770, but it is 'historically not factual' that Captain Cook visited the inner part of the Northern Territory.

As I have explored in Chapter 5, it should be noted that there are many different variations of Captain Cook's historical narratives among the Gurindji people. According to Jimmy Mangayarri, Captain Cook came to Darwin and came down to the south, to places such as Timber Creek station, and later, the Gurindji country. Mick Rangiari's story started with Captain Cook coming to Sydney Harbour. Later, not Captain Cook himself, but his followers came to the Gurindji country. Dandy Danbayarri said Captain Cook first came from 'Big England' to Sydney by boat. He then came to the Gurindji country by horse.

Even though there are contradictions between the stories, different variations of historical knowledge easily co-exist in the Gurindji country. I found no will among the Gurindji people to find or determine a single authentic historical knowledge of Captain Cook's acts. However, no one ever told me that Captain Cook had been a good person. Captain Cook is the evil figure of the settlers who came to Aboriginal countries (Australia) and 'shoot 'em people'.

A historian who is willing to sincerely 'listen to' and 'learn from' Aboriginal people's own experiences has to face a serious dilemma. Here, I would argue, is the voice of the subaltern or the 'dangerous history' which would never be welcomed as a 'good history' by academic historians. However seriously and enthusiastically the Gurindji people tell a history of Captain Cook's invasion of Australia, their histories are rendered unacceptable by academic historians. This is precisely because *academic historians know that Captain Cook never came to the Gurindji country*! Referring to Gayatri Spivak's words, 'even when the subaltern makes an effort to the death to speak, she is not be able to be heard',[51] Yoshinobu Ota argues, 'without shifting the knowledge/power relationship which produces subalternity', the subaltern cannot make 'a speech which deserves to be listened to by us'.[52] That is, because it is not based on accepted historicity, the history of Captain Cook's invasion of the Gurindji country will not be welcomed to the history-space in and from which academic historians produce knowledge. The academic politeness of 'we respect your story as "memory" or "myth"' does not solve the problem I raise here.[53] Rather, the real problem rests in the very knowledge/power structure that tries to categorise the Gurindji people's historical knowledge as myth or memory instead of and in opposition to 'history'.

*

'Localised history', which I want to discuss here, is not 'local history'. Local history is a part of what is viewed as 'good history', as that which can 'enrich the subject matter of history and make it more representative of society as a whole'.[54] In other words, it tends to be integrated within 'universal' history. A fragment called 'local history' which presupposes an implicit whole may demonstrate the diversity and complexity of the whole, but it does not threaten the very idea of wholeness. Local history is reducible to the history-space of the universal. On the other hand, what I call 'localised history' is a fragment which does *not* refer to the whole, but is a history that is irreducible to the 'universal' history-space.[55] Such a localised history is 'dangerous' because it refuses to be universalised. This is a history that one can understand and share only if one patiently stays with its nature/culture of locality.[56]

John F. Kennedy's visit to Wave Hill station before the Gurindji walk-off is a good example of 'localised history'. It is easy to say that we know JFK never visited Wave Hill station. But such a statement becomes logical and reasonable *only if* we stand and rely on Western/universal-oriented historical consciousness. As I discussed in Chapter 7, the Gurindji's history of JFK has its singularity within the local context in their country. Their history is not universalisable, but has its unquestionable *reality* within the local context.

Colonial histories narrated by the Gurindji people are *localised Australian history* whose 'fragmentary' nature is fated to be denied by academic 'universal' historiography. This is not just the Gurindji people's history. Many Aboriginal people in different regions have a localised history of Captain Cook's invasion across the northern part of Australia.[57] I would argue, however, that localised history has to be understood within the specific local context and that we cannot naively call it a 'wrong history' simply because it does not have a place in the universalised/Westernised history-space. Rather, if someone calls it a 'wrong history', we may need to pay attention to the conditions of the knowledge system from which this person makes such a statement. Are historians who speak only from the academic history-space standing on a ground from which they can judge whether Gurindji people's histories are right or wrong? Or, in the first place, do academic historians really know what the Gurindji people's historical practice is like?

What such Aboriginal people's historical practice demonstrates is the fundamental plurality of the history-spaces, or the limits of '(conventional academic) history', which has long been obsessed by universalising modern-Westernness.[58] It is nothing but a continuation of colonial practice if 'dangerous histories' from various history-spaces are excluded as 'wrong histories' by the academic power/knowledge agents. In the era of globalisation and its inevitable accompanying politics of difference, what historical disciplines are required to do is, I believe, acknowledge the limits of their universality, and seek the possibility of communication with histories which lie beyond these limits. This communication, by definition, must be facilitated without either the exclusion or inclusion of 'dangerous histories' within the academic history-space. Rose's remark is relevant to this point:

> (Even though this Aboriginal) account is at odds with Western knowledge of Captain Cook's journeys, the more interesting point is that this difference is irrelevant. Invasion did happen, people did get shot, they did have their lands stolen. Varying accounts of Captain Cook only matter to those who are *determined not to listen.*[59] (emphasis added)

Can we find a chance to practise what Spivak calls the 'systematic unlearning' of postcolonial intellectual privilege here?[60] Academic historians or privileged intellectuals *know* that Captain Cook never came to the Gurindji country. Without unlearning this privilege of 'knowingness', there are no ways for academic historical writings to open themselves up to deeply plural history-spaces.

For further exploration of this point, I want to discuss another limit of academic history. That is a closure towards the 'supernatural' agents which appear in many historical narratives of the Gurindji people.

## POST-SECULAR HISTORY

In this book, I have tried to 'convince' readers that Dreaming beings have been as active as human agents throughout the colonial history of the Gurindji country. Here, I pick up a story of how *kurraj* [rainbow snake] caused the Wave Hill flood at Lipananyku (Chapter 6) as an example to discuss the problem related to the history of non-human agents. The Gurindji people's history of the Wave Hill flood probably perplexes many academic historians. This is because their historical understanding that 'the Wave Hill flood in 1924 was caused by a Gurindji man who used rainstones' – a historical analysis based on supernatural beings or phenomena – is not permitted in academic historical disciplines.

Giving an example of Ranajit Guha's study of the revolt of the Santal people, who claimed that Thakur [god] was the main instigator of their rebellion, Chakrabarty argues about a similar problem. This is the dilemma that the academic historian cannot sincerely 'listen to' the subaltern voices:

> But in spite of Guha's desire to listen to the rebel voice
> seriously, his analysis cannot offer Thakur the same place of
> agency in the story of the rebellion that the Santal's statements
> had given him. A narrative strategy that is rationally defensible
> in the modern understanding of what constitutes public life –
> and the historians speak in the public sphere – cannot be based
> on a relationship that allows the divine or the supernatural a
> direct hand in the affairs of the world.[61]

Therefore, academic historians interpret the Santal's 'beliefs' in an anthropological manner, and then 'produce "good," not subversive, histories, which conform to the protocols of the discipline'.[62] However, such an interpretation does not change the situation where academic historians do not (even try to) believe that the Wave Hill flood was caused by the Gurindji man and the rainbow snake. Moreover, anthropologists have come across this problem as well. For example, Mitsuru Hamamoto points out the dilemma that ethnographers cannot help but confess after their analysis of magical beliefs:

> After all, I really don't understand this belief. This is because
> even though I give some explanations of it, I myself do not at
> all feel as if I believe it as they do. I don't even know how one
> could manage to believe it.[63]

This is the uncrossable gap we face. Since the academic disciplines of history and anthropology must comply with their 'universality', they have to face the limits of historicising or anthropologising. Chakrabarty pays attention to this very impossibility of assimilating the Santal people's experience into academic disciplines and argues, '[W]e have to stay with both, and with the gap between them that signals an irreducible plurality in our own experiences of historicity.'[64]

What does Chakrabarty mean by 'staying with the gap'? This idea is certainly related to the aim of this chapter: seeking the possibility of communication between deeply plural history-spaces. In terms of the Gurindji people's rainbow snake or the Santal people's god, this is about the limits of secularism. Chakrabarty argues, '"disenchantment" is not the only principle by which we world the earth'.[65] In other words, we (including academic historians) all live not only in the secular and homogenous time-space, but also in the times-spaces of gods and spirits even though such realms have been carefully excluded from the modern public sphere and become 'fragmentary' in our life world.[66]

It is not just the rainbow snake that was active throughout the colonial history of the Gurindji country; it is also many other so-called Dreaming (ancestral creative) beings. What is crucial here is that the fact that such supernatural beings existed in the Gurindji people's life world before colonisation never means that they do not live in the modern world today. This is because, as Mircea Eliade repeatedly pointed out, spirituality or the sacred is not a dead past unrelated to society today.[67] The Gurindji people's historical analysis of Australian colonisation, including supernatural agents, demonstrates *Indigenous modern thoughts* of Australia. Australian Indigenous modernity cannot be called 'pre-modern' just because it does not reflect Western modernity.[68]

It seems unavoidably true that academic historical disciplines do not have a language with which to articulate the existence of supernatural beings in their writings. On the other hand, however, supernatural beings can be as common as they are for the Gurindji or Santal people in our everyday life world. Here Chakrabarty claims the importance of 'doubled consciousness'. Both the secularised time-consciousness which Western modernity requires of us, and the supernaturalised time-consciousness which is familiar in our everyday life, exist in people's consciousness at the same time. We all live in the plural world with doubled consciousness(es) which are seemingly contradictory but also connected to each other.[69] That is, we may not be able to 'believe' the Gurindji people's historical consciousness, but we also know that our everyday life is not necessarily disconnected from such non-secular times-spaces. Even though the 'gap' is inevitable between the 'dangerous history' of the supernatural and the academic 'universal' history, this does not have to mean that 'communication over the gap' is impossible.[70]

What all of this may imply is the possibility of 'post-secular historical writings'. Post-secularism is a relatively new phrase, and it has been creating a chain reaction without definitive conceptualisation. In this article, I use the term as an approach to probing the limits of the politics of secularism which Western modernity has promoted in order to disenchant the (public) world.[71] 'Doubled consciousness' does not require us, unlike 'New Age science', to bring the supernatural 'dangerous histories' to the fore of a single history-space by universalising them. Rather it encourages us to write a history in which we demonstrate the inevitability of 'universalising (secularising)' the Gurindji histories while at the same time accepting the deeply plural history-spaces by denying our own universalisation.

With the example of the history of the Wave Hill flood we, on the one hand, can (and probably need to) secularise the Gurindji historical narratives. That is, it is not too difficult to find in these narratives the Gurindji people's desire to criticise the colonial power structure. The different versions of the Wave Hill flood stories all reveal some aspects of race relations in the cattle stations of colonial Australia: settlers did not trust Aboriginal people, settlers needed Aboriginal people's labour, and Aboriginal people generally did not like settlers. By demonstrating that the Gurindji people had the power to control the rain, which was far beyond the settlers' ability, they give evidence that settlers could not run the station without Aboriginal help, and provide an example of Aboriginal people having had the intention of keeping out the settlers.

Consequently, we understand that the Gurindji historians are trying to discursively invert the power structure of Australian colonialism. However, at the same time, we are also asked to (try to) accept the 'dangerous history' of a rainbow snake *without antidote* as 'real/true history' that is impossible to universalise. It seems to me that the only way of not abandoning communication over the gap for academic historians is to struggle to maintain these two contradictory historical narratives at the same time.

In *Why I am not a Secularist* (1999), William E. Connolly calls for 'deep pluralism'[72] and says, 'the formation of multiple lines of connection across these spaces of difference is crucial to a generous ethos of engagement in a post-secular society'.[73] In my understanding, what post-secularism aims for is neither excluding the supernatural or spirituality from the public sphere as secularists do, nor including them for the purpose of universalising them as fundamentalists do, but opening the horizon on which we can interact with each other among the deeply plural worlds.

## CROSS-CULTURALISING HISTORY

It is probably true that such 'dangerous histories' have not been ignored by academia but 'respected' and discussed by anthropologists and historians in the context of mythology or memory studies. Nevertheless, however much one tries to 'rescue' these localised or supernatural histories as 'myths' or 'memory', the power relationship between 'historians who respect and rescue Aboriginal knowledge' and 'Aboriginal knowledge which is respected and rescued by academics' remains unchanged. Such a strategy cannot effectively destabilise the colonial-modernity of academic historical disciplines, but rather is at risk of covering it up. Using a famous quotation from Spivak, we must say, '(r)epresentation has not withered away'[74] in academic historical writing today.

I may need to emphasise a distinction between the issues I raise in this chapter and those which have been influential within so-called historical anthropology or ethnohistory over the last few decades. I do not suggest the importance of an anthropological analysis of past events or mentality (historical anthropology), and I strongly disagree with making a distinction between histories of the West and of the non-West (ethnohistory).[75] Separating his approach from what is usually implied in 'ethnohistory', Greg Dening calls for 'a poetic for histories' and suggests:

> History is a human universal. Knowledge of the past is
> expressed by all human beings according to their different
> cultural and social systems ... There are histories, like
> cultures, that need an ethnographic description for their
> forms and structures and functions. A poetic for histories is
> that ethnographic description.[76]

We should not necessarily understand his reference to 'ethnographic description' as an anthropological interpretation or analysis. Rather, I prefer reading his idea of 'a poetic for histories' as an approach to writing histories multidimensionally by staying in-between plural history-spaces. Our task is therefore to seek ways of writing histories that can facilitate the interplaying and co-existing of various histories from deeply plural history-spaces by alerting us to the limits of modern-rational academic history and by making the universalising desire of academic historiography visible. In this context, I am suggesting a project of 'cross-culturalising history' which stands at the crossroads of Chakrabarty's 'provincialising Europe' and Dening's 'poetic for histories'.[77]

Decades have passed since 'minority histories' entered the front stage of academic historiography and challenged their exclusion from the master (often nationalistic) narrative, calling for pluralism in historical writings. However, historical pluralism within the scope of 'good histories' tends to produce what Tessa Morris-Suzuki calls 'cosmetic multiculturalism'.[78] However much a cultural or cross-cultural history tries to write a history revealing the historical complexity of the past by introducing the minority's pasts, this does not necessarily mean that they are successful in critiquing the power structure inherited in the nature of academic historical narratives. Seeking ways of writing histories of cross-cultural agents is not good enough. What is more important is to *cross-culturalise history itself.* We can never listen to the subaltern voices as long as our writings of 'minority histories' are situated within a cosmetic multiculturalism. This is why academic historians must face the gap between 'good histories' within the limits and 'dangerous histories' beyond the limits.

The project of cross-culturalising history does not necessarily follow the trajectory of discourse analysis or deconstruction. This program is instead a new historical 'experientialism' that seeks possibilities of connecting (to borrow Morris-Suzuki's phrase) the 'historical truthfulness'[79] through communication over the gap. The Gurindji historians do not consider their historical practice as something called 'infinite play/jest of the text'. Historical practice maintained by the Gurindji people can be called postmodern in terms of the ambivalent nature of their narratives, which interplay and disperse without a definitive, central or authentic narrative. In other words, academic historians may be able to learn ways of operating historical knowledge from the Gurindji people, who prefer to localise rather than universalise their knowledge. It is also worthwhile learning how to make seemingly contradictory historical narratives co-exist without much conflict. However, I want to reiterate here that the Gurindji people tell histories of Captain Cook's invasion, President Kennedy's visit to the Gurindji country, and the rainbow snake of the Wave Hill flood as histories which *really happened.* In other words, the Gurindji people's historical practice has been maintained on the obvious assumption that the histories they tell are stories they or their ancestors *experienced.*

In case I receive a criticism saying, 'Are you essentialising "the Gurindji historical practice" and emphasising the fixed binary between academic and the Gurindji people's history?', it may be worth submitting my response to this criticism in advance. First, regarding strategic essentialism: I want to suggest that the elite intellectuals who criticise colonial power relations sometimes need to 'unlearn' their privileged tools of 'discourse analysis'. The Gurindji people often emphasised to me the clear binary between *ngumpin* [Aboriginal] and *kartiya* [non-Aboriginal], and repeatedly said that 'they' never seriously listened to what 'we' said to them. Therefore, I must, at least partly, suspend 'enlightening deconstruction' of the Gurindji people's narratives. What the Gurindji historians expect me to do is not (only) treat their stories as counter-colonial discourses, but convey them to the wider audience as the '*real history* of what they experienced'.

However, this attitude of mine may privilege the Gurindji male elders with whom I worked closely. Therefore, my second response to the question above relates to hybridity. How do I justify my ethnographic writings of 'the Gurindji history' if they are based on my learning mainly from male elders who never had Western school education? Am I totalising such narratives as the authentic and static 'Gurindji history' by excluding the dynamic negotiations among, for example, young or female Gurindji people over the past events? In other words, am I ignoring the possibility of the hybridisation of the Gurindji history through, for example, the attendance of young Gurindji men or women at school where they learn that Captain Cook 'discovered' mainly the southeastern part of the Australian continent?

To respond to this criticism, I want to say that Aboriginal analysis of their *colonial experience* is, by definition, already/always hybrid. Without the influx of Western/colonial knowledge and materials, it is impossible for Aboriginal people to articulate histories such as 'Captain Cook', 'President Kennedy' or 'Wave Hill station'. It is also true that the younger generation of Indigenous Australians gradually learn more Western-universal history at school. Therefore, the Gurindji people – and probably many other Indigenous peoples – are constantly facing the inflow of Western practice and its information. This hybridisation happening in the Gurindji country is so powerful and continuous that I personally think it is unavoidable; it is not really a matter of choice. Since I am not a Gurindji person, I am not in a position to judge if the influx of Western culture is desirable or not for them. Likewise, I cannot tell if the history of Captain Cook's 'discovery' of the eastern part of Australia in 1770 would 'exclude' the history of Captain Cook's invasion of the Gurindji country or could 'co-exist' without conflict in future.

What I would like to suggest here instead is that such flows of hybridisation are not well balanced, but are largely *one-way traffic.* Western/academic 'liberal democratic' history, which is supposed to represent Indigenous/minority agency, often still refuses to be hybridised. Or more precisely, academic history has continuously *held onto its power* to determine whether or not it should be hybridised. This unbalanced hybridisation clearly reveals the global and national power structure of Western/secularist hegemony. Therefore any critique of cosmetic multiculturalism should not be confined to within the academic structure but should be directed towards the political economy of national and global power relations.[80] We also cannot overlook the importance of Ghassan Hage's work on fantasies of white supremacy in a multicultural society. Hage argues that *both* racists *and* multiculturalists take the 'white nation' for granted and try to treat Aboriginal and migrating populations as their controllable objects through white authority/supremacy.[81] As long as academic historical narratives of minority people are framed within the scope of 'good history', minorities' (in fact, any people's) 'dangerous history' will be either excluded as a 'wrong history' or detoxified as a 'controllable object' of myth or memory.

## EXPERIENTIAL HISTORICAL TRUTHFULNESS

What we – academic historians – have to ask ourselves is why we *understand* Captain Cook's invasion and the rainbow snake of the Wave Hill flood even though we may not *believe* them. The Gurindji historians are not saying, for example, 'Captain Cook went to the moon and enjoyed surfing.' They are saying, 'Captain Cook came to the Gurindji country and shot people.' Academic historians cannot understand what the former means in any sense. We cannot connect ourselves to this history by sharing historical truthfulness. However, as Rose pointed out, academic history can *relate* to the latter because within the truthfulness of academic practice, invasion of Australia did happen and Aboriginal people did get shot. In a similar way, the history of the rainbow snake of the Wave Hill flood is not particularly unfamiliar, for supernatural beings or phenomena never disappear from our everyday life world. In other words, even though there is a clear gap between 'good history' and 'dangerous history', we can connect ourselves to the Gurindji people's 'dangerous histories' by sharing their 'historical truthfulness'. This probably suggests that Gurindji history is a *truthful* but *different* mode of history. And more importantly, it also indicates that academic historians can relate to the Gurindji people's histories precisely because we 'understand' them. The gap is there, but communication over the gap is possible. This is because the Gurindji people's history is experiential – it is not a history based on modern-Western empiricism, but it is still based on experiential truthfulness.

Morris-Suzuki calls for making a distinction between 'historical truth' and 'historical truthfulness'.[82] 'Historical truth' has been assumed to be externally (and objectively) 'out there' and accessible by the historian. She argues that this is illusory 'not because there is no historical truth but because historical truth is inexhaustible'.[83] On the other hand, historical truthfulness is situated within 'a relationship between the enquiring subject and the object of enquiry'.[84] Therefore, the *process* of historical enquiry as well as the *positionality* and *biases* which every historian holds become the focus of critical attention.[85] I would argue that communication between history-spaces can be facilitated through this historical truthfulness.

Although ways of connecting historical fact and truth are different between academic empirical disciplines and the Gurindji people's practices, both consciously deal with 'what really happened' rather than the 'narrative's discursive nature'. The Gurindji people's localised and 'supernatural' historical analyses are produced within the nature of experiential historical truthfulness. It is this experiential truthful nature of the Gurindji people's histories that clearly separates them from the 'wrong history' argued by revisionists who, for example, deny the history of the Holocaust. Revisionists are not seeking truthful communication across the plural history-spaces but rather demonstrate their fantasy and desire to exclusively universalise their own 'historical (un)truth'. In contrast, the Gurindji people's histories have been practised and negotiated in a local context by promoting inter-play and co-existence among different historical understandings. Rose argues:

> (K)nowledge, in all Aboriginal systems of information, is specific to the place and to the people. To put it another way: one of the most important aspects of Aboriginal knowledge system is that they do not universalise. Moreover, the fact that knowledge is localised and specific is one of the keys to its value.[86]

'Historical truth' can be exclusive and colonial, but 'historical truth-fulness' is open to the Other. Academic historical disciplines need to learn how to negotiate with 'dangerous history' through experiential historical truthfulness. In the same way as Chakrabarty's project is not a denial of the West, the program of cross-culturalising history does not aim to deny the modern/Western/rational/secular/universal his-torical writings either. What I instead want to emphasise is that since academic historians owe so much to the 'universal-West', *they should not pretend they can escape from it*. However, as such academic historical dis-ciplines have been repeatedly criticised as the product of the 19th cen-tury colonial West, we cannot be content with our present position any more. Therefore, what is critically important for academic historians today is, I believe, to stop mystifying the 'limits of history', and instead to demonstrate them openly and honestly. If Chakrabarty's 'provin-cialising Europe' is a way of philosophising about such a problem of history, and Dening's 'poetic for histories' is an ethnographic descrip-tion of it, the project of cross-culturalising history stands at the cross-roads by making 'dangerous history' visible. Through the process of learning to *listen deeply* to the 'dangerous histories' and sharing their experiential historical truthfulness, it may be possible to seek ways of connecting such deeply plural history-spaces.

# CHAPTER 10

# CHILL OUT: BUT THE JOURNEY NEVER ENDS

*An Eschatological Laundry List:*

*1. This is it!*
*2. There are no hidden meanings.*

*33. All important decisions must be made on the
basis of insufficient data.*
*34. Yet we are responsible for everything we do.*
*35. No excuses will be accepted.*
*36. You can run, but you can't hide.*

*41. You are free to do whatever you like. You need
only face the consequences.*
*42. What do you know ... for sure ... anyway?*
*43. Learn to forgive yourself, again and again
and again and again ...*
SHELDON KOPP 1972

## FEEDBACK FROM THE GURINDJI PEOPLE

Having written the first draft of this book, I went back to the Gurindji country with the draft. I decided to show my draft and explain what I wrote to the Gurindji elders, and hopefully receive their feedback and approval.[1]

There was a certain degree of anxiety among some academics with whom I discussed this idea. Some said 'my analysis' of their history does not need approval from the storytellers; academic freedom, perhaps? Others called it unreal or were concerned that it would just be lip service because they would not read through my thesis and understand my academic arguments. On the other hand, some academics strongly supported this idea. The supporters said such feedback is important because even though my analysis belongs to me, the stories I learned belong to the Gurindji people; I needed to consult the storytellers about the way I use them.

Overall, I liked this idea because I knew I would feel more comfortable and confident about my project if I could show the Gurindji elders my draft and explain it as much as I could, and also as much as they wanted. However, there were still problems with this idea: what if the Gurindji people disagreed with my writings? Before giving up on publishing, I would probably try to negotiate with them. What if they said they could not judge my writings unless they are able to read through the text? What if they were not interested in listening to my presentation? Should I encourage them to listen? Maybe not. 'They said they could not judge my thesis' or 'they were not interested in my thesis' would be their feedback as well. I believe what a researcher can do is to make their feedback and negotiation visible in their text, whatever the feedback is.

## PRESENTATION AND REACTION

On 17 July 2000 I returned to the Gurindji country. I was warmly welcomed by the Gurindji people again. Considering my restricted schedule, I planned to show and explain the draft primarily to my three main teachers – Jimmy Mangayarri, Mick Rangiari and Billy

Bunter – as well as the Daguragu Community Government Council members at their official meeting, which is held fortnightly.

When I explained what I was going to do, Mick Rangiari said to me, 'OK, I listen what you got here. If I agree, you take 'em university.' The others were simply curious about what kinds of stories I wrote.

I knew I had no talent for explaining the Aboriginal historiography or postcolonial theories to them. Instead, I explained the politics which this book inevitably had to face: the difference between *kartiya* and *ngumpin* ways of historical practice. I emphasised that I tried to tell *kartiya* how to learn and share the Gurindji people's history.

I also realised that they did not want to sit next to me just listening for too long. Each time, my presentation took about 15 to 30 minutes. I explained chapter by chapter what stories I wrote. For example, Billy Bunter was very excited when I told of my argument that the idea of the walk-off originated from the Gurindji consciousness. He told me that I learned the Gurindji history 'from inside us'. After hearing my presentation, Mick Rangiari said, 'Good one. Good one this one. *Punyu* [good], *punyu* … If you make 'em book, you can bring it back here.' Old Jimmy said, '*Jarrakap* [stories] like that make 'em people happy. Everything I bin tell you (is) good story … That book [my draft] make me happy.' I also showed them photos that I intended to use for publication. I explained to them that anyone could access these photos once my thesis was lodged in the university library. The Gurindji elders confirmed to me that there were no secret photos among them.

I presented the draft to the community council meeting as well. Some of the council members asked where my publications would be circulated (place-oriented history!). I told them that I would try to publish a book in Japanese as well as English. Therefore, stories would be circulated in Japan, Australia, and possibly other overseas countries.

Spending time with the Gurindji elders, I naturally learned more new stories as well. Once again, I want to emphasise that the Gurindji people's history is alive and organic. There is no way of learning 'the entire Gurindji history'. It would be fair to say that there is no such thing as 'the entire Gurindji history' – the Gurindji history should be open-ended. My purpose for this visit was to confirm the Gurindji people's acceptance of my draft. I still needed to edit the draft, but I wondered if I should change the context or add new stories after their confirmation. They probably would not mind. But I decided not to do so.

## DID I DO A GOOD JOB?

In the end, I did not receive any serious objections to my draft from the Gurindji people. I got the impression that they were, even before my presentation, confident that I had done a good job. They certainly liked hearing my talk as well as looking at the photos. However, they basically picked up the parts which they understood from my talk and showed their approval rather than carefully examining my presentation. I realised that, for the Gurindji people, this whole process was an opportunity for them to show their trust in me, rather than to examine my draft.

Did I really do a good job? To be honest, I don't know. I do not know because there are still difficult questions left over: did I present my draft to them in a fair manner? Is it acceptable that I did not present my draft to everybody who contributed to this project? Is it inevitably just lip service unless they read through the thesis? I am just hopeful that I did my best at this stage.

On the one hand, I concluded that expressing their trust in me rather than thoroughly examining the draft was the Gurindji way of showing their approval. However, at the same time, I cannot help hoping that the Gurindji people of the 'New Generation' will read through my thesis in the future and provide their – possibly more critical? – feedback.

## PLACE-TIME AND HISTORY

I shall summarise here the Gurindji mode of history, which I have tried to characterise as 'place-oriented history'.

It was clear that the Gurindji historians generally see two major discontinuities in their history: (1) before and after Captain Cook, thus precolonial and colonial, and (2) before and after the walk-off, thus colonial and postcolonial. These are major periodic blocks that the Gurindji historians are conscious of. However, what is not clear, or is not too strict, is the Gurindji historians' application of seemingly chronological periodisation within each block, especially in the colonial part of their history, such as 'shoot 'em time', 'Vestey time' or 'hungry time'.

I discovered that one should not simply understand the Gurindji people's notion of '(––) time' in a strictly chronological sense. There were events where *ngumpin* were shot by *kartiya*, and there was also a story about when *kartiya* stopped shooting and started to attract *ngumpin* to the station as stockworkers. They sometimes mentioned that the shooting had happened 'before Vestey time'. Therefore, the Gurindji history seems to give us a certain sequence: from 'shoot 'em time' to 'Vestey time'.

However, we also need to remember that Captain Cook came to the Gurindji country in order to set up cattle stations, and therefore the Vestey mob appeared in the Gurindji country from the very beginning of colonisation. When people told me the story of 'stop shooting and start working for *kartiya*', they never said it occurred at the 'beginning of the Vestey time'. The stories of Old Jimmy's mother and granny getting shot by *kartiya* were clearly narrated as events that happened in Limbunya station – this was during the 'Vestey time'. The stories of *ngumpin* stealing cattle also overlap with the 'shoot 'em time' and the 'Vestey time'. Notions of 'shoot 'em time' and 'Vestey time' are *not* as clearly chronological as they appear at first glance. Rather, there were events of 'shooting' as well as of 'not shooting', both of which overlap within a category of *larrapa* or 'olden time'.

Although academic historians emphasise the gradual process of the transition 'from bush to station', it seems to me that they still try to pinpoint the year of this shift. They generally agree that the Aboriginal people in the Victoria River district settled down at the stations as workers by the late 1920s,[2] the killing of Aboriginals by Europeans had ceased by the 1930s,[3] and many Aboriginal people lived in both the bush and on stations until the 1940s.[4] I do not disagree with all these indexes in terms of their accuracy, but I would also like to emphasise that for the Gurindji historians, 'more shooting in earlier days and more working for *kartiya* in later days' is enough information in terms of the temporal structure of the Gurindji history.

In order to understand the Gurindji sense of '(––) time' we need to shift our attention from chronological order to spatial order. In his *Land is Life* (1999), Richard Baker says his major purpose is to illustrate:

> the value of considering Indigenous notions of history and
> geography. An understanding of how Aboriginal people
> classify periods of their pasts and perceive their environment
> is fundamental to the study of cultural contact.[5]

Thus, unlike many other academic historians, Baker applies the periodisation used by the Yanyuwa people, such as 'wild times', 'police times', 'welfare times', 'cattle times', 'land rights (Gough Whitlam) times' and 'these (tourist) times'.[6] He also warns us that such times 'should not be seen as neatly divided periods, as they are often overlapping'.[7]

However, since the Indigenous notion of 'history' and that of 'geography' are argued in a relatively separate manner, the intricate *relationship* between 'history and geography' is not fully focused on in Baker's work. I share with Baker the value of using the Aboriginal notion of '(––) times' as well as acknowledging its overlapping quality. Nevertheless, even though he gives an excellent analysis of the cultural geography or landscape of the Yanyuwa people within the framework of 'contact history', the very concept of periodisation and history still remains purely 'temporal' in Baker's discussion.

Here I need to remind you once again of Howard Morphy's notion of 'time being subordinated to space' in Aboriginal cosmology.[8] If we want to explore the Indigenous notion of history and geography, I believe we should look into the *connection* between 'time' and 'space', 'history' and 'geography'. In the Gurindji cosmology, time *is* space, and history *is* place, which leads us to the framework of a 'place-oriented history'.

In place-oriented history, the very concept of 'history' is not purely temporal any more. In the Gurindji historical practice, history is more about locality than periods. In other words, history is *more spatial than temporal*. Obviously, the Gurindji historians are conscious that more shooting happened in the earlier days, and more 'working for *kartiya*' happened later. Therefore it is not wrong to say, 'from shoot 'em time to Vestey time'. However, for the Gurindji people, this temporal order seems less important than the spatial order or *localised context* of the events.

I believe I showed enough examples to confirm the above idea. First of all, you have to connect yourself to places to explore the history. Such place-oriented historical practice leads you to place-oriented historical knowledge. Therefore the historical questions are not so much about 'when' but more about 'where' or 'which direction'. For instance, Blackfella Knob *is the history* of 'shoot 'em time', and Lipananyku *holds the history* of starting stockwork for *kartiya*. The spatial direction from north down to south *is the history* of Captain Cook, and the Major's history *is his movement* from east to west outside the Gurindji country. 'Vestey time' is *localised* in cattle stations, but 'holiday time' is *not located* in 'Vestey time', but has its places in the bush. In contrast, 'hungry time' is *localised* in cattle stations. Furthermore, the history of Jacky Pantamarra is strongly connected to the Gurindji moral geography. And the story of the Gurindji walk-off would not be understood without knowing the important connections between places (the Gurindji country, 'union country' and 'America') as well as the spatial movement from Jimparrak to Daguragu.

'Place' is a much more fundamental element than 'time' in the Gurindji historical practice. It is not chronology but places that construct and form the 'backbone' of the Gurindji mode of history.

## PERFORMING HISTORIES

Following is how Greg Dening describes 'writing':

> ... writing is theatre and the writer a performer. The writer's goal, in the words of the theatre, is to 'produce effects'. Make someone laugh, make someone cry, make someone angry. And

the writer does it in performance. All the possibilities, all the perfectibilities are closed down in a performance to one 'there you have it'. The writer is vulnerable at this moment. Writing, I said to a friend, is like dropping a stone into a deep well and waiting for the splash. No, he replied, it is like dropping a rose petal into the Grand Canyon and waiting for the bang.[9]

Whatever I say about the Gurindji historical practice and cross-cultural communication, there is no doubt that, ultimately, this book is a product of my writing – my performance.

I have no intention of comparing the 'quality' of my study with the great historians' works. However, as an 'effects producer', I wanted to combine Henry Reynolds' *The Other Side of the Frontier* (1981) and *Why Weren't We Told?* (1999);[10] the interaction between 'the other side' and my personal search for Aboriginal history. I also intended to combine Ann McGrath and Deborah B. Rose; the interaction between bright/positive and dark/negative narrations of Aboriginal history. Furthermore, I tried to combine Dipesh Chakrabarty and Greg Dening; the interaction between 'provincialising Europe' and 'a poetic for histories' in current historiography.

But I remind you: these desires of mine as a writer originate not simply from my readings, but rather from my interaction with the Gurindji people. To be precise, my readings of the above works helped and encouraged me to realise my desire to set up a theatre in which I can perform the dialogue between the Gurindji historians, heterogeneous pasts and presents, places, Dreaming, and myself.

I feel that I have been writing a long letter to whoever you are, reader. I wanted to share with you how challenging but enjoyable it is to perform cross-cultural practice. I also wanted to share with you how apparently impossible but still possible it is to 'communicate over the gap'. Above all, I wanted to share with you the teachings from the Gurindji country. Now, I post it to you – *the writer is vulnerable at this moment.*

It is up to you whether you shift your being fully into the Gurindji historical reality (if you think you can), or firmly reject it. An alternative choice is what I have been struggling with throughout this book: trying to find a way of being cross-cultural and sharing the experiential historical truthfulness. I believe cross-cultural practice, by definition, cannot avoid the risk of destabilising one's own cultural framework. Otherwise, what is the point of calling it 'cross-cultural'?

As a student of the Gurindji historians, I would like to close this book by quoting Jimmy Mangayarri. I believe this statement tells us something terribly important about history: 'You never kill history. (If) you break it, history kill you!'

I threw a petal.

Let's wait for the bang.

# NOTES

## CHAPTER 1

1   Hokari 1996b.
2   Aboriginal Land Commissioner 1982: 3.
3   This includes Malgin and Wanyjirra. The even broader context includes Mudburra and Ngarinman. However, Warlpiri people living in Daguragu and Kalkaringi often identify themselves as Warlpiri, not Gurindji.
4   McConvell & Hargen 1981.
5   Among many Aboriginal societies, including the Gurindji, 'country' refers to the land on which they live as well as the land with which they have genealogical, ancestral and spiritual connections.
6   Berndt & Berndt 1987: 72–73.
7   Berndt & Berndt 1987: 286.
8   See Chapter 7.
9   To be fair, I want to emphasise that it was only Old Jimmy who said Dreaming told me to visit the Gurindji country.
10  Attwood 1989: 142–45.
11  Klaus Neuman makes a similar criticism of Richard Broome. See Neumann 1998: 10–12.
12  Attwood 1989: 145; McGrath 1995a: 385.
13  A similar point can be found in Ota 1996: 301.
14  Examination of the Gurindji understanding of Christianity requires another book. However, briefly speaking, most Gurindji *do not* regard Christianity or '*Ngaji* [Father/God] way' as European Dreaming; some say *Ngaji* way is for 'everybody', and others say *kartiya* [whites] do not know/ understand the *Ngaji* way.
15  A leader of the political party One Nation, which attacks multiculturalism, Aboriginal rights, and the 'Asianisation' of Australia.

16 On the resurgence of racism in Australia, see, for example, Gray & Winter 1997.
17 I wish to express my gratitude to Ann McGrath, Ann Curthoys and all the participants of the Visiting Scholar Program held by the Centre for Cross-Cultural Research, ANU in 1999. Without their encouragement, I would never have dared to write my thesis and later this book in such an experimental way.

## CHAPTER 2

1 A similar point is made by Rose 1999.
2 Rose 1996: 23.
3 See Chapter 3.
4 Kolig 1987: 128.
5 See, for example, Yengoyan 1968; Rose 1987.
6 Chatwin 1987.
7 *Holy Bible: New International Version*, John 1: 1–4.
8 Strehlow 1970: 129. See also Rose 1996: 35–47.
9 Rose describes it as 'a non-human being-centred cosmos'. See Rose 1992: 105.
10 Similar points are discussed in Myers 1986; Rose 1992.

## CHAPTER 3

1 See, for example, Strehlow 1947; Mountford 1965; Eliade 1973; Biernoff 1978; Myers 1986; Munn 1986; Morphy 1991, 1995; Layton 1995.
2 See, for example, Clarke 1991; Morphy 1993; Swain 1993; Rose 1996; Magowan 1997.
3 Swain 1993.
4 Similar criticism of Swain's work is to be found in Keen 1993. A review symposium on *A Place for Strangers* is in *Social Analysis* no. 40. See Austin-Broos 1996; Beckett 1996; Lattas 1996; Morton 1996. Swain's reply is in Swain 1996.
5 Rudder 1993: Chapter 6.
6 Morphy 1995: 188.
7 Swain 1993: 2.
8 Morphy 1995.
9 Sutton 1988.
10 See, for example, Morphy & Morphy 1984; Beckett 1994; Rumsey 1994.
11 Kolig 1980a; Rose 1984, 1989, 1991: Chapter 3, 1992: Chapter 11; Mackinolty & Wainburranga 1988.
12 See, especially, Rose 1984.
13 One of the exceptions may be the story of Ned Kelly. Among the Aboriginal people in the Victoria River district, Ned Kelly is a moral European. It is important to note that Ned Kelly's story is a Dreaming story for local

people. Ned Kelly is even located in a geographical space at Crawford knob in Karangpuru country (Rose 1994). Immoral Europeans, such as Captain Cook, cannot be Dreaming, but if he/she is regarded as a moral European, even a European can be Dreaming. Likewise, some Christian or Bible-oriented stories are also filtered into Dreaming in Aboriginal cosmology (Kolig 1978, 1980b; Swain 1988).

14  I am not permitted to discuss the specific *Jurntakal* stories here because many of these stories are men's secrets.
15  See Chapter 2.
16  Rose 1992: 57.
17  Rose 1996: 9. See also Rose 1992: Chapter 3.
18  Old Jimmy's view of European education reflects the schooling program in the community. It is very rare for a person from the community to go to a high school or even higher education which is away from the community.
19  Rose 1991: 265.
20  This word may be 'Ireland' instead of 'island' because they sound very similar. However, since I did not learn any stories about 'Ireland' from Gurindji historians, I do not have the necessary information to explore why Old Jimmy might have said 'Ireland' in this context.
21  Tommy Vincent Lingiari was a leader of the Gurindji walk-off. See Chapter 7.

## CHAPTER 4

1   Rose 1992: 186.
2   Rose 1992: 186.
3   Rose 1992: 186.
4   Concerning the situation of such sexual relations at the Wave Hill station, see Hokari 1996b: 72–74. McGrath argues that Aboriginal women hold different perspectives on this 'problem'. See McGrath 1987a: Chapter 4.
5   About Macassans and Aboriginal interactions, see, for example, Macknight 1976; Cole 1975: 8–9, 1979: Chapter 6. About crocodile hunters, see, for example, Ronan 1966; Cole 1988.
6   Riddett 1985: 206.
7   Berndt & Berndt 1987: 58.
8   Rose 1991: 8. On Aboriginal ceremonial networks, see also McCarthy 1939; Thomson 1949; Mulvaney 1976.
9   On Dutch explorers, see, for example, Yarwood & Knowling 1982: Chapter 2; Mulvaney 1990: 2–7.
10  See Cole 1979: Chapter 7.
11  Davidson et al. 1998: 355.
12  Rose 1992: 186.
13  This name also can be spelt 'Kin Loos' or 'King Louis'. However, I do not have the information necessary to further explore the origin of Jacky Pantamarra's English name.
14  Hokari 2002a.

15  Hokari 1996a, 1996b.
16  Attwood 1989. See also Attwood & Arnold 1992; Reece 1987.
17  Stanner 1979: 24.
18  Elkin 1964: 234.
19  Rose 1992: 205.
20  Swain 1993: 22–28.
21  Hobbles Danayarri, quote from Rose 1991: 265.
22  Rose 1992: 205.
23  See Chapter 9.
24  McGrath 1995a: 361–62, 386.
25  McGrath 1995a: 389.
26  McGrath 1995a: 389.


## CHAPTER 5

1  See also quote from Jimmy Mangayarri, in Rose 1991:  265.
2  Buchanan 1997: Chapter 12.
3  Buchanan 1997: 140.
4  See, for example, Middleton 1979: 114.
5  On the establishment of Bow Hill police station (1913) and the later shift
   to Wave Hill (1918), see Rose 1991: 71.
6  See also Rose 1991: 41–42.
7  I could not figure out why Ronnie holds such high authority regarding this
   particular story.
8  Since this story of the first *ngumpin* living with *kartiya* is disconnected from
   the sequence of a later story about two *ngumpin* who helped *kartiya* bring
   the Gurindji mob into the station, I suspect there is a connection between
   this japarta and Old Jimmy's story of 'japarta buluki-waji', which I will
   discuss in the next chapter. Both stories tell us about the first contact with
   settler society (cattle/settlers) that occurred west of the Gurindji country.
   And in both stories the key Aboriginal person's skin name was japarta. It is
   nothing more than speculation, but it seems these two japarta could have
   been the same person, who bravely and peacefully approached settlers and
   stayed with them for a while in the very early stages of colonisation. It is
   reasonable to assume that the japarta's stories of eating beef and learning
   English have been separately narrated among the Gurindji historians
   because of the 'separate roles' of *kartiya* and *buluki* in Gurindji historical
   practice.
9  McGrath 1987a: 114–15.
10  NTAS F292 *Police Station – WAVE HILL (Commonwealth)*, Police Journals
   1916–1977. 19-7-1956.
11  'Native Situation at Wave Hill' (1947) in NAA (Darwin) F1 1946/450
   *Ill-treatment of Aboriginals*.
12  See, for example, 'Murderous Blacks in the Territory', *Northern Territory
   Times and Gazette*, 10-6-1895; 'Attack by Blacks at Wave Hill', *Northern
   Territory Times and Gazette*, 20-1-1899. However, since the incidents

happened mainly in the northern part of Wave Hill station – on the border between the Ngarinman and the Gurindji countries – it is not clear if the attack was conducted by the Gurindji people.

13  Read & Read 1991: Chapter 3; Rose 1991: Chapters 7, 14, 23.
14  Chisholm 1973; Webster 1980; Turnbull & Broadhurst 1983; Roderick 1988.
15  Old Jimmy did not know which country they were working in.
16  Here, I mainly use an account from Shaw 1983. See also Shaw & Sullivan 1979: 104–07; Sullivan & Shaw 1983: 70–74, 215–19; Durack 1983: 197–200.
17  Shaw 1983: 11.
18  Shaw 1983: 11.
19  Shaw 1983: 13–14.
20  Shaw 1983: 14–16.
21  Shaw 1983: 16.
22  Shaw 1983: 17–19.
23  Quote from Jack Sullivan, in Shaw 1983: 19; Shaw & Sullivan 1979: 107; Sullivan & Shaw 1983: 74.
24  Read & Read 1991: 55–62.
25  Rose 1991: 55–56.
26  Rose 1991: 57–58.
27  Rose 1991: 59.
28  Rose 1991: 58, 61.
29  Rose 1991: 62.
30  Ruby Roney, interview with Monica Weedon and Joy Collins, NT Archives Service, NTRS 226, TS 517, n.d., pp. 9–10.
31  Rose 1991: 62.
32  See Rose 1991: Chapters 7, 14; Read & Read 1991: Part 1, Chapter 3.
33  Out of respect for the feelings of his family, I do not specify the name of the deceased person or dates of the episode.
34  NTAS F292 *Police Station – WAVE HILL (Commonwealth)*, Police Journals 1916–1977. 13-9-1961.


**CHAPTER 6**

1  McGrath 1987a: 149.
2  Buchanan 1997: Chapter 12; Buchanan 1933: 70.
3  McGrath 1987a: 13.
4  McGrath 1987a: 16.
5  McGrath 1987a: 13–16, 180.
6  May 1994: 38.
7  McConvell & Hargen 1981: 85–86.
8  McGrath 1987a: 6–9.
9  Rose 1996: Chapter 7.
10  McGrath 1987a: 149–50.
11  McGrath 1987a: 149.
12  Personal communication with Deborah B. Rose.

13 McGrath 1987a: 47.

14 McGrath 1987a: 40.

15 Discussion on *kaya* is also to be found in Rose 1992: 92–93.

16 I have not met this lucky person who survived a *kaya*'s kidnapping.

17 Banjo said he could not speak this old person's name.

18 Hobbles Danayarri told Rose his experience with *mungamunga* at a stock camp. See Rose 1992: 96–97.

19 See also Fitzherbert 1989: 6.

20 'The Flood at Wave Hill', in NTAS F589 *Wave Hill Police Letter Book 1919–1931*, 11-2-1924.

21 A brief version of this story was documented in Fitzherbert 1989: 6.

22 McConvell & Hargen 1981: 84.

23 Hokari 1996a: 23–24; 1996b: Chapter 5.

24 Rowse 1988b: 72. See also McGrath 1987a: 153–60.

25 Wightman et al. 1994: 54–55.

26 Berndt & Berndt 1987: 75.

27 Berndt & Berndt 1987: 70.

28 McGrath 1987a: 159.

29 See, for example, McGrath 1987a: 38, 158; Rose 1992: 20; Meggitt 1955: 45–50; Riddett 1985: 206.

30 In Chapters 5 and 6 I *tacitly* challenge the previous historical understanding of cattle stations and Aboriginal labour in northern Australia. For those who are interested in its background, see Hokari 2001, in which I *explicitly* explore and criticise previous studies on this issue.


## CHAPTER 7

1 There are numerous articles related to this event. Here I select some articles from newspapers and magazines: On the news of the Gurindji walk-off, see, for example, *The Northern Territory Times* 26-8-1966; *Sydney Morning Herald* 27-8-1966; *The Age* 27-8-1966; *The Australian* 18-10-1966; *Tribune* 21-6-1967; *Smoke Signals* 1967. On the returning of their land, see, for example, *The Australian* 24-1-1972; *Canberra Times* 24-1-1972; *The Advertiser* 1-27-1972; *ABM Review* vol. 63, no. 3, 1973; *Northern Territory Newsletter* August 1975.
For a more historical or encyclopaedic retrospective, beyond what I discuss later, see, for example, Maddock 1972: 7–27; Broome 1982: 141, 177; Kijngayari 1986; Lingiari 1986; Read 1995: 291–92; Horton et al. 1994: 443, 1164–65; Davison et al. 1998: 6, 296.

2 Hardy 1968.

3 Macintyre 1985: 127.

4 Riddett 1997: 50.

5 Attwood 2000: 8.

6 Attwood 2000: 4–5.

7 Previously, I argued that the Gurindji walk-off was not a 'strike' but it was, in a sense, a 'land rights movement' (Hokari 2000). However, I developed

my understanding further and am now convinced it was not even a 'land rights' or 'land claim' in the Western sense of these terms.

8    Middleton 1972, 1978, 1979.
9    Briscoe 1986: Chapter 5.
10   On the theory of internal colonialism, see, for example, Wolpe 1980a. For applying the theory to Aboriginal history, see, for example, Beckett 1977; Hartwig 1978.
11   Jowett 1990.
12   On the theory of articulation of mode of production, see, for example, Clammer 1975; Foster-Carter 1978; Wolpe 1980b. For applying the theory to Aboriginal history, see, for example, May 1994: 3–4; McConvell 1989.
13   Hokari 1996a, 1996b.
14   Doolan 1977.
15   McConvell & Hargen 1981: 81–127.
16   Aboriginal Land Commissioner 1982: 3–7.
17   McGrath 1995b: 44.
18   Riddett 1997.
19   Jowett 1990; Riddett 1990: Chapters 8–9; 1997.
20   McConvell & Hargen 1981: 81–127. See, for other examples, Neilley 1970; NTAS: NTRS 226 TS 485; Bernard 1996.
21   Aboriginal Land Commissioner 1982.
22   Rose 1991: Chapter 24.
23   Quote from Hobbles Danayarri, in Rose 1991: 229.
24   Quote from Vincent Lingiari, in Hardy 1968: 71.
25   Quote from Captain Major, in Hardy 1968: 30–31.
26   Quote from Dexter Daniels, in Hardy 1968: 28.
27   Rose 1991: 226. According to the census report, 1962, Sandy Moray was born in 1905. See NAA: E944/0 WAVE HILL 4.
28   Hardy 1968: 161.
29   I also found his name in the Aboriginal employment records at Wave Hill station. For example, Sandy Moray had worked for 29 weeks in 1952, zero weeks in 1953, and 14 weeks up to July in 1954. He earned £1 per week, as most of the other male Aboriginal workers did. See 'Employment of Aboriginals in the Pastoral Industry, Wave Hill Station', in NAA: F1 52/736; NAA: F1 53/674.
30   See also McGrath 1987: a photo page between 84–85; Cole 1988: 196.
31   Wightman et al. 1994: 50–51.
32   I personally think another walk-off leader, Captain Major, could have been there as well. Peanut told me that Bob Warriyawun passed away before the walk-off began.
33   Quote from Riley Young, in Rose 1991: 226.
34   Personal communication with Patrick McConvell.
35   Quote from Captain Major, in Hardy 1968: 30.
36   McGrath's interview with Captain Major, in A. McGrath's Fieldnote 20-6-77, Daguragu.
37   Rowley suggests that they may have had contact with the Pilbara people (Rowley 1971b: 338). On the Pilbara walk-off, see, for example, Stuart 1959;

Wilson 1980: 151–68; McLeod 1984; Hess 1994. Hess argues that it was 'a tribal law meeting' that initiated the Pilbara strike (Hess 1994: 71). This view certainly corresponds to my argument about the Gurindji's initiative for the Wave Hill walk-off.

38  Hardy 1968: 21, 24, 64–65.
39  Attwood 2000: 5–8.
40  Rowley 1971b: 338.
41  Quote from Captain Major, in Hardy 1968: 30.
42  Dexter Daniels indicated to Hardy that he had been to many stations and 'they are ready to fight' (Hardy 1968: 24–26). Aborigines from Brunette Downs went on strike, but they soon went back to work (Hardy 1968: 27). As we know, successful actions have only been led by the Gurindji men, i.e. Newcastle Waters and Wave Hill.
43  Hardy 1968: 27.
44  Quote from Captain Major, in Hardy 1968: 31.
45  Quote from Captain Major, in Hardy 1968: 32.
46  See Chapter 3.
47  See Chapter 8.
48  Rose 1992: 194.
49  Rose 1992: 193.
50  Rose 1992: 193. Rose does not refer to the 'Big American Boss' as President Kennedy.
51  Quote from Hobbles Danayarri, in Rose 1992: 193.
52  Hardy 1968: 68–69, 72.
53  Jowett 1990: 44.
54  See, for example, Thomson 1949; Yengoyan 1968; Kolig 1984; Rose 1987.
55  See, for example, Young & Dooham 1989.
56  Hardy 1968: 111.
57  Hardy 1968: 156.
58  Hardy 1968: 93.
59  Rose 1991: 227.
60  Hardy 1968: 109–10.
61  Hardy 1968: 166.
62  Hardy 1968: 166–67.
63  See, for example, Attwood 2000.
64  Hardy 1968: 74.
65  Hardy 1968: 74, 78–79.
66  Hardy 1968: 70–71.
67  Doolan 1977; McConvell & Hargen 1981: 123; Rose 1991: 229.
68  Rose 1991: 229.
69  Rose 1991: 229–30.
70  Quote from Vincent Lingiari, in Hardy 1968: 158.
71  Quote from Vincent Lingiari, in Hardy 1968: 159.
72  Quote from Captain Major, in Hardy 1968: 34.
73  Hardy 1978: 111.
74  Jowett 1990: 60. See, for other examples, Hardy 1968: 167; Forest 1985: 13; Department of Aboriginal Affairs 1986: 5.

75 Petition to the Governor-General, 19 April 1967, in McConvell & Hargen 1981: 109; Attwood & Markus 1999: 223–25.
76 McConvell & Hargen 1981: 58.
77 Strehlow 1970: 129.
78 See Chapter 2. See also Rose 1996: Chapter 4.
79 Department of the Interior 1968.
80 McConvell & Hargen 1981: 117; Department of Aboriginal Affairs 1986; Jowett 1990: 72.
81 Quote from Pincher Nyurrmiyari (Manguari), in Northern Territory Council for Aboriginal Rights 1968.
82 Middleton 1979: 116; Jowett 1990: 73.
83 Jowett 1990: 73.
84 Jowett 1990: 59.
85 Department of Aboriginal Affairs 1975; McConvell & Hargen 1981: 120–24.
86 On Abschol activities at Wattie Creek see, for example, Oke & Oke 1969; Abschol 1970; Franklin 1976: 183.
87 Rose 1991: 228.
88 Rose 1991: 229.
89 Doolan 1977: 107.
90 Goodall 1996: 324–27.
91 Quote from Vincent Lingiari, in Hardy 1968: 101.
92 Quote from Pincher Nyurrmiyari (Manguari), in Hardy 1968: 111.
93 Quote from Long Johnny Kitgnaari, in Hardy 1968: 112.

## CHAPTER 8

1 Rose 1996: Chapter 7.
2 Berndt & Berndt 1987: 72–73. The Berndts' research in Wave Hill station was done in 1944. The medical survey conducted at Wave Hill station in 1953 also described a similar amount of rations. It shows that there was not much improvement in Aboriginal rations after the Berndts' report. See 'Report on the Medical Survey of the Wave Hill Station, July, 1953', in NAA (Darwin), F1 1952/736.
3 Berndt & Berndt 1987: 73–74.
4 Berndt & Berndt 1987: 75.
5 See also Rose 1991: Chapter 17.
6 See Chapter 7. See also Hardy 1968: 30, McGrath 1987a: 141.
7 'Native Situation at Wave Hill' (1947), in NAA (Darwin) F1 1946/450 *Ill-treatment of Aboriginals*. Similar discussions can be found in 'Native Affairs Branch Report on Inspection Aboriginals (Pastoral Industry) Regulations 1918–1947 Wave Hill Station', in NAA (Darwin), F1 1952/736; 'Report on Patrol Western Stations Alice Springs, 29th June, 1945', in NAA (Darwin), F1 1944/275; 'Report on Medical Survey of the Wave Hill Station, July 1953', in NAA (Darwin), F1 1952/736.
8 See also Rose 1991: Chapter 27.
9 Doolan 1977: 110.

10 Chakrabarty 2000; Hardt & Negri 2000.
11 See Chapter 4.
12 Billy is also a member of the Daguragu Community Government Council.
13 Billy Bunter appears in Hardy's *The Unlucky Australians* as schoolteacher at Wattie Creek: Hardy 1968: 206, 230.

## CHAPTER 9

1 Chakrabarty 2000: 98.
2 Chakrabarty 2000: 97.
3 Chakrabarty 2000: 97.
4 Foucault 1970, 1976.
5 Perheentupa 1998.
6 Stanner 1968. See also McGrath 1995a: 365–66.
7 Rowley 1970, 1971a, 1971b.
8 Biskup 1973.
9 Evans, Saunders & Cronin 1975.
10 McGrath 1995a: 367.
11 Urry 1979; Cowlishaw 1992.
12 Major anthropological studies of 'ahistorical' 'traditional' Aboriginal societies are Spencer 1914; Spencer & Gillen 1938; Elkin 1945, 1964; Strehlow 1947, 1971; Thomson 1949; Stanner 1964; Meggitt 1965; Hiatt 1965.
13 Reynolds 1981.
14 See, for example, Robinson & York 1977; Loos 1982.
15 See, for example, McGrath 1987a; May 1983, 1994; Reynolds 1990, 2000; Ganter 1994; Grimshaw et al. 1994.
16 Perks & Thomson 1998: ix.
17 Ngabidj & Shaw 1981.
18 See, for example, Sullivan & Shaw 1983; Shaw 1992.
19 Read 1988.
20 See, for example, Read & Read 1991; Read 1984, 1999.
21 McGrath 1987a.
22 Human Rights and Equal Opportunity Commission 1997. See also Mellor & Haebich 2002.
23 Review articles on McGrath's *Born in the Cattle* highlight this issue. See, for example, Rowse 1988a, 1988b; Attwood 1988. McGrath's response is in McGrath 1988.
24 Attwood 1989; Attwood & Arnold 1992. See also Reece 1987.
25 See, for example, Cowlishaw 1992.
26 Quote from Smith 1980, in Attwood 1992: xvi.
27 See, for example, Perkins 1975; Barker & Mathews 1977; Morgan 1988; Langford 1988.
28 Morgan 1992.
29 See, for example, Briscoe 1986, 1989, 1993, 1994, 1996, 2003.
30 See, for example, Maynard 1987, 1988.

31 See, for example, Huggins & Huggins 1994; McGrath et al. 1995; Huggins et al. 1997; Huggins 1998.
32 See, for example, Birch 1992, 1993, 1995.
33 Goodall 1992: 119. See also McGrath 1987b. Footnotes 63–66 provide further examples.
34 Benterrak, Muecke & Roe 1984.
35 Rose 1991.
36 Baker 1999.
37 Evans 1997: 3–4.
38 Joyce 1997: 247.
39 Spiegel 1997: 184.
40 Friedlander 1992.
41 Appleby, Hunt & Jacob 1994. Chakrabarty's review article helped me understand this point (Chakrabarty 1996).
42 Curthoys & Docker 1996.
43 Eliade 1954.
44 Lévi-Strauss 1966.
45 *Representations*' special issues on 'memory' (no. 26, 1989) and 'remembering' (no. 69, 1995) are good examples of historians' attention to this topic.
46 Typically and famously, see Nora 1989.
47 See, for example, Hutton 1993.
48 See, for example, Davis & Starn 1989; Le Goff 1992; Darian-Smith & Hamilton 1994.
49 Curthoys & Docker 1999: 6.
50 Evans, 1997: 124–28.
51 Spivak 1996: 292.
52 Ota 2001: 19, 117.
53 Chakrabarty points to a similar problem. See Chakrabarty 2000: 105.
54 Chakrabarty 2000: 97.
55 I owe the notions of 'fragments (not referring to an implicit whole)' and 'irreducible (plurality)' to Chakrabarty. See Chakrabarty 2000: 107–08, 2002: 34–35.
56 The idea of 'localised history' has already been briefly discussed in Hokari 2002b: 4–7.
57 For other examples of localised Captain Cook history, see Kolig 1980a: 2; Rose 1984; Mackinolty & Wainburranga 1988.
58 Not to mention that one should not overlook the danger of exaggeration of 'academic historiography' as a mode of 'Western' 'universality'. For example, historical studies organised in Japanese universities may not necessarily detach themselves from 'non-Western' 'traditional' modes of historical writing and purely rely on 'Western' academic framework. Or, more fundamentally, as for example Naoki Sakai repeatedly points out, the notion of the 'West' itself is already highly problematic (Sakai 2001). In addition, the inevitably ambivalent nature of the notion of 'universality' is also repeatedly discussed by, for example, Judith Butler, Ernesto Laclau and Slavoj Zizek (Butler, Laclau & Zizek 2000). However, as Sakai correctly argues, 'curiously, nowhere in the world does the term "the West" seem to

have lost its universal appeal and immediate intelligibility' (Sakai 2001: 87). Therefore, I intentionally dare to use the term 'universal' as the extension of 'the West' in order to make the problems around these terms visible.

59  Rose 1991: 17.
60  Spivak 1988: 295.
61  Chakrabarty 2000: 104.
62  Chakrabarty 2000: 106.
63  Hamamoto 1984: 283.
64  Chakrabarty 2000: 108.
65  Chakrabarty 2000: 111.
66  Chakrabarty 2000: 108–13.
67  See, for example, Eliade 1954, 1959. Eliade's following statements seem to me the most relevant to my argument: '"(M)odern man" is such in his insistence upon being exclusively historical; i.e., that he is, above all, the "man" of historicism, of Marxism, and of existentialism. It is superfluous to add that not all of our contemporaries recognize themselves in such a man' (Eliade 1954: 156). On Chakrabarty's critique of historicism, see Chakrabarty 2000: 3–23.
68  In a similar manner, Chakrabarty criticises Eric Hobsbawm's category of 'pre-political'. Chakrabarty 2000: 11–13.
69  Chakrabarty 2000: 240, 254–55. See also Goodall & Cowlishaw 2001: 2–3.
70  Following Stephen Muecke's suggestion, I use the term 'communication' not in the sense of 'ideal sameness through "effective", "skilful" or "smooth" communication' but based on '*relative* difference' (italics in original). See Benterrak, Muecke & Roe 1984: 18.
71  I thank John Docker, who told me the term 'post-secularism'. For literature, see, for example, Docker 2001; Connolly 1999; Bond 1998.
72  Connolly 1999: 184–87.
73  Connolly 1999: 16.
74  Spivak 1988: 308.
75  Dening 1996: 45.
76  Dening 1996: 36–37. A similar point can be found in Cohen 1994.
77  The idea of 'cross-culturalising history' first appeared in my PhD thesis. See Hokari 2001.
78  Morris-Suzuki 2002a.
79  Morris-Suzuki 2001, 2002b.
80  In fact, Morris-Suzuki uses the term 'cosmetic multiculturalism' in the context of the political economy of a nation. See Morris-Suzuki 2002a.
81  Hage 1998.
82  Morris-Suzuki 2001.
83  Morris-Suzuki 2001: 304.
84  Morris-Suzuki 2001: 304.
85  Morris-Suzuki 2001: 303–04.
86  Rose 1996: 32.

## CHAPTER 10

1   I acknowledge Peter Read, who suggested I receive approval from the Gurindji people before publication.
2   McConvell & Hargen 1981: 87.
3   Rose 1991: 73.
4   McGrath 1987a; Riddett 1985: 205.
5   Baker 1999: 7.
6   Baker 1999: 65–124.
7   Baker 1999: 61.
8   See Chapter 3.
9   Dening 1998: xix–xx.
10  Reynolds 1999.

# BIBLIOGRAPHY

## ARCHIVAL SOURCES

### National Archives of Australia (NAA), Darwin

E944/0 WAVE HILL 4. Census Report – Wave Hill 4.
F1 1944/275. Patrol Officer WE Harney Patrol & Reports.
F1 1946/450. Ill-treatment of Aboriginals.
F1 1952/736. Wave Hill Station.
F1 1953/674. Native Affairs Branch – Wave Hill Station – Maintenance of
Government Dependants (Aboriginals).

### Northern Territory Archival Service (NTAS)

F292. Police Station – WAVE HILL (Commonwealth), Police Journals
1916–77.
F589. Wave Hill Police Letter Book (1919–31).
NTRS 226. TS 485 Mick Rangiari, interview by Jack Doolan, 1986.
NTRS 226. TS 517 Ruby Roney, interview by Monica Weedon and Joy Collins.

## GOVERNMENT PUBLICATIONS

Aboriginal Land Commissioner 1982. *Gurindji Land Claim to Daguragu Station*.
Canberra: Australian Government Publishing Service.
Department of Aboriginal Affairs 1975. Transfer of Part of Wave Hill Pastoral
Lease to Gurindji Community at Wattie Creek (Daguragu). Canberra:
Department of Aboriginal Affairs.
Department of Aboriginal Affairs 1986. *Daguragu: An Historical Perspective of the
Daguragu Land Claim*. Canberra: Department of Aboriginal Affairs.

Department of the Interior 1968. Statement of Aboriginals at Wave Hill,
    Northern Territory. Canberra: Department of the Interior.
Human Rights and Equal Opportunity Commission 1997. *Bringing Them Home:*
    *Report of the National Inquiry into the Separation of Aboriginal and Torres Strait*
    *Islander Children from Their Families.* Sydney: Human Rights and Equal
    Opportunity Commission.

## NEWSPAPERS AND MAGAZINES

*ABM Review*, vol. 63, no. 3, 1973.
*The Advertiser*, 1972.
*The Age*, 1966.
*The Australian*, 1966, 1972.
*Canberra Times*, 1972.
*The Northern Standard*, 1924.
*Northern Territory Newsletter*, August 1975.
*Northern Territory Times*, 1895, 1899, 1924, 1966.
*Smoke Signals*, 1967.
*Sydney Morning Herald*, 1966.
*Tribune*, 1967.

## SECONDARY SOURCES

Abschol 1970. *What Now at Wattie Creek: Report of Abschol Field Team May – June*
    *1970.* Melbourne: Abschol.
Appleby, Joyce, Hunt, Lynn and Jacob, Margaret 1994. *Telling the Truth About*
    *History.* New York: W.W. Norton.
Attwood, Bain 1988. 'Understandings of the Aboriginal Past: History or Myth'.
    *Australian Journal of Politics and History*, vol. 34, no. 2, pp. 265–71.
Attwood, Bain 1989. *The Making of the Aborigines.* Sydney: Allen & Unwin.
Attwood, Bain 1992. 'Introduction', in Bain Attwood amd John Arnold (eds),
    *Power, Knowledge and Aborigines.* Bundoora, Vic.: La Trobe University Press,
    pp. i–xvi.
Attwood, Bain and Arnold, John (eds) 1992. *Power, Knowledge and Aborigines.*
    Bundoora, Vic.: La Trobe University Press.
Attwood, Bain and Markus, Andrew 1999. *The Struggle for Aboriginal Rights: A*
    *Documentary History.* Sydney: Allen & Unwin.
Attwood, Bain 2000. 'The Articulation of "Land Rights" in Australia: The Case
    of Wave Hill', *Social Analysis*, no. 44, pp. 3–39.
Austin-Broos, Diane J. 1996. 'What's in a Time, or a Place?: Reflections on
    Swain's Hypothesis', *Social Analysis*, no. 40, pp. 3–10.
Barker, Jimmie and Mathews, Janet 1977. *The Two Worlds of Jimmie Barker:*
    *The Life of an Australian Aboriginal 1900–1972, as told to Janet Mathews.*
    Canberra: Australian Institute of Aboriginal Studies (AIAS).

Baker, Richard M. 1999. *Land is Life: From Bush to Town: The Story of the Yanyuwa People*. Sydney: Allen & Unwin.

Beckett, Jeremy 1977. 'The Torres Strait Islanders and the Pearling Industry: A Case of Internal Colonialism', *Aboriginal History*, vol. 1, pp. 77–104.

Beckett, Jeremy 1994. 'Aboriginal Histories, Aboriginal Myths: An Introduction', *Oceania*, vol. 65, pp. 97–115.

Beckett, Jeremy 1996. 'A Comment on Tony Swain's A Place for Stranger: Towards a History of Australian Aboriginal Being', *Social Analysis*, no. 40, pp. 11–19.

Benterrak, Krim, Muecke, Stephen and Roe, Paddy 1984. *Reading the Country: Introduction to Nomadology*. Fremantle, WA: Fremantle Arts Centre Press.

Bernard, Ida 1996. *An Oral History from the Wave Hill Strike*. Website: http://jinx.sistm.unsw.edu.au/~greenlft/1996/251/251p15.htm.

Berndt, Ronald M. (ed.) 1970. *Australian Aboriginal Anthropology: Modern Studies in the Social Anthropology of the Australian Aborigines*. Nedlands, WA: University of Western Australia (UWA) Press.

Berndt, Ronald M. (ed.) 1977. *Aborigines and Change: Australia in the '70s*. Canberra: AIAS.

Berndt, Ronald M. and Berndt, Catherine H. (eds) 1980. *Aborigines of the West: Their Past and Their Present*. Nedlands, WA: UWA Press.

Berndt, Ronald M. and Berndt, Catherine H. 1987. *End of an Era: Aboriginal Labour in the Northern Territory*. Canberra: AIAS.

Biernoff, David 1978. 'Safe and Dangerous Places', in L.R. Hiatt (ed.), *Australian Aboriginal Concepts*. Canberra: AIAS, pp. 93–105.

Birch, Tony 1992. 'Nothing Has Changed: The Making and Unmaking of Koorie Culture', *Meanjin*, vol. 51, no. 2, pp. 244–46.

Birch, Tony 1993. 'Real Aborigines – Colonial Attempts to Re-imagine and Re-create the Identities of Aboriginal People', *Ulitarra*, no. 4, pp. 13–21.

Birch, Tony 1995. 'A Mabo Blood Test', *Australian Journal of Anthropology*, vol. 6, no. 122, pp. 32–42.

Biskup, Peter 1973. *Not Slaves, Not Citizens: The Aboriginal Problem in Western Australia, 1898–1954*. Brisbane: University of Queensland Press (UQP).

Bond, Phillip (ed.) 1998. *Post-Secular Philosophy: Between Philosophy and Theology*. London, New York: Routledge.

Briscoe, Gordon 1989. 'Class, Welfare and Capitalism: The Role Aborigines Have Played in the State-building Processes in Northern Territory History', in Richard Kennedy (ed.), *Australian Welfare: Historical Sociology*. Melbourne: Macmillan, pp. 197–215.

Briscoe, Gordon 1993. 'Aboriginal Australian Identity: The Historiography of Relations Between Indigenous Ethnic Groups and Other Australians, 1788 to 1988', *History Workshop Journal*, no. 36, pp. 133–61.

Briscoe, Gordon 1994. 'The Struggle for Grace: An Appreciation of Kevin John Gilbert', *Aboriginal History*, vol. 18, pp. 13–31.

Briscoe, Gordon 2003. *Counting, Health and Identity: A History of Indigenous Health and Demography in Western Australia and Queensland 1900–1940*. Canberra: Aboriginal Studies Press.

Broome, Richard 1982. *Aboriginal Australians: Black Response to White Dominance 1788–1980*. Sydney: Allen & Unwin.

Buchanan, Bobbie 1997. *In the Tracks of Old Bluey*. Central Queensland University Press.

Buchanan, Gordon 1933. *Packhorse and Waterhole: With the First Overlanders to the Kimberleys*. Sydney: Angus & Robertson.

Butler, Judith, Laclau, Ernest and Zizek, Slavoj 2000. *Contingency, Hegemony, Universality: Contemporary Dialogues on the Left*. London: Verso.

Chakrabarty, Dipesh 1996. 'Small Workable Truths', *UTS Review*, vol. 2, pp. 159–63.

Chakrabarty, Dipesh 2000. *Provincializing Europe: Postcolonial Thought and Historical Difference*. Princeton, NJ: Princeton University Press.

Chakrabarty, Dipesh 2002. *Habitations of Modernity: Essays in the Wake of Subaltern Studies*. Chicago: University of Chicago Press.

Charlesworth, Max et al. (eds) 1984. *Religion in Aboriginal Australia: An Anthology*. Brisbane: UQP.

Chatwin, Bruce 1987. *The Songlines*. London: Cape.

Chisholm, Alexander H. 1973. *Strange Journey: The Adventures of Ludwig Leichhardt and John Gilbert*. Adelaide: Rigby.

Clammer, John 1975. 'Economic Anthropology and the Sociology of Development: "Liberal" Anthropology and its French Critics', in Ivar Oxaal, Tony Barnett and David Booth (eds), *Beyond the Sociology of Development: Economy and Society in Latin America and Africa*. London: Routledge & Kegan Paul, pp. 208–28.

Clarke, Philip A. 1991. 'Adelaide as an Aboriginal Landscape', *Aboriginal History*, vol. 15, no. 1, pp. 54–72.

Cohen, David W. 1994. *The Combing of History*. Chicago: University of Chicago Press.

Cole, Keith 1975. *A History of Oenpelli*. Darwin: Nungalinya Publications.

Cole, Keith 1979. *The Aborigines of Arnhem Land*. Adelaide: Rigby.

Cole, Tom 1988. *Hell West and Crooked*. Sydney: Collins.

Connolly, William E. 1999. *Why I am not a Secularist*. Minneapolis: University of Minnesota Press.

Curthoys, Ann and Docker, John 1996. 'Is History Fiction?', *UTS Review*, vol. 2, no. 1, pp. 12–37.

Curthoys, Ann and Docker, John 1999. 'Time, Eternity, Truth, and Death: History as Allegory', *Humanities Research*, no. 1, pp. 5–26.

Cowlishaw, Gillian 1992. 'Studying Aborigines: Changing Canons in Anthropology and History', in Attwood and Arnold (eds), *Power, Knowledge and Aborigines*, pp. 20–31.

Darian-Smith, Kate and Hamilton, Paula (eds) 1994. *Memory and History in Twentieth-Century Australia*. Melbourne: Oxford University Press (OUP).

Davis, Natalie Z. and Starn, Randolph 1989. 'Introduction', *Representations*, no. 26, pp. 1–6.

Davison, Graeme, Macintyre, Stuart and Hirst, John (eds) 1998. *The Oxford Companion to Australian History*. Melbourne: OUP.

de Certeau, Michel 1984. *The Practice of Everyday Life* (trans. Steven Rendall). California: University of California Press.

Dening, Greg 1996. *Performances*. Chicago: University of Chicago Press.

Docker, John 2001. *1492: The Poetics of Diaspora*. London, New York: Continuum.

Doolan, Jack K. 1977. 'Walk-off (and later return) of Various Aboriginal Groups from Cattle Stations: Victoria River District, Northern Territory', in Berndt (ed.) *Aborigines and Change: Australia in the '70s*, pp. 106–13.

Durack, Mary 1983. *Sons in the Saddle*. London: Constable.

Eliade, Mircea 1954. *The Myth of the Eternal Return*. New York: Pantheon Books.

Eliade, Mircea 1959. *The Sacred and the Profane: The Nature of Religion*. New York: Harcourt Brace.

Eliade, Mircea 1973. *Australian Religions: An Introduction*. Ithaca, NY: Cornell University Press.

Elkin, Adolphus P. 1945. *Aboriginal Men of High Degree*. Sydney: Australasian Pub. Co.

Elkin, Adolphus P. 1964. *The Australian Aborigines: How to Understand Them*. Sydney: Angus & Robertson.

Evans, Raymond, Saunders, Kay and Cronin, Kathryn 1975. *Exclusion, Exploitation and Extermination: Race Relations in Colonial Queensland*. Sydney: Australia & New Zealand Book Co.

Evans, Richard J. 1997. *In Defence of History*. London: Granta.

Fitzherbert, Sarah 1989. *My Dreaming is the Christman Bird*. Gosford, NSW: Bookshelf Publishing Australia.

Forest, Peter 1985. *An Outline of the History of Daguragu and Locality*. F.A.C.T.S., unpublished.

Foster-Carter, Aiden 1978. 'Can We Articulate "Articulation"?', in John Clammer (ed.), *The New Economic Anthropology*. London: Macmillan, pp. 210–49.

Foucault, Michel 1970. *The Order of Things: An Archaeology of the Human Sciences*. New York: Pantheon Books.

Foucault, Michel 1976. *The Archaeology of Knowledge*. New York: Harper & Row.

Franklin, Margaret A. 1976. *Black and White Australians*. Melbourne: Heinemann Educational Australia.

Friedlander, Saul (ed.) 1992. *Probing the Limits of Representation: Nazism and the 'Final Solution'*. Cambridge, MA: Harvard University Press.

Ganter, Regina 1994. *The Pearl-Shellers of Torres Strait: Resource Use, Development and Decline 1860s–1960s*. Melbourne: Melbourne University Press (MUP).

Gilbert, Kevin (ed.) 1988. *Inside Black Australia: An Anthology of Aboriginal Poetry*. Melbourne: Penguin.

Goodall, Heather 1992. 'The Whole Truth and Nothing but …: Some Intersections of Western Law, Aboriginal History and Community Memory', *Journal of Australian Studies*, vol. 35, pp. 104–19.

Goodall, Heather 1996. *Invasion to Embassy: Land in Aboriginal Politics in New South Wales, 1770–1972*. Sydney: Allen & Unwin.

Goodall, Heather and Cowlishaw, Gillian 2001. 'Editors' Introduction', *UTS Review*, vol. 7, pp. 1–5.

Gray, Geoffrey and Winter, Christine (eds) 1997. *The Resurgence of Racism: Hanson, Howard and the Race Debate*. Clayton, Vic: Department of History, Monash University.

Grimshaw, Patricia et al. 1994. *Creating a Nation*. Melbourne: McPhee Gribble.

Hage, Ghassan 1998. *White Nation: Fantasies of White Supremacy in a Multicultural Society*. Sydney: Pluto Press.

Hamamoto, Mitsuru 1984. 'Genshou-gaku to Jinrui-gaku', in Ayabe, Tsuneo (ed.), *Bunka Jinruigaku 15 no Riron*. Tokyo: Chukou Shinsho, pp. 281–98.

Hamilton, Paula 1994. 'The Knife Edge: Debates About Memory and History', in Darian-Smith and Hamilton (eds), *Memory and History in Twentieth-Century Australia*, pp. 9–32.

Hardy, Frank 1968. *The Unlucky Australians*. Melbourne: Thomas Nelson.

Haris, Hyllus 1988. 'Spiritual Song of the Aborigine', in Gilbert (ed.), *Inside Black Australia: An Anthology of Aboriginal Poetry*, p. 60.

Hartwig, Mervyn 1978. 'Capitalism and Aborigines: The Theory of Internal Colonialism and its Rivals', in E.L. Wheelwright and K.D. Buckley (eds), *Essays in the Political Economy of Australian Capitalism*. Sydney: Australia and New Zealand Books, pp. 119–41.

Hercus, L.A. and Sutton, Peter (eds) 1986. *This is What Happened: Historical Narratives by Aborigines*. Canberra: AIAS.

Hess, Michael 1994. 'Black and Red: The Pilbara Pastoral Workers' Strike, 1946', *Aboriginal History*, vol. 18, pp. 65–83.

Hiatt, L.R. 1965. *Kinship and Conflict: A Study of an Aboriginal Community in Northern Arnhem Land*. Canberra: Australian National University (ANU).

Hirsch, Eric and O'Hanlon, Michael (eds) 1995. *The Anthropology of Landscape: Perspectives on Place and Space*. Oxford: Clarendon Press.

Hokari, Minoru 1996. 'Aboriginal Economy and Cattle Labour: History of the Gurindji People', *Journal of Australian Studies, Australian Studies Association of Japan*, vol. 9, pp. 14–28 (in Japanese).

Hokari, Minoru 2000. 'From Wattie Creek to Wattie Creek: An Oral Historical Approach to the Gurindji Walk-off', *Aboriginal History*, vol. 24, pp. 98–116.

Hokari, Minoru 2002a. 'Reading Oral Histories from the Pastoral Frontier: A Critical Revision', *Journal of Australian Studies*, vol. 72, pp. 21–28.

Hokari, Minoru 2002b. 'Localised History: "Dangerous" Histories from the Gurindji Country', *Locality*, Autumn issue, pp. 4–7.

Horton, David et al. (eds) 1994. *The Encyclopaedia of Aboriginal Australia: Aboriginal and Torres Strait Islander History, Society and Culture*. Canberra: Aboriginal Studies Press.

Huggins, Jackie, Huggins, Rita and Jacobs, Jane M. 1997. 'Kooramindanjie: Place and the Postcolonial', in Richard White and Penny Russell (eds), *Memories and Dreams: Reflections on Twentieth-century Australia*. Sydney: Allen & Unwin, pp. 229–45.

Huggins, Jackie 1998. *Sister Girl: The Writings of Aboriginal Activist and Historian Jackie Huggins*. Brisbane: UQP.

Huggins, Rita and Huggins, Jackie 1994. *Auntie Rita*. Canberra: Aboriginal Studies Press.

Hughes, Selwyn 1988. 'Home On Palm', in Gilbert (ed.), *Inside Black Australia: An Anthology of Aboriginal Poetry*, p. 154.

Hutton, Patrick H. 1993. *History as an Art of Memory*. London: University Press of New England.

Joyce, Patrick 1997. 'History and Postmodernism', in Keith Jenkins (ed.), *The Postmodern History Reader*. London, New York: Routledge, pp. 244–49.

Keen, Ian (ed.) 1988. *Being Black: Aboriginal Cultures in 'Settled' Australia*. Canberra: Aboriginal Studies Press.

Keen, Ian 1993. 'Ubiquitous Ubiety of Dubious Uniformity', *Australian Journal of Anthropology*, vol. 4, no. 2, pp. 96–110.

Kerouac, Jack 1957. *On the Road*. New York: Viking Press.

Kijngayari, Long J. 1986. 'The Gurindji Story: The Wave Hill Strike', in Hercus and Sutton (eds), *This is What Happened: Historical Narratives by Aborigines*, pp. 305–11.

Kolig, Erich 1978. 'Dialectics of Aboriginal Life-Space', in Michael C. Howard (ed.), *'Whitefella Business': Aborigines in Australian Politics*. Philadelphia: Institute for the Study of Human Issues, pp. 49–79.

Kolig, Erich 1980a. 'Captain Cook in the Western Kimberleys', in Berndt and Berndt (eds), *Aborigines of the West: Their Past and Their Present*, pp. 274–82.

Kolig, Erich 1980b. 'Noah's Ark Revisited: On the Myth–Land Connection in Traditional Thought', *Oceania*, vol. 51, pp. 118–32.

Kolig, Erich 1984. 'The Mobility of Aboriginal Religion', in Charlesworth et al. (eds), *Religion in Aboriginal Australia: An Anthology*, pp. 390–416.

Kolig, Erich 1987. *The Noonkanbah Story: Profile of an Aboriginal Community in Western Australia*. Dunedin: University of Otago Press.

Kopp, Sheldon 1972. *If You See the Buddha on the Road, Kill Him!* London: Sheldon Press.

Langford, Ruby 1988. *Don't Take Your Love to Town*. Melbourne: Penguin.

Lattas, Andrew 1996. 'Colonialism, Aborigines and the Politics of Time and Space: The Placing of Stranger and the Placing of Oneself', *Social Analysis*, no. 40, pp. 20–42.

Layton, Robert 1995. 'Relating to the Country in the Western Desert', in Hirsch and O'Hanlon (eds), *The Anthropology of Landscape: Perspectives on Place and Space*, pp. 210–231.

Le Goff, Jacques 1992. *History and Memory, European Perspectives*. New York: Columbia University Press.

Lévi-Strauss, Claude 1966. *The Savage Mind*. Chicago: University of Chicago Press.

Lingiari, Vincent 1986. 'The Gurindji Story: Vincent Lingiari's Speech', in Hercus and Sutton (eds), *This is What Happened: Historical Narratives by Aborigines*, pp. 313–15.

Loos, Noel 1982. *Invasion and Resistance: Aboriginal–European Relations on the North Queensland Frontier 1861–1897*. Canberra: ANU Press.

Mackinolty, Chips and Wainburranga, Paddy 1988. 'Too Many Captain Cooks', in Tony Swain and Deborah B. Rose (eds), *Aboriginal Australians and Christian Missions: Ethnographic and Historical Studies*. Bedford Park, SA: Australian Association for the Study of Religions, pp. 355–60.

Macintyre, Stuart 1985. *Winners and Losers: The Pursuit of Social Justice in Australian History*. Sydney: Allen & Unwin.

Macknight, Campbell C. 1976. *The Voyage to Marege: Macassan Trepangers in Northern Australia*. Melbourne: MUP.

Maddock, Kenneth J. 1972. *The Australian Aborigines: A Portrait of Their Society*. London: Penguin.

Magowan, Fiona 1997. 'Crying to Remember: Memory and Identity in Yolngu Landscape and Seascape', paper presented for the conference, Northern Landscape in Story and History. Darwin: Museum and Art Gallery of the Northern Territory.

Mamak, Alexander and Ali, Ahmed (eds) 1979. *Race, Class and Rebellion in the South Pacific*. Sydney: Allen & Unwin.

May, Dawn 1983. *From Bush to Station: Aboriginal Labour in the North Queensland Pastoral Industry, 1861–1897*. Townsville: James Cook University.

May, Dawn 1994. *Aboriginal Labour and the Cattle Industry: Queensland from White Settlement to the Present*. Cambridge, Melbourne: Cambridge University Press (CUP).

Maynard, John 1997. 'Fred Maynard and the Australian Aboriginal Progressive Association (AAPA): One God, One Aim, One Destiny', *Aboriginal History*, vol. 21, pp. 1–13.

Maynard, John 1988. 'Aboriginal Stars of the Pigskin', *Aboriginal History*, vol. 22, pp. 116–42.

McCarthy, Frederick D. 1939. 'Trade in Aboriginal Australia, and Trade Relationships with Torres Strait, New Guinea and Malaya', *Oceania*, vol. 9, no. 4, pp. 405–438; vol. 10, no. 1, pp. 80–104, no. 2, pp. 171–95.

McConvell, Patrick and Rod Hargen 1981. *A Traditional Land Claim by the Gurindji to Daguragu Station*. Alice Springs: Central Land Council.

McConvell, Patrick 1989. 'Workers and "Camp-Mob": Aborigines and the Discourse of Cattle Stations'. Darwin: Northern Territory University, unpublished.

McGrath, Ann 1987a. *Born in the Cattle: Aborigines in Cattle Country*. Sydney: Allen & Unwin.

McGrath, Ann 1987b. '"Stories for Country": Oral History and Aboriginal Land Claims', *Oral History Association of Australia Journal*, vol. 9, pp. 34–46.

McGrath, Ann 1988. 'Born or Reborn in the Cattle?', *Meanjin*, vol. 47, pp. 171–77.

McGrath, Ann (ed.) 1995. *Contested Ground: Australian Aborigines Under the British Crown*. Sydney: Allen & Unwin.

McGrath, Ann and Saunders, Kay with Huggins, Jackie (eds) 1995. *Aboriginal Workers*. Sydney: The Australian Society for the Study of Labour History.

McGrath, Ann 1995a. 'Contested Ground: What is 'Aboriginal History'?', in McGrath (ed.), *Contested Ground: Australian Aborigines Under the British Crown*, pp. 365–366.

McGrath, Ann 1995b. '"Modern Stone-Age Slavery": Images of Aboriginal Labour and Sexuality', in McGrath and Saunders with Huggins (eds), *Aboriginal Workers*, pp. 30–51.

McLeod, D.W. 1984. *How the West Was Lost: The Native Question in the Development of Western Australia*. Port Hedland, WA: private publication.

Meggitt, Mervyn J. 1955. 'Notes on the Malngjin and Gurindji Aborigines of Limbunya, N.W. Northern Territory', *Mankind*, vol. 5, pp. 45–50.

Meggitt, Mervyn J. 1965. *Desert People: A Study of the Walbiri Aborigines of Central Australia*. Chicago: University of Chicago Press.

Mellor, Doreen and Haebich, Anna (eds) 2002. *Many Voices: Reflections on Experiences of Indigenous Child Separation*. Canberra: National Library of Australia.

Middleton, Hannah 1978. 'A Marxist at Wattie Creek: Fieldwork among Australian Aborigines', in Sol Encel and Colin Bell (eds), *Inside the Whale: Ten Personal Accounts of Social Research*. Sydney: Pergamon Press, pp. 238–69.

Middleton, Hannah 1979. 'Aboriginal Resistance: The Gurindji at Wattie Creek', in Mamak and Ali (eds), *Race, Class and Rebellion in the South Pacific*, pp. 114–26.

Morgan, Sally 1988. *My Place*. Fremantle, WA: Fremantle Arts Centre Press. (Morgan, Sally 1992. *Mai Preisu*. Japanese translation, Saimaru Publishing.)

Morphy, Howard and Morphy, Frances 1984. 'The "Myths" of Ngalakan History: Ideology and Images of the Past in Northern Australia', *Man*, vol. 19, no. 3, pp. 459–78.

Morphy, Howard 1991. *Ancestral Connections: Art and an Aboriginal System of Knowledge*. Chicago: University of Chicago Press.

Morphy, Howard 1993. 'Colonialism, History and the Construction of Place: Politics of Landscape in Northern Australia', in Barbara Bender (ed.), *Landscape: Politics and Perspectives*. Providence, NJ: Berg, pp. 85–106.

Morphy, Howard 1995. 'Landscape and the Reproduction of the Ancestral Past', in Hirsch and O'Hanlon (eds), *The Anthropology of Landscape: Perspectives on Place and Space*, pp. 184–209.

Morris-Suzuki, Tessa 2001. 'Truth, Postmodernism and Historical Revisionism in Japan', *Inter-Asia Cultural Studies*, vol. 2, pp. 297–305.

Morris-Suzuki, Tessa 2002a. 'Immigration and Citizenship in Contemporary Japan', in Javed Maswood, Jeffrey Graham and Hideaki Miyajima (eds), *Japan: Change and Continuity*. London: Routledge Curzon, pp. 163–78.

Morris-Suzuki, Tessa 2002b. *Hihanteki Souzou Ryoku no Tameni*. Tokyo: Heibon-sha.

Morton, John 1996. 'A Place for Strangers and a Stranger out of Place: Towards a History of Tony Swain's Aboriginal Being', *Social Analysis*, no. 40, pp. 43–50.

Mountford, C.P. 1965. *Ayers Rock: Its People, Their Beliefs, and Their Art*. Honolulu: East-West Center Press.

Mulvaney, Derek J. 1976. '"The Chain of Connection": The Material Evidence', in Nicolas Peterson (ed.), *Tribes and Boundaries in Australia*. Canberra: AIAS, pp. 72–94.

Mulvaney, Derek J. 1990. 'The Australian Aborigines 1606–1929: Opinion and Fieldwork', in Susan Janson and Stuart Macintyre (eds), *Through White Eyes*. Sydney: Allen & Unwin, pp. 1–44.

Munn, Nancy D. 1986. *Walbiri Iconography: Graphic Representation and Cultural Symbolism in a Central Australian Society*. Chicago: University of Chicago Press.

Murakami, Haruki 1997. *The Wind-up Bird Chronicle*. London: Harvill Panther.

Myers, Fred R. 1986. *Pintupi Country, Pintupi Self: Sentiment, Place and Politics Among Western Desert Aborigines*. Canberra, Washington: AIAS, Smithsonian Institution Press.

Neilley, Warwick 1970. 'An Interview with Pincher Numiari'. Sydney: ABSCHOL and Save the Gurindji Campaign.

Neumann, Klaus 1998. 'Remembering Victims and Perpetrators', *UTS Review*, vol. 4, no. 1, pp. 1–17.

Ngabidj, Grant and Shaw, Bruce 1981. *My Country of the Pelican Dreaming: The Life of an Australian Aborigine of the Gadjerong, Grant Ngabidj, 1904–1977 as told to Bruce Shaw*. Canberra: AIAS.

Nora, Pierre 1989. 'Between Memory and History: Les Lieux de Mémoire', *Representations*, vol. 26, pp. 7–25.

Northern Territory Council for Aboriginal Rights 1968. Circular Letter on the Gurindji at Wave Hill Station. Darwin: Northern Territory Council for Aboriginal Rights (Inc.)

Oke, Robert and Oke, Kay 1969. *Wattie Creek: Present and Future*. Melbourne: ABSCHOL.

Ota, Yoshinobu 1996. 'Posutokoroniaru Hihan wo Koeru tameni', in Akitoshi Shimizu et al. (eds), *Shisouka Sareru Shuuhen Sekai*. Tokyo: Iwanami, pp. 283–307.

Ota, Yoshinobu 2001. *Minzokushi teki Kindai heno Kainyu: Bunka wo Kataru Kenri ha Dareni Arunoka*. Tokyo: Jinbun Shoin.

Oxaal, Ivar, Barnett, Tony and Booth, David (eds) 1975. *Beyond the Sociology of Development: Economy and Society in Latin America and Africa*. London: Routledge & Kegan Paul.

Perkins, Charles Nelson 1975. *A Bastard Like Me*. Sydney: Ure Smith.

Read, Peter 1984. *Down There with me on the Cowra Mission: An Oral History of Erambie Aboriginal Reserve, Cowra, New South Wales*. Sydney: Pergamon Press.

Read, Peter 1988. *A Hundred Years War: The Wiradjuri People and the State*. Sydney: ANU Press.

Read, Peter 1995. 'Northern Territory', in McGrath (ed.), *Contested Ground: Australian Aborigines Under the British Crown*, pp. 269–305.

Read, Peter 1999. *A Rape of the Soul So Profound: The Return of the Stolen Generations*. Sydney: Allen & Unwin.

Read, Peter and Read, Jay 1991. *Long Time, Olden Time: Aboriginal Accounts of Northern Territory History*. Alice Springs: Institute for Aboriginal Development Publications.

Reece, Bob 1987. 'Inventing Aborigines', *Aboriginal History*, vol. 11, pp. 14–23.

Perks, Robert and Thomson, Alistair (eds) 1998. *The Oral History Reader*. London: Routledge.

Reynolds, Henry 1981. *The Other Side of the Frontier: An Interpretation of the Aboriginal Response to the Invasion and Settlement of Australia*. Townsville, Qld: History Department, James Cook University.

Reynolds, Henry 1990. *With the White People*. Melbourne: Penguin.

Reynolds, Henry 1999. *Why Weren't We Told?: A Personal Search for the Truth About Our History*. Melbourne: Viking.

Reynolds, Henry 2000. *Black Pioneers*. Melbourne: Penguin.

Riddett, Lyn A. 1985. 'Aboriginal Employment in the Pastoral Industry (N.T. 1930–1966)', in Deborah Wade-Marshall and Peter Loveday (eds), *Employment and Unemployment: Collection of Papers*. Darwin: ANU North Australia Research Unit, pp. 199–207.

Riddett, Lyn A. 1990. *Kine, Kin and Country: The Victoria River District of the Northern Territory, 1911–1966*. Darwin: ANU North Australia Research Unit.

Riddett, Lyn A. 1997. 'The Strike That Became a Land Rights Movement: A Southern "Do-Gooder" Reflects on Wattie Creek 1966–74', *Labour History*, no. 72, pp. 50–65.

Robinson, Fergus and York, Barry 1977. *The Black Resistance: An Introduction to the History of the Aborigines' Struggle Against British Colonialism*. Melbourne: Widescope.

Roderick, Colin A. 1988. *Leichhardt, the Dauntless Explorer*. Sydney: Angus & Robertson.

Ronan, Tom M. 1966. *Once There Was a Bagman: A Memoir*. Melbourne: Cassell.

Rose, Deborah B. 1984. 'The Saga of Captain Cook: Morality in Aboriginal and European Law', *Australian Aboriginal Studies*, no. 2, pp. 24–39.

Rose, Deborah B. 1989. 'Remembrance', *Aboriginal History*, vol. 13, no. 2, pp. 135–47.

Rose, Deborah B. 1991. *Hidden Histories: Black Stories from Victoria River Downs, Humbert River and Wave Hill Stations*. Canberra: Aboriginal Studies Press.

Rose, Deborah B. 1992. *Dingo Makes Us Human: Life and Land in an Aboriginal Australian Culture*. Cambridge, Melbourne: CUP.

Rose, Deborah B. 1994. 'Ned Kelly Died for Our Sins', *Oceania*, vol. 65, pp. 175–86.

Rose, Deborah B. 1996. *Nourishing Terrains: Australian Aboriginal Views of Landscape and Wilderness*. Canberra: Australian Heritage Commission.

Rose, Deborah B. 1999. 'Taking Notice', *Worldviews: Environment, Culture and Perspectives*, vol. 3, no. 2, pp. 93–103.

Rose, Frederick G.G. 1987. *The Traditional Mode of Production of the Australian Aborigines*. Sydney: Angus & Robertson.

Rowley, C.D. 1970. *The Destruction of Aboriginal Society*. Canberra: ANU Press.

Rowley, C.D. 1971a. *Outcasts in White Australia*. Canberra: ANU Press.

Rowley, C.D. 1971b. *The Remote Aborigines*. Canberra: ANU Press.

Rowse, Tim 1988a. 'Tolerance, Fortitude and Patience: Frontier Pasts to Live with?', *Meanjin*, vol. 47, pp. 21–29.

Rowse, Tim 1988b. 'Paternalism's Changing Reputation', *Mankind*, vol. 18, no. 2, pp. 57–73.

Rumsey, Alan 1994. 'The Dreaming, Human Agency and Inscriptive Practice', *Oceania*, vol. 65 pp. 97–115.

Russell, Bertrand 1958. *The ABC of Relativity*. London: Allen & Unwin.

Sakai, Naoki 2001. 'Dislocation of the West and the Status of the Humanities', *Traces*, vol. 1, pp. 71–93.

Shaw, Bruce and Sullivan, Jack 1979. '"They Same as You and Me": Encounters with the Gadia in the East Kimberley', *Aboriginal History*, vol. 3, pp. 97–107.

Shaw, Bruce 1983. 'Heroism Against White Rule: The "Rebel" Major', in Eric Fry (ed.), *Rebels and Radicals*. Sydney: Allen & Unwin, pp. 8–26.

Shaw, Bruce 1992. *When the Dust Come in Between: Aboriginal Viewpoints in the East Kimberley Prior to 1982*. Canberra: Aboriginal Studies Press.

Spencer, Baldwin 1914. *Native Tribes of the Northern Territory of Australia*. London: Macmillan.

Spencer, Baldwin and Gillen, Francis J. 1938. *The Native Tribes of Central Australia*. London: Macmillan.

Spiegel, Gabrielle 1997. 'History, Historicism and the Social Logic of the Text in the Middle Ages', in Keith Jenkins (ed.), *The Postmodern History Reader*. London, New York: Routledge, pp. 180–203.

Spivak, Gayatri C. 1988. 'Can the Subaltern Speak?,' in Cary Nelson and Lawrence Grossberg (eds), *Marxism and the Interpretation of Culture*. Urbana: University of Illinois Press, pp. 271–313.

Spivak, Gayatori C. 1996. 'Subaltern Talk', in Donna Landry and Gerald MacLean (eds), *The Spivak Reader*. London, New York: Routledge, pp. 287–308.

Stanner, W.E.H. 1964. *On Aboriginal Religion*. Sydney: University of Sydney.

Stanner, W.E.H. 1968. *After the Dreaming: Black and White Australians – An Anthropologist's View*. Sydney: ABC (Boyer Lectures).

Stanner, W.E.H. 1979. *White Man Got No Dreaming: Essays 1938–1973*. Canberra: ANU Press.

Strehlow, T.G.H. 1947. *Aranda Traditions*. Melbourne: MUP.

Strehlow, T.G.H. 1970. 'Geography and the Totemic landscape in Central Australia: A Functional Study', in Berndt (ed.), *Australian Aboriginal Anthropology: Modern Studies in the Social Anthropology of the Australian Aborigines*, pp. 92–140.

Strehlow, T.G.H. 1971. *Songs of Central Australia*. Sydney: Angus & Robertson.

Stuart, Donald 1959. *Yandy*. Melbourne: Australian Book Society.

Sullivan, Jack and Shaw, Bruce 1983. *Banggaiyerri: The Story of Jack Sullivan*. Canberra: AIAS.

Sutton, Peter 1988. 'Myth as History, History as Myth', in Keen (ed.), *Being Black: Aboriginal Cultures in 'Settled' Australia*, pp. 251–68.

Swain, Tony and Rose, Deborah B. (eds) 1988. *Aboriginal Australians and Christian Missions: Ethnographic and Historical Studies*. Bedford Park, SA: Australian Association for the Study of Religions.

Swain, Tony 1988. 'The Ghost of Space: Reflections on Warlpiri Christian Iconography and Ritual', in Swain and Rose (eds), *Aboriginal Australians and Christian Missions: Ethnographic and Historical Studies*, pp. 452–469.

Swain, Tony 1993. *A Place for Strangers: Towards a History of Australian Aboriginal Being*. Cambridge, Melbourne: CUP.

Swain, Tony 1996. 'Play and Place', *Social Analysis*, no. 40, pp. 51–58.

Thomson, Donald F. 1949. *Economic Structure and the Ceremonial Exchange Cycle in Arnhem Land*. Melbourne: Macmillan.

Turnbull, Henry and Broadhurst, Francis J. 1983. *Leichhardt's Second Journey: A First-hand Account*. Sydney: John Ferguson.

Urry, James 1979. 'Beyond the Frontier: European Influence, Aborigines and the Concept of "Traditional" Culture', *Journal of Australian Studies*, no. 5, pp. 2–16.

Webster, E.M. 1980. *Whirlwinds in the Plain: Ludwig Leichhardt – Friends, Foes, and History*. Melbourne: MUP.

White, Richard and Russell, Penny (eds) 1997. *Memories and Dreams: Reflections on Twentieth-Century Australia*. Sydney: Allen & Unwin.

Wightman, Glenn et al. 1994. *Gurindji Ethnobotany: Aboriginal Plant Use from Daguragu, Northern Australia*. Darwin: Conservation Commission of the Northern Territory.

Wilson, John 1980. 'The Pilbara Aboriginal Social Movement: An Outline of its Background and Significance', in Berndt and Berndt (eds), *Aborigines of the West: Their Past and Their Present*, pp. 151–68.

Wolpe, Harold 1980a. 'The Theory of Internal Colonialism: The South African Case', in Harold Wolpe (ed.), *The Articulation of Modes of Production: Essays from Economy and Society*. London: Routledge & Kegan Paul, pp. 229–52.

Wolpe, Harold (ed.) 1980b. *The Articulation of Modes of Production: Essays from Economy and Society*. London: Routledge & Kegan Paul.

Yarwood, A.T. and Knowling, M.J. 1982. *Race Relations in Australia: A History*. Sydney: Methuen Australia.

Yengoyan, Aram A. 1968. 'Demographic and Ecological Influences on Aboriginal Australian Marriage Sections', in Richerd B. Lee and Irven DeVore (eds), *Man the Hunter*. Chicago: Aldine Publishing, pp. 185–99.

Young, Elspeth and Dooham, Kim 1989. *Mobility for Survival: A Process Analysis of Aboriginal Population Movement in Central Australia*. Darwin: ANU North Australia Research Unit.

## Theses

Briscoe, Gordon 1986. *Aborigines and Class in Australian History*. BA Thesis (Hons), Canberra: ANU.

Briscoe, Gordon 1996. *Disease, Health and Healing: Aspects of Indigenous Health in Western Australia and Queensland, 1900–1940*. PhD Thesis, Canberra: ANU.

Hokari, Minoru 1996b *Aboriginal Economy and Cattle Labour: Economic History of the Gurindji People*. MA Thesis (English translation), Tokyo: Hitotsubashi University.

Hokari, Minoru 2001. *Cross-Culturalizing History: Journey to the Gurindji Way of Historical Practice*, PhD thesis, Canberra: ANU.

Jowett, Tina 1990. *Walking to Wattie Creek: The History of the Strike by the Gurindji People and Their Struggle for Land Rights, 1966–1986*. BA Thesis (Hons), Sydney: University of New South Wales (UNSW).

Middleton, Hannah 1972. *The Land Rights and Civil Rights Campaign of the Gurindji at Wattie Creek: An Australian Manifestation of the World-Wide National Liberation Movement*. PhD Thesis, Germany: Humboldt University.

Perheentupa, Johanna 1998. *'Those Poor Creatures – The Children of the Soil':*
*Aborigines in Australian Historiography 1798–1883.* Pro Gradu Dissertation,
Finland: University of Turku.

Rudder, John 1993. *Yolngu Cosmology: An Unchanging Cosmos Incorporating a*
*Rapidly Changing World?* PhD Thesis, Canberra: ANU.

## MINORU HOKARI'S WORK

### Photography exhibition catalogue

Being Connected with HOKARI MINORU 2010. 'The Call of the Living
Earth: Photographs of Indigenous Australians by Minoru Hokari' (text in
English and Japanese).

### Book

Hokari, Minoru 2004. 'Radical Oral History: Historical Practice of Indigenous
Australians'. Ochanomizushobo (in Japanese).

### Japanese translations

[Rose, Deborah B. 2003. *Seimei no Daichi: Aborijini Bunka to Ekoroji* (trans.
Hokari Minoru). (Tokyo: Heibonsha Publishing)]. Original: Rose, Deborah
Bird 1996. *Nourishing Terrains: Australian Aboriginal Views of Landscape and*
*Wilderness* (Canberra: Australian Heritage Commission).

[Hage, Ghassan 2003. *Howaito Neishon* (trans. Minoru Hokari and Y. Shiobara).
(Tokyo: Heibonsha Publishing)]. Original: Hage, Ghassan 2000. *White*
*Nation: Fantasies of White Supremacy in a Multicultural Society* (Sydney: Pluto
Press).

### Articles

Hokari, Minoru 2006. 'Re-enchantment of History: Writing Aboriginal
Spiritualities', in L.R. Bennett and M. Hokari (eds), *Locations of Spirituality:*
*Conference Proceedings.* Melbourne: Australian Research Center in Sex
Health and Society, La Trobe University (CD-ROM).

Hokari, Minoru 2005. 'Gurindji Mode of Historical Practice', in Luke Taylor
(ed.), *AIATSIS Conference 2002: Power of Knowledge and the Resonance of*
*Tradition.* Canberra: AIATSIS Press, pp. 214–23.

Hokari, Minoru 2003. 'The Living Earth: The World of the Aborigines' [first
published in Japanese in *Niigata Nippo* newspaper, 17 June–7 October].
English trans. Kyoko Uchida, published in *Conversations*, vol. 6, no. 2,
Summer 2006 (Canberra: Pandanus Books, Research School of Pacific and
Asian Studies, ANU).

Hokari, Minoru 2003. 'History Happening in/between Body and Place: Journey
to the Aboriginal Way of Historical Practice', in J.R. Stephens (ed.), *Habitus:*
*A Sense of Place: Proceedings of the Habitus 2000 Conference.* Perth: Curtin
University of Technology (CD-ROM).

Hokari, Minoru 2003. 'Anti-Minorities History: Perspectives on Aboriginal-
Asian Relations', in Penny Edwards and Shen Yuanfang (eds), *Lost in the*

*Whitewash: Aboriginal-Asian Encounters in Australia, 1901–2001*. Canberra: Humanities Research Centre, ANU, pp. 85–101.

Hokari, Minoru 2003. 'Globalising Aboriginal Reconciliation: Indigenous Australians and Asian (Japanese) Migrants', *Cultural Studies Review*, vol. 9, no. 2, pp. 84–101.

Hokari, Minoru 2002. 'Localised History: "Dangerous" Histories from the Gurindji Country', *Locality*, Autumn, pp. 4–7.

Hokari, Minoru 2002. 'Maintaining History: The Gurindji People's "Truthful" Histories', *Cultural Survival Quarterly*, vol. 26, no. 2, pp. 26–27.

Hokari, Minoru 2002. 'Reading Oral Histories from the Pastoral Frontier: A Critical Revision', *Journal of Australian Studies*, vol. 72, pp. 21–28.

Hokari, Minoru 2002. 'Images of Australian Colonialism: Interpretation of Colonial Landscape by an Aboriginal Historian', in Henry Stewart, Alan Barnard and Keiichi Omura (eds), 'Self- and Other-Images of Hunter-Gatherers: Papers Presented at the Eighth International Conference on Hunting and Gathering Societies (CHAGS 8), National Museum of Ethnology, Osaka, October 1998', *Senri Ethnological Studies* (*English Journal of National Museum of Ethnology*), no. 60, pp. 153–69.

Hokari, Minoru 2000. 'From Wattie Creek to Wattie Creek: An Oral Historical Approach to the Gurindji Walk-off', *Aboriginal History*, vol. 24, pp. 98–116.

## PhD Thesis

Hokari, Minoru 2001. 'Cross-Culturalizing History: Journey to the Gurindji Way of Historical Practice'. PhD Thesis, Canberra: ANU.

# INDEX

cowboy hats 184
Crew, Teddy 185
cross-cultural history 4, 83–86, 248, 258–262
cultural relativism 37
Curthoys, Ann 7, 249

Daguragu Aboriginal Land Trust 78
Daguragu community
　　cattle station 182, 186–187
　　establishment of 35, 77–78, 219–220, 223–225
　　feedback from 267
　　history in 42
　　MH's work at 8, 86
Daguragu Community Government Council 33, 78, 86
Danayarri, Hobbles 120, 156, 204, 213–214
Danbayarri, Dandy 161, 251
'dangerous history' 244, 251, 258, 264
Daniels, Dexter
　　meets Tommy Vincent Lingiari 214–215
　　on planned Victoria River Downs walk-off 221
　　role in Wave Hill walk-off 205, 210–212
Darwin (NT), MH's stay in 74–75
De Certeau, Michel 243
deep pluralism 50
denialism 45, 249
Dening, Greg
　　as examiner for Hokari Minoru 4
　　on 'poetic for histories' 259, 264
　　on writing 271–272
　　thesis advice 7, 87–88
diagrams drawn on ground see sand drawings
discourse analysis 260
Docker, John 7, 249
Docker River trip 82–83, 100, 109
doctorate research 4, 29, 57–58
Donald, Violet 231
Doolan, Jack K. 203, 235–236
doubled consciousness 51, 256–257
'Double-O' (Aboriginal man) 211
drawings see sand drawings

Dreaming stories 180–198 see also supernaturalism
　　connection to landscape 156–157
　　cosmology 96–99
　　for anthropologists 149
　　methodology of 155–159
　　paying attention to 90
　　place-oriented 80
　　tracks in 103
dreams 81–82, 121–122

earth
　　as entity 95
　　law from 79, 119
　　listening to 36
　　paper not from 133–134
　　punishment from 177–179
　　sand drawings 93, 118–119, 122–131
education
　　Aboriginal attitudes to 239
　　European 122–123
　　Lingiari supports 228
Edwards, Harry 173
Edwards, Roy 211
'effective cultural interchange' 247–248
Eliade, Mircea 50, 250, 256
Elkin, A.P. 155
'enduring time' 111–112
England, Aboriginal views of
　　see also kartiya
　　law from 134–135
　　morality in 129–131, 147–148, 157
　　people descended from monkeys 141
equality in rights 51–52
ethics of spatial movement 19, 102–104
ethnohistory 258–259
European education 122–123
Evans, Raymond 245
Evans, Richard 249
evolutionary theory 149–150, 153
Exclusion, Exploitation and Extermination 245
experientialism 59

All royalties from the sale of this book will be donated to the Minoru Hokari Memorial Scholarship for Fieldwork in Indigenous History, hosted by the Australian Centre for Indigenous History at the Australian National University.

http://history.cass.anu.edu.au/minoru-hokari-scholarship

Donations to the fund can be directed to:
    Minoru Hokari Memorial Scholarship Fund
    Director, Foundation and Alumni Relations
    Block 1, Building 003
    The Australian National University
    Canberra ACT 0200
    Australia

    Tel: (61)-2-6125-0462/7814
    Fax: (61)-2-6125-9698
    Email: endowment@anu.edu.au